Jesus *Loves* Canaanites

♥

Biblical Genocide in the Light of Moral Intuition

2 Cup Press

Canada

Jesus Loves Canaanites

Copyright © 2021 Randal Rauser

All Scripture quotations, unlss otherwise indicated, are taken from The Holy Bible: New International Version®, NIV®. Copyright © 1973, 1978, 1984, 2011 by Biblica, Inc.™ Used by permission of Zondervan. All rights reserved.

Printed in the United States of America.

All rights reserved. No part of this book may be reproduced in any form or by any electronic or mechanical means, including information storage and retrieval systems, without permission in writing from the publisher, except by reviewers, who may quote brief passages in a review.

ISBN: 978-1-7750462-4-0
ISBN: 978-1-7750462-5-7

Book cover design by Darryl Frayne - steadydigital.ca

*For every Christian who ever said,
"I don't know what this means,
but it can't mean that."
You were right.*

Thou shalt not follow a multitude to do evil.

(Exodus 23:2 KJV)

Jesus Loves Canaanites

Acknowledgements vii

Parable of the Good Canaanite ix

Foreword: A Harvest of Tears xi

Introduction: The Blood-Soaked Soil of Canaan xiii

1. Killing the Joneses: Coming to Terms with Biblical Violence 1

2. Joshua and the International Criminal Court 13

3. How We Learn *Not* to Read the Text 21

4. Moral Intuition and the Divine Will 39

5. Moral Knowledge and Intimate Acquaintance 79

6. On the Canaanites of Central Africa 99

7. Interpreting the Bible: Five Guiding Principles 127

8. The Genocide Apologists 163

9. The Just War Interpreters 187

10. The Spiritualizers 215

11. The Providential Errantists 275

12. The Ethics of Authorial Ambiguation: Why isn't God clearer? 313

Acknowledgements

On December 22, 2020, I participated in a debate with atheist Dan Barker on the topic "Is the Christian God Worthy of Worship?" The debate was hosted by Cameron Bertuzzi of Capturing Christianity. In preparation for it, I mapped out several points I wanted to address, points which were the culmination of my thinking on the topic of biblical violence, theology, and hermeneutics dating back to 2008. A few days later, on December 26, I decided to turn those rough notes into a book and so I started writing. I kept writing through January and finally completed the manuscript two months later, in late February.

At this point, nobody has read the manuscript, and that means that I don't have a long list of people to thank who made the book better. But I'd be deluded if I thought that meant I had nobody to thank. Former Democratic chairman Bob Strauss famously said that the typical politician wants you to think he was born in a log cabin that he built, but it doesn't work like that. Nobody is an island and over the last thirteen years I have formed my views through countless books, essays, and conversations with more interlocutors than I can possibly remember. To them, I am grateful. I still don't have everything figured out: far from it. But I do know this: I no longer need to sacrifice my conscience when I read the Bible. For that, I am grateful, indeed.

Parable of the Good Canaanite

But he wanted to justify himself, so he asked Jesus, "And who is my neighbor?"

In reply Jesus said: "An Israelite soldier was marching toward Jericho, when he was attacked by robbers. They stripped him of his clothes, beat him and went away, leaving him half dead. A priest happened to be going down the same road, and when he saw the man, he passed by on the other side. So too, a Levite, when he came to the place and saw him, passed by on the other side. But a [**Canaanite**], as he traveled, came where the man was; and when he saw him, he took pity on him. He went to him and bandaged his wounds, pouring on oil and wine. Then he put the man on his own donkey, brought him to an inn and took care of him. The next day he took out two denarii and gave them to the innkeeper. 'Look after him,' he said, 'and when I return, I will reimburse you for any extra expense you may have.'

"Which of these three do you think was a neighbor to the man who fell into the hands of robbers?"

The expert in the law replied, "The one who had mercy on him."

Jesus told him, "Go and do likewise."

Foreword:

A Harvest of Tears

One summer evening some twenty-five years ago, I happened upon a haunting story in a newspaper about a man who decapitated his son because he believed God told him to. As I read of the horrifying scene that unfolded beside a U.S. interstate my eyes blurred with tears of anger. I couldn't begin to understand why God would allow such a terrible thing to occur. But one thing I did know and I knew it immediately and with every fiber of my being: I knew that God would never ask a man to sacrifice his son, not *really*. That moral truth radiated out for me with the same force as any truth that I have ever known.

What I didn't realize at the time was how that direct, powerful acquaintance with an undeniable moral truth was my first step on a long journey toward a new understanding of the Bible. As the tears of rage rolled down my cheeks, I knew that God was a god of love and peace, not a god of violence and carnage.

The tears that fell into the dust on that summer evening twenty-five years ago were the seeds. For better or for worse, this book is the harvest.

Introduction:
The Blood-Soaked Soil of Canaan

I have seen many violent films over the years, but *The Stoning of Soraya M.* is definitely among the most disturbing. There are several reasons that this film has never left me. To begin with, this tragic story of a spiraling marriage in rural Iran culminates in a horrific scene in which a woman is stoned to death by the residents of her village with her husband and father leading the way. It is a truly awful, extended display of inexplicable cruelty and sickening violence. There are few more vicious ways to die than to be pelted to death with rocks. Yet, through it all there is no compassion or mercy displayed by the villagers; once friendly neighbors have now become stone-cold executioners. Right before this haunting murder begins to unfold, Soraya, buried up to her waist, screams desperately at the gathered villagers glaring back at her with a mixture of hatred and curiosity. "How can you do this to *anybody*?" she cries. And without missing a beat, one man bellows back at her: "It's God's law!"

God's law.

How many atrocities of history have been justified by an appeal to those words? "It's God's law!" "God wills it!" "God commands it!" "God approves of it!" How often have those very words been bellowed just loud enough to silence the voices of protest? And I speak not only of the audible voice of protest from a desperate victim buried up to her waist in sand. I speak also of the still small voice deep within, that piercing voice of conscience that says "No, this isn't right".

One of the most disturbing aspects of that scene from *The Stoning of Soraya M.* is that it is not drawn from ancient history. Rather, the film tells the story of an actual killing which unfolded in 1980. It is one thing to reconstruct bare traces of archaeological evidence of a stoning in ancient Mesopotamia or to read legislative directions for stoning in ancient Greece. But it really brings home the visceral nature of the violence when the setting is a contemporary crime scene investigation.

Any Christian that witnesses that scene in the film will surely share my utter shock and revulsion at the brutality of the killing. They will wince at every rock that slices into Soraya's forehead, causing a spray of blood. They will sense a deep moral impulse within, one that gives voice to an unqualified moral condemnation of the act. And they will balk at the idea that any action so vicious and cruel could be God's law.

But for every Christian who experiences such an immediate and visceral moral condemnation of the scene—as I hope all do—there is a problem nearby. Ironically enough, stoning is mentioned nowhere in the Qur'an, but it *is* a fixture of "God's law" as it is recorded in the Bible. In his article on stoning, Paul Simmons summarizes the range of actions outlined in Torah that would warrant a fate like that of Soraya M:

> worshiping pagan deities (Deut 17:2-7); sacrificing a child to Molech (Lev 20:2-5); prophesying in the name of pagan gods (Deut 13:1-5); spirit divinations (Lev 20:27); blasphemy (Lev 24:15-16); and Sabbath breaking (Num 15:32-36). Insofar as the ban (*herem*) was a ritual sacrifice to Yahweh, the stoning of Achan for taking booty can be added (Josh. 7:25). A killer ox (Exod 21:28-32), adulterers (Deut 22:22-24), and rebellious children (Deut 21:18-21) were also to be stoned.[1]

---

1 Paul Simmons, "Stoning," *Mercer Dictionary of the Bible*, edited by Watson E. Mills (Macon, GA: Mercer University Press, 1991), 858. For my discussion see

Adultery, Sabbath breaking, rebellious children, and much else: if we followed these dictates faithfully today, how many people would face the same grisly fate as Soraya M? If we react with moral revulsion at her death, what about the people that would be pelted to death with rocks under these countless other circumstances? And if the Israelite holding the stone turned to us and bellowed "It's God's law!" to silence our moral concerns, what would be our reply?

The case of punitive stoning is but one example of the conflict between the moral intuitions of a contemporary reader and divinely sanctioned violence in Scripture. There are other cases of biblical violence as well, cases that are deeply disturbing on their own terms. For example, the beloved Psalms, the spiritual home of so many lost souls, are full of shockingly violent rhetorical lightning bolts. Consider this awful wish: "The righteous will be glad when they are avenged, when they dip their feet in the blood of the wicked" (58:10).[2] And then there is the violence of the end of history. For example, according to Revelation 14:20, God's final return will be accompanied by a vast winepress of divine wrath that will produce a tsunami of blood for 1,600 stadia [300 km].

As disturbing as these nightmarish images of rhetorical and eschatological violence may be, one can at least appeal to the fact that such language in the Psalms and Revelation is heavy with symbol. But not all biblical violence is like that. Arguably, the most troubling of all instances of violence in Scripture occurs in the narrative of God's actions in history and it involves accounts of God commanding and directing his people to undertake brutal

---

my book *Conversations with My Inner Atheist: A Christian Apologist Explores Questions that Keep People Up at Night* (Two Cup Press, 2020), chapter 6.

2 For some other examples, the psalmist hates the wicked and he says God does too (11:5). The Lord laughs at their destruction (37:13) as will the righteous (52:6). The psalmist longs for the children of the wicked to be orphaned beggars (109:9-10) and he relishes bludgeoning their infants to death (137:8-9).

wars and then empowering the Israelites to carry out these grisly tasks.³ And of the many wars fought in God's name, the most troubling of all would surely be those which begin with the direct command to eradicate completely entire peoples. That is the divine word we find against the Canaanites (Deuteronomy 20:10-20), Midianites (Numbers 31:17-18), and Amalekites (1 Samuel 15:3).⁴ Such actions take the singular horror of one impromptu execution by stoning and raise it to an unimaginable level of shock and carnage. If our moral intuitions are violated by the notion of one woman being pelted to death with rocks, what should we think of an entire nation of men, women, and children reduced to fleshy pulp by rock, sword, and spear? If we want to think through the problem of biblical violence at its agonizing core, we should begin here, at ground Zero, standing on the blood-soaked soil of Canaan.

From the perspective of contemporary international law, Canaan appears to tell a story of genocide. And given that the conquest of the Canaanites in Joshua is the most notorious of all biblical genocides, it is on this series of events that we will focus. Our attention will be directed to Deuteronomy 7 and 20 in which God appears to command the genocidal eradication of Canaanites, as well as the subsequent chronicle of Joshua 1-12 where the Israelites seek to carry out the divine wishes. In particular, I will give special attention to the early chapters of Joshua that present the entry of Israel into the land culminating in the wholesale slaughter of the people of Jericho in Joshua

---

3 Gregory Boyd begins his survey of biblical violence with these texts of total war because he rightly recognizes them as constituting the most horrifying and disturbing problem of biblical violence. See *The Crucifixion of the Warrior God: Interpreting the Old Testament's Violent Portraits of God in Light of the Cross*. Volume 1: *The Cruciform Hermeneutic* (Fortress Press, 2017), 294.

4 In the case of the Midianites in Numbers 31, God only stipulates that Moses "take vengeance" (31:2) so it is Moses, in fact, who articulates the directives to slaughter the men, women, and boys and to spare only the virginal girls (15-18).

6. If we are to hope to make sense of any instances of biblical violence, we would be wise to begin here.

With the invocation of genocide, our problem has now grown immensely. An instance of capital punishment by way of pelting a person to death with rocks offends our deep moral sensibilities. Not surprisingly, it is even more horrific to countenance the eradication of an entire society by methods no less brutal. When we consider the wholesale slaughter of entire communities can we simply silence the voice of conscience within with an appeal to 'God's law'?

I have framed the problem as consisting of a conflict with our moral intuitions, and it is indeed that. But for the Christian, the resulting cognitive dissonance also extends to additional theological questions. In short, how do we reconcile the genocidal destruction of entire people with the idea that the image of God is revealed in the visage of every precious human being? And how do we reconcile it to the fact that we are called to love each other in the manner of Jesus? How do we reconcile the command to kill all living things with God who comes to us in the story of the Prodigal Son? How do we relate the hatred of the Canaanites with the call to love our neighbor in the manner of the Good Samaritan? And how do we make it all fit with the love and kindness of Jesus who shows the Father heart of God by dying for us while we were yet sinners? How do we make sense of it all?

Concern over biblical violence has taken on a new urgency in the last twenty years. The initial catalyst, not surprisingly, was the horror of 9/11 and its link to a particular religious ideology. This shocking event heightened the age-old connection between religion and violence in the public imagination.[5] Not surprisingly,

---

5 However, it is important to recognize that almost all terrorist violence is motivated by geopolitical rather than simply religious concerns. See Randal Rauser and Justin Schieber, *An Atheist and a Christian Walk into a Bar* (Prometheus, 2016), 68-70.

soon afterward, this event prompted an important address from noted biblical scholar John Collins in which he stressed the need for fellow scholars to confront the issue of biblical violence.[6] Even more significantly, 9/11 spawned the new atheists who entered the public square distinguished by a novel rhetorical stridency in their attacks on the Bible, Christianity, and organized religion in general. Populists like Richard Dawkins, Sam Harris, and Christopher Hitchens published bestselling books in which they vocally called out the violence in the Bible. This only served to magnify the problem for a new generation of doubters, skeptics, and troubled Christians.[7]

The recent emphasis on the problem might lead some people to think that this is an issue newly discovered. Indeed, some Christians seem to believe that the problem with biblical violence is the product of uniquely *modern* sensibilities rather than human *moral* sensibilities. But this assessment is misguided at best. While awareness of the issue and critical responses to it have reached a fever pitch in recent years, Christians have struggled for centuries to understand biblical violence and to reconcile it to their understanding of the life and teaching of Jesus. So it must always be borne in mind that the challenges of our current day are hardly unique even if they do present us with a new urgency in sensing the problem and seeking a solution.

In this book I will aim to develop an honest and direct appraisal of the problem of biblical violence and to propose a way forward. But many books have already been written on the topic, particularly in the last fifteen years or so, so what justifies

---

6 See John J. Collins, "The Zeal of Phineas: the Bible and the legitimation of violence," *Journal of Biblical Literature*, 122 (2003), 3-21. Cf. John J. Collins, *Does the Bible Justify Violence* (Augsburg Fortress, 2004).

7 Dawkins opens chapter 2 of *The God Delusion* (Mariner, 2008) with a rambling sentence impugning the biblical God. This sentence has been quoted by others too many times for me to bother citing it here. But if you want to read it, turn to page 51 of *The God Delusion*.

adding one more to the already crowded bookshelf? From my perspective, the primary distinctive of this book resides in my commitment to identify and defend the central role of *moral intuition* and *moral perception* in theology and hermeneutics along with the determination to apply these insights to one specific case: the Canaanite conquest. After clearing the ground in the first three chapters with a suvey of the problem and how Christians seek to avoid it, in chapter 4 I will present the foundation of my moral case. I will argue that moral intuitions provide a powerful tool for the reader to identify which texts present the most serious moral problems.

Given that fact it seems to me a gross oversight that so many contributors to the discussion pay comparatively little attention to moral intuition or the way that it should inform our thinking about biblical violence. This book aims to address that gap by articulating a simple methodology in chapter 5 that seeks to clarify moral knowledge rooted in bedrock intuitions which can, in turn, guide our reading of the Bible and subsequent theological reflection. I believe these intuitions provide invaluable (though obviously not infallible) guides for reading and interpreting morally problematic texts, thereby helping us to understand which possible readings of the Canaanite conquest are, and are not, defensible.

The starting point is to come to terms with precisely what kind of moral action is being described in the text. In order to grasp the implications of the Canaanite conquest, in chapter 6 I will develop an extended model for moral reflection based on a closely analogous modern case of genocide, that of Rwanda in 1994. Just as concrete reflection on the experience of an actual stoning victim like Soraya M. provides invaluable insight into the moral status of stoning as a mode of capital punishment, so concrete reflection on the Rwandan genocide will provide invaluable insight into the prospect that God commanded similar genocidal actions in ancient Canaan as a way to secure the land and protect the moral integrity of God's people. And just as our visceral response to the wrongness of stoning provides powerful *prima facie* evidence that action of this type is intrinsically wrong, so that much more will it be the case that our moral intuition categorically condemns the targeted mass civilian slaughter that occurred in Rwanda.

This will bring us to the second part of my methodology in chapter 7 wherein I will seek to outline a theological-hermeneutical lens by way of five moral principles. Collectively these principles will aim to guide our reading of texts which appear to violate our most basic moral deliverances. They include the following:

1. **Perfect God Principle**: the Bible is the product of a perfect God;
2. **Two Authors Principle**: every biblical text has both a human author with human authorial meaning (that which we refer to as the 'literal sense') and a divine author (i.e. God) and the divine meaning (that which we refer to as the 'plenary sense'); while these two senses may be identical, they may also differ and to the extent that they do differ, the divine plenary sense is the controlling and authoritative sense of the passage and the one by which the literal sense should be understood;
3. **Canon Principle**: the entire biblical text should be interpreted as a unified whole such that some individual texts within the entire canon should be interpreted in light of other texts which serve as interpretive control passages; one identifies which texts should serve as control passages by way of a careful theological interpretation of the whole canon, its meaning and purpose;
4. **Jesus Principle**: the primary control texts for interpreting all of Scripture, including morally problematic violence like the Canaanite conquest, are those that comprise the life and teachings of Jesus;
5. **Love Principle**: in light of the Jesus Principle, all texts should

be interpreted in such a way that they increase the love of God and neighbor; consequently, any reading of a text which diminishes love of God and/or neighbor (e.g. by encouraging the dehumanization and othering of particular groups) should be rejected as an incorrect reading of the passage.

Once we have established our method of intuitive moral reflection based on a concrete case and our five basic hermeneutical principles, we can turn to evaluate the four main responses to the Canaanite conquest.

In Chapter 8 we meet the Genocide Apologists. These folk accept that these are historically accurate narratives and that God commanded actions which would qualify as genocide by legal definition and the Israelites carried out those actions against the Canaanites. Since God commanded those actions, it follows that at least in some circumstances, genocide may be a morally laudable and even obligatory action.

Chapter 9 is devoted to the Just War Interpreters. This group agrees with the Genocide Apologists that these texts are historically accurate accounts of God sending his people to conquer Canaan; however, they insist that 'genocide' is an incorrect description of the actions described in Deuteronomy and Joshua and that when these passages are read properly, it becomes clear that they more closely approximate the standards of just war.

Chapter 10 introduces us to the Spiritualizers, a group that expresses skepticism about (if not rejecting outright) the moral justification of these actions; as a result, Spiritualizers commonly reject the claim that God ever commanded such actions or that the Israelites ever carried them out. Instead, they propose that these narratives are best interpreted by way of a plenary spiritual message consistent with the revelation of Jesus that can be derived from a careful reading attendant to the deeper meaning of the narratives.

In Chapter 11 we meet our final group: the Providential Errantists agree with the Spiritualizers that one cannot defend the morality of the texts when read as historical and thus that one must deny the historical reference. While they are open to finding spiritual meaning in the plenary sense in the manner suggested by the Spiritualizers, Providential Errantists also emphasize the importance of developing a moral critique of the literal sense, while recognizing that this very act places the reader in a prophetic engagement with Scripture which serves the end of becoming like Jesus and loving God and neighbor.

My sympathies in this book lie with the Providential Errancy approach supplemented with key insights gleaned from the Spiritualizers. However, this book is less about proposing a simple solution to the problem than it is about rejecting the shared approach of the Genocide Apologists and Just War Interpreters. As I see it, our moral intuitions demonstrate how *not* to read these texts while leaving open or indeterminate the question of how precisely we *should* read them. The key, thus, is to seek to develop plausible interpretations consistent with our moral intuitions and the formative spiritual ends of Scripture and I believe the space explored by the Spiritualizers and Providential Errantists together provides the best way forward.

Finally, I will conclude the book in chapter 12 by considering the problem of miscommunication. If, as I claim, the purpose of the Bible is to cultivate disciples of Jesus who love God and neighbor, why does the biblical text offer so much room for errant interpretation in the first place? In short, isn't it a problem that seemingly reasonable people ranging from the untutored layperson to the sophisticated scholar can read these passages and end up believing that God really did command genocide? And if it is, doesn't that entail that the Bible *fails* in the transformative ends for which God allegedly purposed it? I believe this is an important issue and so I shall conclude the book by suggesting some thoughts in response.

This book does not seek to provide a definitive answer to all the questions one might have about biblical violence generally or even the Canaanite conquest, in particular. The truth is that I don't believe there is any one simple solution for these difficult topics. On the cover of my previous book, *Conversations with My Inner Atheist*, I quoted the great physicist Richard Feynman: "I would rather have questions that can't be answered than answers that can't be questioned." That sentiment describes this book as well. We need to ask some hard questions, even if we aren't entirely satisfied with all the answers we find. Through it all, I trust one thing will become clear: the attempt to defend moral atrocities by a stentorian invocation of 'God's law' is not the end of conversation. Rather, it is only the beginning.

1

Killing the Joneses:
Coming to Terms with Biblical Violence

For more than fourteen centuries, if you were traveling in the isolated Bamyan Valley in northwest Afghanistan, you would come upon two stunning statues of the Buddha carved into the side of a cliff. At 38 meters, the Eastern Buddha towered over the surrounding valley while the Western Buddha reached an even higher 55 meters, the equivalent of a 13 story building. For more than a millennium, the Bamyan Buddhas stood as a majestic monument to devout religious conviction. However, the centuries-old history of those revered statues came to an abrupt end in early March 2001 when these monuments to religious devotion were unceremoniously dynamited into rubble and dust by the Taliban.[8] Since then, the debris of these once glorious icons has provided a tragic monument to another kind of devout religious conviction, one that expresses itself in violent intolerance and destruction.

---

8 "Cultural Landscape and Archaeological Remains of the Bamiyan Valley," UNESCO, https://whc.unesco.org/en/list/208/

Christians in the West joined a universal chorus in condemning the appalling, intolerant actions of the Taliban. The fact is, however, that I suspect few of those Christians paused to reflect on the fact that the Bible itself records God issuing commands for the destruction of competing religious cultural expressions of their day, commands which would be very much in line with the actions of the Taliban: "Break down their altars, smash their sacred stones and cut down their Asherah poles." (Exodus 34:13)[9] Just as the Taliban viewed Buddhism in their region as a dangerous affront to proper piety, so apparently did the ancient Israelites view the competing religions of their day. One can only imagine what they might have done to a 55 meter Buddha.

A religious impulse that can fuel frenzied violence against the sacred cultural products of another belief community is distressing enough. It is even more disturbing when that impulse to exterminate shifts from the cultural products to the civilian populations of those religious communities. Think back to the last time you heard in the news of a suicide bombing in the Middle East: shop keepers, diners, and people just out for an evening stroll and in a moment blown to bits by a terrorist seeking to promote a particular cause. Were you not immediately appalled? Did you need a moment to consider the circumstances before you rendered your moral condemnation of the bomber's actions? When a terrorist detonates a bomb at a busy marketplace in Baghdad or Jerusalem, the action rightly receives a universal chorus of condemnation. Yet, while Christians in the West often associate such actions with Islam, as Philip Jenkins points out, the Qur'an actually offers no precedent for suicide bombing, as such. If you want to find a religious text providing a justification for this type of action, you need to turn to the *Bible*, and specifically the story of Samson killing himself in an

---

[9] Jenkins, *Laying Down the Sword: Why We Can't Ignore the Bible's Violent Verses* (HarperOne, 2011), 69.

act intended to inflict maximal carnage and terror on the civilian population of the Philistines while they are gathered for a public celebration (Judges 16:23-31). As Jenkins provocatively asks, "Could a text offer better support for a modern-day suicide attack, in Gaza or elsewhere?"[10]

It seems to me that the Christian who criticizes the violence of Islam and the Qur'an has not yet learned the lesson that he who lives in a glass house should not throw stones. From pelting an allegedly unfaithful wife to death with rocks to destroying the icons and implements of another religious culture to suicide bombing, the Bible provides a potential source of justification for all manner of overtly violent behaviors, actions which stand in profound, deep tension with ostensibly Christian devotion to the peaceable savior.

As disturbing as all these instances of violence are, however, arguably the very worst example of biblical violence and thus the one that presents the starkest challenge to the Christian resides in divinely commanded and approved actions that appear to target entire civilian populations *in toto* for violent displacement and outright destruction. If we really want to get our arms around the problem in its darkest manifestation, it will be here. And so it is on this specific topic that we will focus going forward. If we can make sense of passages that target civilian populations for expulsion and destruction, we will likely be well on our way to addressing other instances of biblical violence as well.

Even with this limited focus we cannot give the same detailed attention to all the biblical war texts that inflame our moral sensibilities. But before we narrow our scope further, we can at least take note of a couple of other significant and very disturbing cases. These include the Bible's profoundly troubling description of the hated Amalekites culminating in 1 Samuel 15. In verse 3 Yahweh speaks through Samuel to command King Saul to destroy every last Amalekite, man and woman, child and infant.

---

10 Jenkins, *Laying Down the Sword: Why We Can't Ignore the Bible's Violent Verses*, 7.

Saul is then described as faithfully carrying out this command with one exception: he spares the king. Incredibly, the moral problem within the narrative is not that Saul slaughtered children and infants but rather that after doing so he failed to *finish the job* by killing King Agag as well. Enter Samuel who indignantly takes matters into his own hands. And so, as we read in the admirably straightforward KJV, Samuel "hewed Agag in pieces before the LORD in Gilgal" (1 Samuel 15:33) as if he were piling a grisly stack of human cordwood.

One other case worthy of our attention should be noted here and it is the shocking fate faced by the Midianites in Numbers 31. The stage is set in Numbers 25:8 when Phineas, grandson of Aaron the priest, consumed by religious fervor and outrage at the Israelites cavorting with Midianite women, summarily enters the tent of an Israelite man and plunges a spear through the man and the stomach of his female companion. This horrific human shish kabob is lauded as a pious act, one sufficiently grisly to avert God's fury. Fast-forward to Numbers 31 where we read that Yahweh directs the Israelites to massacre all the Midianite men, boys, and women, actions that certainly appear to qualify as genocidal. But what sets this text apart for especial ignominy is the fact that Moses then directs the Israelite soldiers to spare the virgin Midianite girls for their own use (verse 18). The irony is striking: shortly before this, Midianite women are presented as dangerously scurrilous seducers of Israelite men. But apparently that threat does not extend to the nubile Midianite virgins.

In addition to the manifold other moral problems presented by Numbers 31, the specter of sexual assault hangs over it all. It hardly needs to be pointed out that when a man comes into your tent, massacres your father, mother, and brother, and then demands that you become his bride, there is no such thing as *consent*. It is very difficult to avoid the implication that Numbers 31 takes us right up to the threshold of divinely sanctioned *rape*. To put this scene into contemporary context, one may draw an obvious, and profoundly disturbing parallel with Boko Haram, the Jihadist terrorist group that is notorious for invading villages in northern Nigeria, massacring civilians, and kidnapping young girls. Once again, we find the Bible providing a disturbing template for some of the greatest moral outrages of our own day.

The horrors inflicted on the Amalekites and Midianites should disturb any reader with a functioning moral conscience. But arguably the most infamous Israelite attack of all is that which is visited upon the Canaanites. And this will be our focus throughout the remainder of the book. In particular, we will keep in mind Deuteronomy 7:1-6 and 20:10-18, two passages that outline the divine will and directives, as well as the summary of the conquest itself in Joshua 1-12 with special attention to the entry to Canaan culminating in the destruction of Jericho in chapter 6.

Getting rid of the Joneses

Going forward, it would make sense to begin by getting the specific texts before us. So let's start with the divine directives that God provides in Deuteronomy 7:1-6:

> When the Lord your God brings you into the land you are entering to possess and drives out before you many nations—the Hittites, Girgashites, Amorites, Canaanites, Perizzites, Hivites and Jebusites, seven nations larger and stronger than you— [2] and when the Lord your God has delivered them over to you and you have defeated them, then you must destroy them totally. Make no treaty with them, and show them no mercy. [3] Do not intermarry with them. Do not give your daughters to their sons or take their daughters for your sons, [4] for they will turn your children away from following me to serve other gods, and the Lord's anger will burn against you and will quickly destroy you. [5] This is what you are to do to them: Break down their altars, smash

their sacred stones, cut down their Asherah poles and burn their idols in the fire. ⁶ For you are a people holy to the Lord your God. The Lord your God has chosen you out of all the peoples on the face of the earth to be his people, his treasured possession.

Thomas W. Mann characterizes the passage as follows: "What Moses recommends is not simply 'keeping apart from the Joneses'; rather, it is getting rid of the Joneses in order to remove the temptation of 'the world.' Canaanite culture is a threat to faith, and thus to life itself."[11] Indeed, in this striking passage, Yahweh provides the directions to Israel as they prepare to enter into Canaan. They are to maintain their purity and avoid being corrupted by the peoples who now occupy the land. To ensure this purity, they need to undertake a shockingly unrestricted policy of total violence against the enemy, one in which Israel seeks to "destroy them totally" and "show them no mercy." The language of total destruction derives from the Hebrew word *herem*, a technical term referring to the complete devotional destruction of objects that are given to the deity. One may commit material objects to the *herem* and indeed that is suggested in verse 5. However, the language does not stop there but instead extends the targeted eradication to human beings and indeed entire societies. The language appears to exhibit both a deep devotion to Yahweh and a profound fear of contamination from the outsider. Indeed, by contemporary standards this kind of fear of corruption by the other would look positively xenophobic. To sum up, as Brueggemann observes, "By any stretch, the modern reader is sure to find this language deeply offensive and problematic."[12]

Our second passage is in Deuteronomy 20:10-18. At this

---

11 Thomas W. Mann, *Deuteronomy* (Westminster John Knox Press, 1995), 65.

12 Walter Brueggemann, *Deuteronomy*, Abingdon Old Testament Commentaries (Abingdon Press, 2001), 94.

point, Yahweh provides detailed outlines for treating two different groups, the tribes near the Promised Land (10-15) and the tribes *within* the Promised Land (16-18):

> ¹⁰ When you march up to attack a city, make its people an offer of peace. ¹¹ If they accept and open their gates, all the people in it shall be subject to forced labor and shall work for you. ¹² If they refuse to make peace and they engage you in battle, lay siege to that city. ¹³ When the Lord your God delivers it into your hand, put to the sword all the men in it. ¹⁴ As for the women, the children, the livestock and everything else in the city, you may take these as plunder for yourselves. And you may use the plunder the Lord your God gives you from your enemies. ¹⁵ This is how you are to treat all the cities that are at a distance from you and do not belong to the nations nearby.
>
> ¹⁶ However, in the cities of the nations the Lord your God is giving you as an inheritance, do not leave alive anything that breathes. ¹⁷ Completely destroy them—the Hittites, Amorites, Canaanites, Perizzites, Hivites and Jebusites—as the Lord your God has commanded you. ¹⁸ Otherwise, they will teach you to follow all the detestable things they do in worshiping their gods, and you will sin against the Lord your God.

There is a striking contrast between the treatment of the neighboring tribes and those living within the land. The offer to the neighboring tribes looks bleak for the only options are total surrender in which case the Israelites will enslave all the men, women, and children, or fight back, an action which will assuredly result in defeat followed by the Israelites' slaughter of all the men and enslavement of all the women and children.[13] As harsh as those terms may be, that offer looks positively benevolent when

---

13 To put this into context, imagine today if China invaded Taiwan and gave the island nation two options: full surrender and enslavement or the massacre of all the men of Taiwan followed by the enslavement of women and children.

compared to the lot of the tribes living *within* the land. In this case, God gives the Israelites one directive: "do not leave alive anything that breathes." Instead, "Completely destroy them". As with Deuteronomy 7:2, the central term is the Hebrew *haram*, to destroy. Thus, the command is absolute: annihilate every living being, human and animal, as you seize the land.

Once again, the putative motivation for this shocking, categorical destruction is to maintain the purity of the Israelites. If the Canaanites are not destroyed, they will continue to pose an ominous threat as they may teach the Israelites false things and potentially dilute their witness or lead them away from their mission. Consequently, in this passage the primary directive is to protect the Israelites from contamination. The neighboring tribes are not a direct influence on the Israelites and so they may be spared, albeit as slaves. But the nearby nations must be completely butchered to ensure that they do not woo the Israelites away from their mission and entice them with false gods. Brueggemann suggests that the warning of verse 18 signals a move from the slaughter as simply evincing an act of devotion to manifesting "a pragmatic step by an exceedingly anxious community to eliminate all threats and seductions that might provide an alternative to YHWH."[14]

We should also note that immediately following these shockingly absolute directives, Yahweh then specifically directs the Israelites in verse 19 to spare the trees, because "Are the trees people, that you should besiege them?" The logic is impeccable, the environmental concern admirable. But one could have wondered why the same logic and concern could not, at least, have been extended to Canaanite livestock, infants and small children.

As you can imagine, such an extraordinarily harsh ultimatum would hardly be viewed as a benevolent concession by the Taiwanese or anyone else.

14 Brueggemann, *Deuteronomy*, 212.

The Conquest to Jericho

As the story picks up in Joshua, Moses has just passed away and the Israelites prepare to take the land that God promised to them (Joshua 1:1-6). Their preparation consists of careful meditation day and night on the book of the Law (v. 8) in order to ensure that their hearts are prepared for battle. Next, we read that two spies enter the land to scope out their target and visit the home of Rahab the Prostitute.[15] Rahab tells the spies that she recognizes the LORD is taking the land because all the people are melting in fear (2:9) given the Israelites' spectacular escape from Egypt and the fact that they subsequently committed the kings of the Amorites—Sihon and Og—to the complete destruction of the *herem*. Rahab is clearly a pragmatist and a survivor and so once she has identified the winning side, she pleads with the spies to spare her family—father, mother, brothers, sisters, and those who live with them—when the Israelites come to destroy Jericho (2:12-13). The spies agree to this bargain and they settle on the sign of a scarlet rope in Rahab's window to ensure that the family cowering inside is spared from the mass carnage that will soon be visited on the entire population of the city.

As the army prepares for the invasion, Joshua says "This is how you will know that the living God is among you and that he will certainly drive out before you the Canaanites, Hittites, Hivites, Perizzites, Girgashites, Amorites and Jebusites." (3:10) Notably, this language of *driving out* the seven tribes from the land contrasts with the command of total eradication recorded in Deuteronomy 7:2 and 20:16-17. The reader might reasonably wonder: which is it? Are the Israelites called to slaughter every living thing or to drive every living thing out of the land?

---

15 Incidentally, there is no shortage of irony that this suggestive story, rich with sexual innuendo, has assumed a relatively high profile in the Sunday school canon of conservative evangelicals. See Jerome Creach, *Joshua,* Interpretation (John Knox Press, 2003), 32.

The army is told to be consecrated (3:5) in preparation for battle. The entire framework of the unfolding events—meditation on the Law, consecration, the Ark preceding the Israelites into battle—drives home the overtly religious/cultic context. This is a form of holy war, of battle as *worship*. Next, they cross the Jordan after a miraculous halt in the flow of water—a sign that God is with them—and continue on as war fervor builds with approximately forty thousand soldiers amassing for battle on the plains of Jericho (4:13). At that point, we receive a glimpse of the psychological terror that is beginning to grip the residents of Canaan as they witness the advancing threat: when the Amorite and Canaanite kings learn of this miraculous crossing, "their hearts melted in fear and they no longer had the courage to face the Israelites." (5:1)

God then commands the circumcision of the Israelite soldiers which is, to say the least, a rather unconventional method of battle preparation (5:2-10). This act both highlights the cultic backdrop of the battle and the consistent theme that it is *God* who is the primary agent of victory. At that point, we read of a particularly mysterious encounter when Joshua meets a mysterious man with sword in hand. When asked if he is with Israel or the Canaanites, the man replies "Neither, but as commander of the army of the Lord I have now come" (5:14). The message could not be clearer: God will be with the Israelites but it is God's battle not theirs and their victory is found as they submit to the divine will. This mysterious being then commands Joshua to remove his sandals for the land where he stands is holy (5:15). Once again, the impending conflict is presented as a holy act of worship.

The Israelites arrive at the famed walls of Jericho and it becomes clear (if it wasn't already) that this is *God's* battle. The soldiers are directed to carry out another unconventional battle plan by marching around the city for six days coupled with the ceremonial blowing of their trumpets. On the final day, Joshua directs them:

"Shout! For the Lord has given you the city! [17] The city and all that is in it are to be devoted to the Lord. Only Rahab the prostitute and all who are with her in her house shall be spared, because she hid the spies we sent. [18] But keep away from the devoted things, so that you will not bring about your own destruction by taking any of them. Otherwise you will make the camp of Israel liable to destruction and bring trouble on it.

At that point, the walls miraculously collapse and the Israelites faithfully carry out these directions: "They devoted the city to the Lord and destroyed with the sword every living thing in it—men and women, young and old, cattle, sheep and donkeys." (6:21) Rahab and her family, however, are spared.

The story carries on with the ill-fated attack on Ai, the killing of Achan and his family and the subsequent destruction of Ai (chapters 7-8), the trickery of the Gibeonites as they succeed in making a pact with Israel that spares their lives (9), the defeat of five Amorite kings in a great battle with a supernaturally extended day (10), and the defeat of the southern and northern kings (10-11).

Conclusion

God commands the enslavement of those in bordering nations and the utter eradication of the people that live in the Promised Land. They are to be committed to the *herem*, that act of setting apart for utter destruction. Once again, the battle is framed in a religious cultic context, one that has been variously described as *Holy War, Yahweh War* or simply *total war*. Regardless, it is a uniquely brutal type of battle and throughout, the emphasis is on the fact that it is the might of Yahweh that accomplishes this destruction. While Joshua does exhibit some military strategy (as in the defeat of Ai), victory is not attributed to Israel's military brilliance, a point made clear by their unconventional methods. Rather it is due to their submission to the will of God: always and throughout, it is God who accomplishes the victory.

I have taken some time to (re)familiarize us with the overall religious-cultic and devotional context of the conquest of Canaan. But of course, for our purposes, the most important factor to note is that which is referenced in the text only in passing. We read that in faithful fulfillment of the directives of Deuteronomy 7 and 20, entire populations of Canaanite settlements, including civilians, are consigned to destruction. As noted above, the narrator of Joshua is restrained in his description: "They devoted the city . . . and destroyed with the sword every living thing in it—men and women, young and old, cattle, sheep and donkeys." (6:21) Nonetheless, the message is unequivocal.

The less time we invest in reflecting on the full implications of the events of that bloody day in Jericho and the other conflicts that constitute the conquest of Canaan, the easier it is to accept the story as written and move on. Conversely, the more time we invest in understanding what those actions looked like on the ground, the more difficult the problem becomes that lies before us. If I may state the matter bluntly, it is far easier to eat a beef burger if you don't look in the slaughterhouse. And it is far easier to accept the directives of Deuteronomy and the narrative of Jericho at face value if we don't take a closer look at the implications of what, precisely, is being proposed.

But we cannot afford to keep the text at arms-length any longer. We cannot afford to look away. We shall have to look closer. The moral imperative of the text and our own moral integrity as readers demand nothing less.

2

Joshua and the International Criminal Court

If we are going to grapple properly with the moral challenge presented by the Israelite conquest of the Canaanites, we shall need to begin with the correct terminology to frame the discussion. There are two terms that are commonly thrown around in contemporary discussion of biblical violence: 'genocide' and 'ethnic cleansing'. Unfortunately, people rarely pause to grapple with the precise legal definitions of these terms and thus to clarify their applicability to this context. With that in mind, this chapter is devoted to identifying the proper legal definitions to guide us going forward. It is also important to keep in mind that even though the legal terms are modern (the concept of genocide dates to the 1940s, that of ethnic cleansing to the 1990s), it is nonetheless perfectly appropriate to apply them retrospectively. For example, the Turkish 1915 assault on the Armenian people is commonly (and properly) classed as genocide.[16] Indeed, if retrospective application were not appropriate, one would not

---

16 See, for example, John Kifner, "Armenian Genocide of 1915: An Overview," *The New York Times* https://archive.nytimes.com/www.nytimes.com/ref/timestopics/topics_armeniangenocide.html?mcubz=1

be able to apply the term to the Holocaust, and that would be absurd given that this was the very event that provided the original catalyst for the formulation of the concept.

Genocide

Raphael Lemkin was an ethnically Jewish Polish lawyer who lost close to fifty relatives in the Holocaust. While the Final Solution involved the killing of millions of individuals, Lemkin observed that the primary goal was not simply the destruction of European Jews but of *European Jewry* as such. In other words, the target was not simply a group of *individuals* but also the group identity itself. Horrified by the Final Solution and recognizing that it entailed a uniquely offensive action deserving of clear and unqualified censure, in 1944 Lemkin proposed a new term to identify this action: genocide. He coined the neologism by combining the Greek noun *genos* (race; kin) with the Latin suffix *cida* (one who kills) to refer to one who attempts to kill/destroy a particular group identity within the human population.[17]

Lemkin's insight that genocide is a unique action requiring specific moral and legal censure was profound, the implications far reaching. The singular nature of genocide is described by a survivor of the Rwandan horror named Edmond who sagely observed, "An animal will kill, but never to completely annihilate a race, a whole collectivity. What does this make us in this world?"[18] Edmond is correct: there is something especially disturbing and vicious about this uniquely human attempt to eradicate group identity. Blaise Pascal famously described human

---

17 Jenkins notes that the closest conceptual antecedent to genocide is the concept of *extirpation*. *Laying Down the Sword*, 113, 118, 127.

18 Cited in Philip Gourevitch, *We Wish to Inform You that Tomorrow We Will Be Killed with Our Families: Stories from Rwanda* (Farrar, Straus, & Giroux, 2002), 239.

beings as the glory and refuse of the universe: it is uniquely glorious that human beings have the ability to cultivate distinct religious, national and ethnic group identities and it is uniquely horrific that we can then seek to eradicate those very same identities *in toto*. That was what prompted Lemkin to seek formal recognition of this disturbing action in international law.[19] After several years of tireless lobbying, that recognition finally came in 1948 when, at the *Convention on the Prevention and Punishment of the Crime of Genocide*, the United Nations adopted the following definition of genocide in article 2:

> In the present Convention, genocide means any of the following acts committed with intent to destroy, in whole or in part, a national, ethnical, racial or religious group, as such:
>
> (a) Killing members of the group;
>
> (b) Causing serious bodily or mental harm to members of the group;
>
> (c) Deliberately inflicting on the group conditions of life calculated to bring about its physical destruction in whole or in part;
>
> (d) Imposing measures intended to prevent births within the group;
>
> (e) Forcibly transferring children of the group to another group.[20]

---

19 See Samantha Powers, *A Problem from Hell: America and the Age of Genocide* (Basic Books, 2013), chapters 3-4.

20 "Convention on the Prevention and Punishment of the Crime of Genocide," United Nations, https://www.un.org/en/genocideprevention/documents/atrocity-crimes/Doc.1_Convention%20on%20the%20Prevention%20and%20Punishment%20of%20the%20Crime%20of%20Genocide.pdf

It is important to note that while genocide is commonly equated with the act of mass killing, actions of mass killing are, of themselves, neither necessary nor sufficient for genocide.[21] Given that the primary nature of this crime is the attempt to eradicate an *identity*, *any* concerted actions which involve the attempt to eradicate that identity may qualify as genocidal. This could include, for example, the attempt to prevent births within the group by way of forced sterilizations or the forcible removal of children from the group so that they do not learn the culture and language of the group.[22]

We should also keep in mind that we should not think of ethnic, national, and religious markers too narrowly. One of the most infamous genocides of the twentieth century, that which was carried out under the Khmer Rouge of Cambodia and which resulted in the death of approximately two million people, primarily targeted an intelligentsia class, even going to the absurd length of identifying the target group as those who wore glasses.[23]

Ethnic Cleansing

While the term 'ethnic cleansing' has also occupied much discussion in recent years, it is a comparatively modern term which

---

21 As we will see later, this is an oft misunderstood point which is evident when, for example, Christians attempt to deflect charges of genocide by saying that not all Canaanites were killed. Mass killing (let alone total eradication) is not necessary for the charge of genocide.

22 The latter point is the primary basis for the charge that the infamous effort of the Canadian government to separate First Nations children from their families and culture by placing them in residential schools constitutes a genocide.

23 For a powerful and harrowing depiction of the Cambodian genocide, see the 2017 film *First They Killed My Father*.

only entered common usage in the early 1990s during the conflict in Yugoslavia. While the term as yet lacks a formally recognized legal definition, Klejda Mulaj provides a working definition of the term in common use which will provide a good starting point for reflection.[24] Mulaj writes:

> Ethnic cleansing is considered to be a deliberate policy designed by, and pursued under, the leadership of a nation/ethnic community or with its consent, with the view to removing an "undesirable" indigenous population of a given territory on the basis of its ethnic, national, or religious origin, or a combination of these by using systematically force and/or intimidation.[25]

The first thing to note is that ethnic cleansing is defined in terms of a 'top-down' policy dimension which is not necessarily present in cases of genocide. In other words, ethnic cleansing is typically understood to be a state-based, or at least state-supported, effort. That said, such a stipulation should not be considered necessary. For example, if guerillas without state authority undertake a policy of seeking to displace an indigenous population, it would also qualify as ethnic cleansing. Indeed, the United Nations appeals to a working definition of ethnic cleansing as the action of ". . . *rendering an area ethnically homogeneous by using force or intimidation to remove persons of given groups from the area.*"[26]

---

[24] Mulaj is a senior lecturer at the Institute of Arab and Islamic Studies at the University of Exeter and did extensive doctoral research on the cases of ethnic cleansing in the Balkans in the 1990s. Thus, she is one uniquely qualified to speak to the issue.

[25] Mulaj, *Politics of Ethnic Cleansing: Nation-State Building and Provision of Insecurity in Twentieth-Century Balkans* (Lexington, 2008), 4.

[26] "Ethnic Cleansing," United Nations-Office on Genocide Prevention and the Responsibility to Protect, https://www.un.org/en/genocideprevention/ethnic-cleansing.shtml

This definition does not require that the actions are undertaken by a recognized governmental authority.

To return to Mulaj's definition, the primary goal in ethnic cleansing is to remove a people from a geographic territory and while this may include killing members of the targeted group, as with genocide it also encompasses other means to remove them from the territory. And as with genocide, the group targeted for displacement may be the subject of expulsion not simply because of ethnicity but also because of national and/or religious identity.[27]

Joshua in The International Criminal Court

The terms 'genocide' and 'ethnic cleansing' are valuable for several reasons. First, they provide clear and widely accepted definitions of actions which, as noted, can be applied retrospectively to classify events throughout history. Second, these terms carry a formidable moral weight and concomitant legal and social censure which is appropriate given the morally abhorrent nature of the actions they describe. As such, the suggestion that the actions commanded by God and carried out by the Israelites might be categorized as genocide or ethnic cleansing should deeply disturb any Christian even as it underscores the moral seriousness of the issues at stake.

Within international law, The International Criminal Court (ICC) in The Hague, Netherlands, which commenced operation

---

27 For clarity sake, it would be more accurate to identify a general type action—'land cleansing'—and then classify various sub-variations or tokens such as ethnic cleansing, religious cleansing, class-cleansing, and so on. But a predictable impact of that added clarity would be a weakening of the emotive force of these various ascriptions. As a result, I would prefer to remain with a single imprecise but emotionally weighty term, ethnic cleansing.

on July 1, 2002, has a particular focus on adjudicating crimes against humanity. The ICC court is an intergovernmental body that is devoted to the prosecution of a range of war crimes including genocide and ethnic cleansing. With that in mind, we can frame the issue as follows: if prosecutors brought a case against ancient Israel before the ICC, accusing God's people of crimes against humanity, crimes that included genocide and ethnic cleansing, and if their evidence consisted of the directions provided by God in Deuteronomy 7 and 20 and the conquest account of Joshua 1-12, would the court have sufficient evidence to find the Israelites guilty of the crime?

On a first read, the evidence would seem to be overwhelming, the answer an unequivocal *yes*. The directives God provides in Deuteronomy 7 and 20 provide policy goals that most certainly appear to meet the definition of genocide in its starkest manifestation: killing all members of the group while showing them no mercy and leaving alive nothing that breathes. And as the Israelites are described as carrying out those actions in the conquest narrative, the image of genocide is again clearly confirmed in the description of an entire population being slaughtered at sites like Jericho (Joshua 6:21) and Ai (8:22-24). The text also includes references to God driving out the Canaanites from the land (e.g. 3:10), language that is clearly suggestive of ethnic cleansing. To be sure, our judgment is at this point only provisional. In chapter 9 we will consider the position of the Just War Interpreters who attempt to rebut such readings. But suffice it to say, a cursory survey of the text appears to be very damning, indeed.

This leaves Christians with a very serious problem. As terrible as actions like capital punishment by stoning, cultural destruction, and suicide attacks on civilian populations may be, the most horrific and terrible crimes in international law are actions like genocide and ethnic cleansing. Such actions surely bring us to the nadir of human moral action. And yet, we are expected to believe that the only way that God could establish his perfect people and protect them from outside corrupting influence was to slaughter all the residents of the land they were forcibly seizing? To put it another way, must we believe that the only means by which the one genuine theocracy in history could establish itself in order to become a blessing for the world (Genesis 12:3) was by carrying out divinely commanded actions which qualify under international law as being among the most heinous crimes against humanity?

One of the most surprising facts about this whole awkward situation is that many Christians have never seriously grappled with the weight of this problem. Instead, somehow they have remained mostly oblivious to it. It does not haunt them. It does not keep them up at night. While they have read these stories in the Bible for years, somehow they have never paused to consider how Israel's actions might be evaluated by the ICC let alone how that, in turn, should affect how we think about those actions. This raises a rather important question which should be addressed before we proceed much further: how is it that many Christians manage to keep the moral problems with these texts at a comfortable arms-length? How is it that Christians succeed in reading these texts without coming to grapple with the moral problems that they present?

3

How We Learn *Not* to Read the Text

Growing up, my daughter loved the story of Cinderella. To be more accurate, she loved the Disney film and all the associated merchandise that came with it straight on down to her own Cinderella dress which she would proudly wear at Halloween and on other special occasions.[28] So it was with particular interest that, after purchasing a copy of the famous 1812 collection of fairytales by Brothers Grimm in a used bookstore, I decided to start by reading the original Grimms' version of this beloved story.

The first difference is the name: the German version refers to our protagonist as 'Ashputtel'. However, the thing that most struck me about reading the Brothers Grimm is not merely superficial differences in the names or plot; rather, it was the shocking and often gratuitous violence that saturates these tales, and Ashputtel is no exception. As a case in point, when the prince comes with the glass slipper, the sisters don't merely try to squeeze their foot into the petite Plexiglas pump. Instead, the

---

28 This discussion of Cinderella and Disneyfication is based on Rauser, *What's So Confusing About Grace?* (Two Cup Press, 2017), chapter 20.

one sister resorts to amputating her big toe before she rams in her mangled tootsies. Not to be outdone, the other sister takes a knife and hives off her heel before sliding in her bleeding, de-heeled stump. In each case, the prince only becomes wise to the trickery when he notices dark red blood squirting out of the shoe. Nor are the Brothers Grimm as yet finished with these poor stepsisters. Later, after Ashputtel finds happiness with her prince, the narrator cannot leave well enough alone and instead has some magpies swoop down out of the trees and viciously peck out their eyes. Look, I get it: we want the stepsisters to get their comeuppance. But was that *really* necessary? Suffice it to say, this is not Cinderella as *I* remember it, that's for sure.

When I shared my shocking results from reading the Brothers Grimm with my daughter, we both concluded that the popular Disney version of Cinderella on which we had both been raised had undergone a process of 'Disneyfication', one in which the especially 'Grimm' bits were all hived off the narrative like the stepsister's whittled heel. The result: an inoffensive, eminently marketable all-ages tale.

A Disneyfied Bible

The interesting thing is that those who begin to read the Bible carefully will typically undergo a similar revelation to my experience with the Brothers Grimm: the way that Christians have often been led to understand, contemplate, hear, and read the stories of the Bible is an end product of a complex process rather akin to Disneyfication. The important thing to recognize is that the processes that shape our reading of the Bible come from many directions. Those forces begin to shape how we hear the text when we are very young. And they do so from many different angles, thereby refashioning the biblical narratives into a suitably family friendly mode.

Consider, for example, the children's choir in which my daughter sang when she was young. The most popular number in their setlist, "100% Chance of Rain," was a playful retelling of the flooding of the earth and drowning of all living things at the time of Noah: "It's gonna rain, rain, rain, rain . . . ." Not exactly child-appropriate material, one might think. But then, given that many children grow up with a range of Noah's ark-themed products, perhaps it isn't that surprising. The performers and audience had long been trained to read the narrative without due consideration to the fact that it centers on the horror of mass capital punishment by way of drowning, which is by any measure a terrible way to die.

To turn back to our present topic, countless Christian youth have been introduced to the horrifying fate of the Canaanites by way of "Joshua Fought the Battle of Jericho," a musical number which has travelled far from its origins as a nineteenth century spiritual expressing the longing of slaves for freedom. When my daughter was young, she was introduced to the song by watching a music video performed by a children's group named 'Cedarmont Kids.' The video features children marching around a fortress made of foam colored bricks as they wield their toy spears. Eventually, the walls are knocked down to gales of laughter and joy. Not surprisingly, no Canaanites ever make an appearance.[29] Presumably, the tear-stained cheeks of terrified civilians pleading for their lives wouldn't fit the ethos of the video.

This practice of retelling exceedingly violent and disturbing Bible stories for a children's audience is so familiar that Christians rarely stop to think about how these narratives are changed when they are radically reedited for popular consumption. Nor do people consider how we shall go about introducing the actual violence of the real narratives at a later date. Instead,

---

29 You can watch the video here: https://www.youtube.com/watch?v=MdQy2l8BegA&ab_channel=CedarmontKids

the reading strategies that are often first invoked in childhood frequently carry on unabated through adulthood thereby perpetually keeping the most troubling moral aspects of the Bible safely at arm's length.

In this chapter, I will briefly summarize four of these common strategies: omission, misrepresentation, distraction, and blunted affect.[30] As you may know, the abbreviation 'OMDB' commonly stands for "over my dead body." You might want to borrow that abbreviation as an acronym for these four strategies, not least because, as we proceed, I hope you will recognize their limitations and become more critically self-aware in your own use of them. As we seek to grasp the function of these strategies, we will gain a fuller understanding as to how Christians often inure themselves and others from the morally problematic content in the Bible. In turn, learning how to identify these strategies will provide an important step in coming to see the depth of the problem before us so that we may learn to read the texts with a new attention to their deep moral complexity.

Omission

The first and perhaps most baldly overt reading strategy is *omission*, a process by which we simply remove, skip or ignore problematic moral content from our relaying of the biblical narrative. For example, we might tell the story of David and Goliath while delicately avoiding the detail that David mutilated Goliath's corpse after he felled the giant (1 Samuel 17:51). Or we exult in Elijah's triumph on Mount Carmel without mentioning the mass slaughter of priests that followed (1 Kings 18:40). Or we delight in the way that God used Esther to save the Israelites from a nefarious attempt at genocide while neglecting to

---

30 This analysis is based upon Rauser, *What's So Confusing About Grace?* 127-29.

mention that the Israelites then received the right to slaughter not only the the men who threatened them but also their wives and children across the empire (Esther 8:11). As with the song "100% Chance of Rain," we share a selected retelling of the Noahic flood which carefully omits any mention of drowning animals or people. And when it comes to Canaan, we describe the Israelites' victory as complete and total. Yet somehow we manage to do so without mentioning a single drop of actual Canaanite blood.

The problem is exacerbated by ministers who studiously avoid dealing with difficult topics. To be sure, that avoidance strategy is understandable: how do you broach the topic of genocide in a twenty minute sermon? As a result, the average pastor who is following their own self-chosen list of topics or books is not likely to spend much time preaching from these passages. To be sure, it isn't that they set out to *ignore* these texts; rather, they will just naturally gravitate to passages that are comfortable and familiar and appear to be more readily preachable. Again, who wants to shoulder the daunting burden of attempting to exposit "Show them no mercy" or "Let nothing that breathes remain alive" for a comfortable suburban congregation?

You might think that matters are better in liturgical churches that follow the Revised Common Lectionary given that the purpose of the lectionary is to guide congregations through the entire counsel of God on a three-year cycle. However, ministers still have the option of deciding which of the weekly passages they will preach. What is more, that three year reading schedule itself is not complete but rather is a partial collection of biblical readings, one which already reflects editorial decisions as to which biblical passages are appropriate for public reading.[31]

The fact is that omissive reading strategies are pervasive in the Christian church. Sometimes omission is a conscious strategy of intentionally deleting or censoring particular biblical passages

---

31 Jenkins, *Laying Down the Sword*, 202-208.

from public or private reading.[32] However, in most cases it consists of an unconscious process of *selective attention* and *confirmation bias* in which readers have unknowingly been trained to read by screening for content that fits particular theological assumptions and interests. In cases like that, it can often be very surprising to discover disturbing moral content in passages that we *thought* we knew. To recall a personal example, when my daughter was being dedicated in church as an infant, my wife and I chose to read from Psalm 139:13-14 which describes God knitting each child in their mother's womb such that they are "fearfully and wonderfully made". In preparation for the service, however, I thought it wise to read the entire psalm. Good call: I will never forget my initial surprise at reading verses 21-22:

> Do I not hate those who hate you, Lord,
> and abhor those who are in rebellion against you?
> I have nothing but hatred for them;
> I count them my enemies.

Despite my familiarity with the psalm generally—I had read it countless times over the years—in all that time I somehow had missed these particular verses. No doubt, I *had* read them, probably many times, but it was equally clear that I had never truly *processed* their content. To read the dark curse of the imprecatory psalmist so close to those familiar verses of God's benevolence and care was a bit of a shock, to say the least.

Omission often occurs in this manner when we simply sidestep problematic moral content. One could see such actions as reflecting a confirmation bias in which we read texts to reinforce our beliefs—such as the belief that God is a loving Father who cares for children—while skipping verses that don't conform to our beliefs—as in the notion that God's disciples ought to hate other people.

---

[32] Jenkins, *Laying Down the Sword*, 198-201.

Again, it should be no surprise that omissive readings are key to keeping the horror of the conquest of the Canaanites at arms-length. When we focus on the faithfulness of the Israelites and rush to apply similar spiritual lessons to ourselves but with nary a thought for the people who were slaughtered in the narrative, we perpetuate the omissive approach that inures the reader from confronting and wrestling with problematic moral content.

Misrepresentation

The strategy of *misrepresentation* occurs when we reframe problematic moral content in the text in a way that illegitimately removes, masks, or otherwise diminishes it. For example, consider again the section in Numbers 31 where Moses directs the soldiers to slaughter men, women, and boys but to keep the young virgins for themselves. As I suggested above, in addition to the horror of mass killing, the capture of virgin girls clearly calls to mind a relationship that we would today call sexual slavery.[33] At the very least, that is a stark concern when we read of Midianite virgin girls who are taken captive after their families are slaughtered. To refer to these terrified children as willing brides is as absurd

---

33 According to the Customary International Humanitarian Law, sexual slavery is defined "as the exercise of 'any or all of the powers attaching to the right of ownership over one or more persons, such as by purchasing, selling, lending or bartering such a person or persons, or by imposing on them a similar deprivation of liberty' combined with the causing of such person or persons 'to engage in one or more acts of a sexual nature'." International Committee of the Red Cross, "Rule 94. Slavery and Slave Trade," *Customary International Humanitarian Law* (IHL), https://ihl-databases.icrc.org/customary-ihl/eng/docs/v1_rul_rule94#:~:text=Under%20the%20Statute%20of%20the,of%20%E2%80%9Cany%20or%20all%20of

and offensive a reframing as to do the same of the terrified girls kidnapped by Boko Haram in northern Nigeria.

When it comes to Jericho, the practice of misrepresentation is evident first in the fact that the act is often described as a *battle*. The term 'battle' suggests a mutuality of combat, but in the encounter with Jericho, at least, there is no mutual combat evident. Rather, the Canaanites are described as being terrified as they lock up their gates and stay in the city (6:1). Meanwhile, Israel prepares for an assault with the aim of slaughtering the entire town. This is a *battle* in the same way that a boy who chases down and then begins assaulting a terrified victim is a *fight*. The truth is that this is a one-sided assault, an invasion, *not* a battle.

The reframing frequently goes much further than this even to the extent of boldly recasting the *Canaanites* as the oppressors. Joshua Ryan Butler presents this audacious perspective when he suggests that the Israelites are like "the weakling who's been getting her lunch money taken every day by the playground bullies."[34] By contrast, he suggests that the real bullies are the Canaanites who were simply living out their lives in their home territory when they were invaded. Butler explains:

> it is almost as if God is intentionally choosing the smallest, weakest, most vulnerable, helpless, and powerless nation he can to demonstrate to the mightiest, wickedest, bloodiest, nastiest powerhouse empires of the day that there is a message he wants to send loud and clear to the ancient world. His message? *"This is who I am!* I am the rightful ruler of the earth, and I stand up for the weak, exploited and oppressed!"[35]

As I said, this is a strikingly bold reframing of the narrative. But

---

34 Joshua Ryan Butler. *The Skeletons in God's Closet: The Mercy of Hell, the Surprise of Judgment, the Hope of Holy War* (Thomas Nelson, 2014), 213.

35 Butler, *The Skeletons in God's Closet: The Mercy of Hell, the Surprise of Judgment, the Hope of Holy War,* 218.

the fact remains that *Israel is presented as having God on their side* while the terrified residents of Jericho are described as utterly helpless to avert their fate. This is *not* a mutual battle, still less one in which the Canaanites are the dominant and bullying aggressors. Rather, it is a wholly one-sided conflict, one which culminates in the attempted eradication of the losers.

Distraction

The third standard device for dealing with morally problematic texts is *distraction*. This approach is exemplified in the practice of invoking general prudential or moral lessons from morally difficult material, often lessons that have only a tangential relationship to the text and which serve to draw attention away from the morally problematic nature of the source material.

The Exodus is an excellent example: readers are rarely troubled by the indiscriminate killing of the firstborn of all Egyptian families, still less by the drowning of the Egyptian army. Instead, the text is read only as an illustration of God's special care for his chosen people and, more generally, a lesson of God's general care for the oppressed as well as his unequivocal defeat of the false gods. All this is well and good, of course, but it leaves unaddressed the moral problems with the narrative. For example, was it really necessary to punish the entire nation, including the poorest of Egyptian families, by pummeling them all with plagues and the death of their children?

When it comes to the Canaanites and Jericho, there are many suggestive lessons to which one might appeal. For example, in a devotional reflection on the passage, Lisa Buffaloe says that Jericho reminds us to look and see what God is doing in the world. The Israelites' defeat of Jericho was unconventional and unexpected: "Not exactly the strategic war plan you'll see used by most generals."[36] But if you pay attention to where God is working, so the lesson goes, you can join him on mission.

Here are some other standard go-to lessons when it comes to Joshua 6:

- **Trust**: The Israelites didn't understand why they had to march around the city for seven days. It didn't make sense in the eyes of the world. But Israel trusted God and he was faithful. We also need to trust God!
- **Devotion**: God told the Israelites to give everything over to him. And they trusted him by doing so. They held nothing back! Do you give everything to God?
- **Care**: The Israelites had nothing, but God gave them a beautiful land in which to dwell. So we can trust God to care for our needs as well.

To be sure, these are all important spiritual truths on their own terms: we *should* pay attention to where God is working; we should trust him, remain devoted to him, and remember that he cares for us and provides for our needs. All this is perfectly true. But we should also recognize that these various general spiritual truths may function to distract the reader from the horrifying detail of a civilian population being slaughtered *in toto*. In this way, the reader is effectively insulated from the troubling aspects of the text and the substantive moral reflection which might've been occasioned by a more honest reading.

Blunted Affect

I refer to the final common strategy as *blunted affect*. In this case, the problematic moral content is simply presented to the

---

36 Lisa Buffaloe, *Living Joyfully Free Devotional* (Westbow Press, 2015), 166.

reader/listener in a mundane, straightforward manner without flagging the fact that it is indeed shocking and naturally invites a properly strident and indignant moral response from the reader. In *A People's History of the United States,* Howard Zinn gives an excellent example of what I am calling blunted affect. Zinn refers to the popular 1954 book by Harvard historian Samuel Eliot Morison: *Christopher Columbus, Mariner.* Morison writes, "The cruel policy initiated by Columbus and pursued by his successors resulted in complete genocide."[37] Zinn then comments that this extraordinarily revealing single sentence is "on one page, buried halfway into the telling of a grand romance."[38] Notably, Zinn points out that Morison does not *lie* about the past: on the contrary, he correctly labels Columbus' actions with the harsh and all-too-accurate word 'genocide'. All well and good: however, that does not exonerate Morison's framing of the issue. As Zinn explains,

> he does something else—he mentions the truth quickly and goes on to other things more important to him. Outright lying or quiet omission takes the risk of discovery which, when made, might arouse the reader to rebel against the writer. To state the facts, however, and then to bury them in a mass of other information is to say to the reader with a certain infectious calm: yes, mass murder took place, but it's not that important—it should weigh very little in our final judgments; it should affect very little what we do in the world.[39]

That is the key to blunted affect: present the truth in a straightforward manner without adornment, but do so with "infectious calm": yes, mass murder of the Canaanites took place, a

---

[37] Cited in Zinn, *A People's History of the United States* (HarperPerennial, 2015), 7.

[38] Zinn, *A People's History of the United States*, 7.

[39] Zinn, *A People's History of the United States*, 8.

genocidal attempt to wipe them and their culture from the face of the earth, but it's not that important—it should weigh very little in our final judgments; it should affect very little what we do in the world.

I can't begin to count the number of times I've seen Christians appealing to blunted affect when relaying extraordinarily violent and ethically problematic material in the Bible, material that would shock and appall the reader if encountered in any other context. Often, when people live with stories, concepts, and images for an extended period of time they cease to shock. But one need only step back and reflect anew on precisely what is being proposed for that shock to begin to grip us as it should. For example, I remember as a child hearing a preacher speaking on 2 Kings 19 and blithely describing how the Angel of the Lord had killed 185,000 Assyrians. There was no pause to reflect on the fact that this was enough people to fill a city the size of Burlington, Ontario or Knoxville, Tennessee. The number was simply listed matter-of-factly before we quickly moved on. Here's another example. From childhood, I recall on multiple times hearing this declaration cited as an illustration of the greatness of King David: "Saul has killed his thousands but David his tens of thousands" (1 Samuel 18:7). Alas, no Sunday school teacher or pastor ever paused to point out how problematic it is in our day to measure political greatness by *the number of people one has killed*. The description was simply shared without irony as evidence for the unparalleled greatness of this Israelite king. To borrow Zinn's astute observation, the message conveyed when extreme biblical violence is communicated by blunted affect is that "it's not that important—it should weigh very little in our final judgments."

For the remainder of the chapter I will survey some ways that these strategies are manifested in children and youth and then how they come to fruition in the distorted and even shocking ways that adults sometimes read and process problematic ethical material within the biblical text.

Surveying One Child's Bookshelf

As I said above, the process of cultivating reading strategies begins with the way these stories are communicated in childhood. Personally, I have long wrestled with the ethics of children's Bibles, and in particular the practice of changing narrative content to make it more palatable or age appropriate. The truth is that the Bible itself has more than enough content to warrant the highest adult rating: it is *not* a children's book. Of course, many book publishers have recognized this fact and so they have undertaken age-appropriate editing of the Bible. But those heavily edited, child-friendly retellings of violent and otherwise morally problematic content raise further ethical problems. Can the bombing of Hiroshima or the liberation of Auschwitz meaningfully be edited for children? I'm not so sure. And yet, it would appear that for many Christians the selected passages that result in Disneyfied reading begin in the earliest years and continue throughout childhood with an endless succession of Bibles adapted for young readers.

One does not need to look far for examples of how young Christians learn to employ these reading strategies. I need only turn to my grown daughter's childhood bookshelf. Her first Bible ever was the *Children's Everyday Bible,* a collection of devotional readings for the toddler complete with a different Bible story for every day of the year. The fall of Jericho is the topic of March 10. The short text briefly summarizes a seven day march around the city followed by a trumpet blast and the crumbling of the walls: "When Joshua gave the signal, the people began to shout, and the city walls crashed to the ground."[40] This brief retelling for small children exhibits the methods of omission and misrepresentation by removing all the violence and killing and presenting the story as a mutual battle in which the Israelites trusted God and won (not that we should *want* the details of

---

40 Deborah Chancellor, *Children's Everyday Bible* (DK Publishing, 2002), 79.

an entire town being massacred to be relayed to a four-year-old audience).

When my daughter was in kindergarten, our church gifted her with a copy of *The Picture Bible*. This is a full cartoon version of the Bible and with over three million copies in print, it has been very successful. The target audience for this version ranges from about six-year-olds to teenagers. The story of Jericho begins to take on more details in this version. The narrative begins by building suspense as the Israelites walk around the city while the citizens and soldiers look on in growing apprehension and fear. One soldier looking down from the high wall ominously wonders, "What are they trying to do—work an evil charm on us?"[41] As the walls collapse Joshua raises his sword and yells "Jericho is ours!"[42] Some soldiers then come to retrieve Rahab as one of them explains: "Everything in the city will be destroyed. But you and your family will be safe . . . ." Rahab understandably breathes a sigh of relief: "Thank God!"[43] Next, we see that Jericho has been set aflame. As two Israelite soldiers stoically look on, one reflects, "Soon there will be nothing left of a once powerful city" while the other replies with a somber moral lesson: "It was so wicked that it had to be destroyed or its evil ways would have spread among our people."[44] The clear message—follow God faithfully or be destroyed—comes through by way of this fast-paced and dramatic storytelling. However, while *The Picture Bible* blithely notes that every *thing* in the city will be destroyed, it notably omits the critical detail that every *living human being* will also be destroyed: in short, this version exhibits blunted affect and omission.

In the popular teen devotional *If God Loves Me, Why Can't I Get My Locker Open?*, Lorraine Peterson includes a few devotional

---

41 Iva Hoth, *The Picture Bible* (Faithkidz, 2004), 200.

42 Hoth, *The Picture Bible*, 201.

43 Hoth, *The Picture Bible*, 202.

44 Hoth, *The Picture Bible*, 203.

reflections based on the book of Joshua. She doesn't discuss the familiar story of Jericho but she does address the case of Israel's surprising defeat at the hand of "the little hick town of Ai."[45] Peterson explains that God was teaching Israel a lesson when they lost the battle to this 'hick town': "God used the occasion to point out that Israel had sinned, and Joshua went tribe to tribe until he found the offender, Achan." Okay, so he finds Achan, *and then what?* Peterson doesn't tell us. More specifically, she doesn't say that Achan's sin was that he retained some of the possessions of Ai despite God's command to *haram* all things: human beings, animals, and material goods. Nor does she say that he and his family were then pelted with rocks until they were all dead. Instead, Peterson simply observes that the lesson of the defeat at Ai is that we should remember to depend on God rather than our own abilities: "Don't let pride create an Ai for you. But if you do suffer a defeat, remember there is a road back to victory. You may have lost a game, but Christ in you can still win the championship."[46] In this case, we have a clear example of omission and distraction: the morally troubling problematic details magically disappear from the text only to be replaced by a perfectly practical lesson: "Put your trust in God, not yourself."

When a Christian is raised in this reading tradition, they learn to focus on particular aspects of the narrative while passing by the morally problematic references to the eradication of entire civilian populations. They look to identify particular life lessons or moral principles which, while perhaps legitimate, may serve in this case to distract from the moral problematic of the text. And when all else fails, morally problematic details may be bluntly relayed shorn of appropriate emotional affect lest the reader be inclined to linger on the horrifying carnage.

---

[45] Peterson, *If God Loves Me, Why Can't I Get My Locker Open?* (Bethany House, 2006), 202.

[46] Peterson, *If God Loves Me, Why Can't I Get My Locker Open?*, 202.

The Zeal of Phineas in Devotional Perspective

For those who have been raised with reading strategies that keep the shock and horror of biblical violence at bay, it is no surprise that these same strategies remain operative in adulthood. To consider a particularly stark example, we can turn to a devotional reflection by a pastor named J. Craig Chaffin based on the infamous story in Numbers 25. In this haunting narrative which I referred to earlier, an Israelite named Phineas, outraged at a fellow Israelite man having a relationship with a Midianite woman, impales both of them with a spear. This is the kind of shockingly violent story that would simply be avoided by many Christians. But with the effective use of these reading strategies, even the most horrific stories can readily be mined for spiritual insight without fear of cognitive dissonance.

In his reflection on this ghastly depiction of spontaneous pious impalement, Chaffin takes us back to his senior year in high school. At the time, he recalls, he was taking a leadership course with Campus Crusade for Christ and seeking to mentor a friend: in short, he was on a devout and promising track of spiritual growth and service. Then a beautiful girl from his school invited him to a dance:

> I was stunned. I forgot about doing any kind of spiritual follow-up with my friend. For the next three months all I could think about was her. Three months later when she broke up with me, the full import of what happened dawned upon me. I had been snared by the enemy, who used what seemed good to me to divert my attention off of the Lord.[47]

Did you get that? Chaffin is comparing himself to the spiritually pure Israelites who are seeking to follow Yahweh. Meanwhile,

---

47 J. Craig Chaffin, *Meditations on the Glory of Christ: Genesis Through 2 Chronicles* (Westbow Press, 2014), 149.

he places his former high school girlfriend in the role of the wicked temptress just like the Midianite damsel that was impaled in a flash of pious devotion by Phineas. One cannot help but wonder how that former girlfriend would receive the comparison! Regardless, Chaffin then goes on to praise the zeal of Phineas as a type of Jesus: just as the zeal of pious Phineas that led him to impale the Israelite and his Midianite temptress with his spear deflected God's wrath away from the people, so Jesus' pious action in dying for our sins deflected God's wrath against us. In short, with a warm glow of piety, Chaffin concludes that Jesus is our Phineas: "His zealous act on my/our behalf at the cross has stayed the wrath of the LORD!"[48]

It truly is extraordinary how a horrifying story of spontaneous punitive impalement can be tamed and transformed by these venerable reading strategies into an inspiring tale of Christ's love and our call to follow him in devotion. But that is the power of blunted affect and distraction when they are pressed into service for pious Christian reading.

What if you were to encounter the story of Numbers 25 in a contemporary context? Imagine, for example, that you read in the news of a story where a Muslim man brought his Christian fiancée home to his village in northern Nigeria. Soon after their arrival, an outraged local imam stormed into their engagement party and plunged a spear into both the man and his fiancée. As they lie writhing on the ground, the imam then preached a fierce sermon to the Muslim village about the need to be religiously pure and reject Christian temptresses. Would your response be *that would have been a pious action if the religious identities were reversed?* Or would you reject the act of that zealot outright as an inherently wrong exhibition of xenophobia, misogyny, and utterly immoral violence?

I am very confident that with properly functioning moral intuitions unencumbered by the numbing effect of these venerable

---

48 Chaffin, *Meditations on the Glory of Christ: Genesis Through 2 Chronicles*, 150.

reading strategies, your response would be the latter. Mine most definitely is. That is an example of how powerfully distortng if not *blinding* these reading strategies can be. And that's why we need to strip them away and allow the church to read these texts anew, perhaps for the first time.

4

Moral Intuition and the Divine Will

Imagine that your friend James, a young man who has been very successful in business, tells you one afternoon that God told him to sacrifice his wealth. "What do you mean 'sacrifice'?" you ask curiously. James then explains that God told him to sell all his possessions (including a sizeable home and three cars) and to give the money to the poor. Assuming that you've had no prior concerns about James' mental health you would likely be cautiously open to the possibility that God had indeed spoken in this way. After all, Jesus famously made a request just like that to the Rich Young Ruler (Mark 10:21). Further, Jesus warned of the spiritually deadening impact of riches (Matthew 19:24) and he called us to care for the poor, the weak, and the vulnerable (Matthew 25:31-46). What is more, other Christians throughout history have concluded that God was likewise calling them to such a radical action. For example, Anthony the Great famously became a monk after he believed God called him to give up his considerable wealth and head into the desert.[49] Given

---

[49] Athanasius writes that on the way to church one day Anthony was reflecting how the apostles gave all they had to the early mission of the church. "He

that there is evidence in scripture and history that God has done things like that in the past you could agree in principle that God might do it again. So while you don't yet know that James has been called to this radical action, you think it is certainly a live possibility that he has.

Now imagine another scenario, one in which your friend Tom, a young man with a wife and young child, comes to you one afternoon and tells you that God told him to sacrifice his son. "Uh, what do you mean 'sacrifice'?" you ask nervously. Tom then matter-of-factly explains that God told him to take his son on a camping trip in the woods and to kill and dismember the boy with a carving knife as an act of faith and devotion. Whether or not you previously had any concerns about Tom's mental health, you would definitely have some very serious concerns now. Indeed, upon hearing his plans, you would likely be prepared to contact the authorities and forcibly restrain him from carrying out his grisly plan. One thing you *wouldn't* consider seriously is that God actually did ask Tom to kill and dismember his son as an act of faith and devotion. If you're like most people, you wouldn't give that scenario even a moment's consideration.

Sacrificing Fortunes and Children

What, precisely, is the difference between our cautious openness to James' belief and our strong opposition and incredulity toward Tom's belief? Many Christians will say that the difference lies

---

went into the church pondering these things, and just then it happened that the Gospel was being read, and he heard the Lord saying to the rich man, *If you would be perfect, go, sell what you possess and give to the poor, and you will have treasure in heaven.* It was as if by God's design he held the saints in his recollection, and as if the passage were read on his account." *The Life of Saint Anthony*, trans. Robert C. Gregg, ed. Emilie Griffin (New York: HarperSanFrancisco, nd), 6.

in the testimony of Scripture: the Bible provides the means by which we distinguish between defensible claims about God's will and indefensible ones. For example, Norman Geisler describes Christians who would object morally to the total slaughter of Jericho (Joshua 6:21) as only being concerned about the act insofar as "It seems contrary to God's command not to kill innocent human beings (see Exod. 20:13)."[50] Notably absent from Geisler's account is the rather obvious fact that the reader would just see such actions as *wrong* in a manner *wholly independent* of any biblical precedent. Geisler seems to assume that our moral views are simply derived from the Bible as if our moral judgment on such scenarios is dependent on being aware of a biblical teaching for or against any particular action.

But is that really an accurate description of how Christians reason? Is it really the case that our very different responses to James and Tom can be explained simply in terms of the weight of scriptural precedent for James' action but not for Tom's? If that idea is to be sustained, it must first be the case that James' action has biblical warrant while Tom's action would lack any warrant. Further, it must be the case that, in terms of our actual cognitive processes, that is, our rational evaluation of each scenario, that we formed our beliefs by way of an evaluation of the total sum of relevant biblical data. Thus, according to this scenario, a Christian would first take note of the total number of examples where Jesus warns against riches and calls for love of neighbor. Then she would evaluate all the passages where the Bible addresses devotional child killing. And after seeing strong condemnations in passages like Deuteronomy 12:31, Jeremiah 7:31, and Ezekiel 20:31 she might then conclude based upon the total survey of Scriptural data that while God might've commanded James' action he certainly did not command Tom's.

There are some obvious problems with this analysis. For

---

50 Norman L. Geisler, *The Big Book of Christian Apologetics: An A-Z Guide* (Baker, 2012), 66.

starters, I am quite sure that most Christians lack a sufficiently comprehensive familiarity with all the possibly relevant passages to which one could appeal for and against Tom's claim. And yet, those individuals still confidently reject the child sacrifice suggestion and they are surely justified in doing so. Moreover, for that small minority who would have that comprehensive knowledge, it seems to me that they too wouldn't need to *reason* to the conclusion that child sacrifice is wrong based on the biblical evidence: rather, their response would be immediate and intuitive. In short, it does not appear at first blush that their rejection of Tom's proposal is based on a discursive process reasoning from biblical evidence at all. It appears, rather, to be immediate and intuitive. Finally, such accounts are flatly falsified by the common moral principles that are found throughout the entire human population, including basic knowledge of such moral actions as the rightness of honoring one's parents, caring for the poor and weak, and telling the truth.[51]

Despite these very serious objections to this Biblicist account of moral knowledge, for the sake of argument, I suggest that we try working with its assumptions for a bit. Let's act for the time being as if the Bible were our sole means of evaluating claims of radical divinely commanded sacrifice. And based on that assumption, let's give Tom an opportunity to lay out his reasoning for child sacrifice *from the Bible.* You might be surprised at how much evidence can be marshalled in favor of the claim that God possibly requested a devotional sacrifice of a child just like he might possibly request a devotional sacrifice of a fortune.

So let's rejoin our exchange in progress: "Not so fast, friend," Tom says. "I am aware that there are Bible passages which condemn child sacrifice. But you need to read closer: several of those passages are specifically condemning sacrifices offered to *false*

---

[51] C.S. Lewis famously gathered together a summary of such commonly held beliefs in "Appendix-Illustrations of the *Tao*" in *The Abolition of Man* (Harper Collins, 2000).

gods like Molech. It's quite another thing if you are offering your child to the one true Lord of the universe. Have you not read of Abraham who faithfully offered up his son Isaac in sacrifice in Genesis 22? Due to his faithfulness, Abraham has been lauded in Hebrews 11:17 as a great man of faith for all time."

"Uh, well okay, technically, that is true," you concede, "but remember that it was *never* God's intent that Abraham would go through with the sacrifice."

"Agreed," Tom says. "But that hardly settles the matter for it is still significant that God *asked* him to do it in the first place, even if he never intended for him to follow through. Think about it. Surely it is wrong to command a person to do an intrinsically *evil* act, right? And that doesn't change even if you don't intend for them to carry out that evil act. Like, for example, it would be *wrong* for God to command you to rape a child, because rape is essentially wrong, correct?"

"Yes, of course!" you reply confidently.

"So then," Tom says, "if it is always wrong for you to rape a child, wouldn't it *also* be wrong for God to tell you to rape a child *even if he never ultimately intended for you to carry out the act?*"

You pause for a moment. "That seems right. Yeah, I guess so."

"Good. And I agree: that seems right. If an action is *intrinsically* wrong, then it is also intrinsically wrong to command someone else to do it, even if you ultimately don't intend to let them go through with it. The idea seems to be that asking them to form the *will* to commit an evil act is itself an evil act. For this reason, I think we can know that God would never command Abraham to *rape* a person as a test of faith. But then if God *did* ask Abraham to *sacrifice Isaac* it must follow that child sacrifice is not essentially wrong like rape. The fact that God subjected Abraham to the test shows us that child sacrifice is not itself always wrong: it depends on the conditions under which you're offering your child."

"No, I can't agree with that," you reply heatedly. "You're making way too much of that case. That was an utterly *unique* one-off event. It's not a guide for the rest of us. When God asked Abraham to offer Isaac, he was providing us with a type of Christ, the once for all sacrifice. And note that God then provided a ram for the sacrifice (Genesis 22:14) so that Abraham would not need to offer his son. The point we can't miss is that this looks forward to the time when God would offer his Son as a once-for-all sacrifice (Hebrews 10:12). So for that reason, we can know that we shall never be asked to offer our children."

Tom is shaking his head: he looks completely unmoved. "Let me be clear," he says, "I'm not claiming that I would offer my son as a sacrifice of *atonement*. That wouldn't make any sense since, as you rightly point out, Jesus fulfilled the requirements of the Law. I am simply speaking of a sacrificial *gift*, like a burnt offering, to show my devotion to my Lord. And by the way, just because the offering of Isaac is a type of Christ does not automatically mean that the command that God gives Abraham will never be repeated. After all, Joseph's exile into Egypt followed by his glorious return to his family 'back from the dead' in Genesis 37-50 is also widely interpreted as a type of Christ. And yet, many other followers have since experienced their own exile and return. So the fact that the offering of Isaac was a type of Christ doesn't entitle us to conclude that God will never again ask a man to sacrifice his son as a devotional gift. And you mentioned that Abraham never carried out his sacrifice. True enough. But in Judges 11 we read of the case of Jephthah who faithfully fulfilled a vow to sacrifice his daughter."[52]

"Jephthah?!" you interject. "Whoa, hold on! Now I *really* need to disagree. His vow was a foolhardy one. And the narrator in Judges *never* commends Jephthah's action."

Tom replies without missing a beat, "Neither does the narrator expressly *condemn* it. But more importantly, you neglect to mention that Jephthah is included alongside Abraham in the

---

52 As John Collins writes, "the assumption is that the offering wins the support of the deity." *Does the Bible Justify Violence?*, 6.

great Hall of Faith in Hebrews 11. If the act for which he is best known—the sacrifice of his own daughter—was such a great moral atrocity, do you really believe he would be included in that exemplary list of stalwarts of faith?"

Tom takes a breath and then continues. "And I think you should also consider 2 Kings 3 where we read that Israel is embattled against Moab. Once the Moabites begin to lose the fight, their king offers his firstborn son 'as a sacrifice on the city wall' and right after that 'the fury against Israel was great . . . .' (3:27) It's quite clear in the context that the fury against Israel is related to a deity accepting the sacrifice and fighting for the Moabites. So choose your deity: either Molech exists and he fought the Israelites based on the king's human sacrifice, or the one true God accepted the sacrifice and *he* fought against the Israelites. Either way, some divine being accepted a human sacrifice and turned the battle against the Israelites."

"Look," you reply cautiously, "Molech doesn't exist except maybe as a pathetic demon."

Tom looks skeptical. "So are you saying that a mere demon accepted the human sacrifice, fought for the Moabites, and defeated the armies of Israel? You can't be serious. *That was God's battle to win or lose*. And that must mean that it is God who accepted the king's sacrifice.

"And then there is the act of *herem* killing practiced by the Israelites in which they turn captured possessions, animals, and human beings over to God for destruction. For example, in 1 Samuel 15 we read that God commanded Saul to slaughter all the Amalekites and that included infants. The sacrificial nature of the *herem* killing, or as it is sometimes called, 'the ban,' is clearly illustrated by the fact that in 1 Samuel 15:33 Samuel hews their king into pieces before the Lord much as one would carve up a Christmas turkey. The framework is of a human sacrifice. As scholar Susan Niditch observes, 'deep in the mythological framework of Israelite thought, war, death, sacrifice, the ban, and divine satiation are integrally associated . . . . To dissociate the

Israelite ban from the realm of the sacred and from the concept of sacrifice is to ignore the obvious . . . .'[53] In other words, to commit a human being to the *herem* just is to participate in *human sacrifice*. The evidence is overwhelming, friend: God certainly *does* accept human sacrifices. It looks like in particular circumstances, human sacrifices 'are a fragrant offering, an acceptable sacrifice, pleasing to God.' (Philippians 4:18) And God doesn't simply accept sacrifices as gifts. Sometimes he *commands* them, too. If the Israelites were willing to be faithful and sacrifice other human beings as a gift to God, why can't I?"

"You're making a big mistake," you reply. "While it is true that ancient Israel practiced the *herem*, we need to keep in mind that we are *Christians* and as Christians we need to read the Hebrew Scriptures in light of the coming of Jesus. And surely Jesus doesn't ask you to commit people to the ban. On the contrary, he said that we should love our neighbor. As for inflicting harm on small children, Jesus said the kingdom of God belongs to such as these (Luke 18:16). And he warned that for those who harm a child, it would be better for a millstone to be tied around their neck and for them to be drowned (Matthew 18:6)."

"Not so fast," Tom interjects. "That's *not* what Jesus said. He was warning those who would cause a child to stumble. I'm not causing *any* child to stumble. On the contrary, I'm modeling total devotion to Jesus. That's the best thing I can do for my children's faith! It's a gift to them."

Now you're getting desperate. "What? *No, Tom, that's crazy!* How could your children be inspired by your willingness to kill them? Can you really imagine Jesus calling you to kill your child? Surely you can see that this is just wrong?!"

Tom shoots you a sympathetic look: "No, I don't 'see' that. Don't take offense," he says, "but I think you have an overly romanticized picture of Jesus. Remember that Jesus also told his disciples that they must hate their family (Luke 14:26). He

---

53 Niditch, *War in the Hebrew Bible* (Oxford University Press, 1993), 41.

said that he came to *divide* households (Matthew 10:35-36; Luke 12:51-53). He called his disciples to leave their family for his sake (Matthew 19:29; Mark 10:29-30; Luke 18:29-30)."

Tom pauses for a long moment and stares intently at you. Then, as his eyes fill with tears, he whispers: "Jesus said in Matthew 10:37 that 'anyone who loves their son or daughter more than me is not worthy of me.' That was *me*, my friend! I have loved my little boy so much that I turned him into an idol. I was choosing my boy over my Jesus and that is idolatry, plain and simple. So today when Jesus spoke to me, it became clear what I needed to do: while meditating on that very verse in my devotions, the Lord told me that if I truly love him, I will be willing to sacrifice my child just like Abraham and Jephthah offered up their children. And if I am faithful then I too may be included within his great hall of faith. And so, that is what I will do. It is what I *must* do! Lord, may I be found faithful!"

Debriefing the Child Sacrifice Case

I believe that this exchange illustrates the manifold problems with the Biblicist claim that one's moral condemnation of child sacrifice is derived wholly from the biblical text. While it is true that the voice of the critic in this exchange attempts to corroborate their moral perception with biblical data, the actual reasoning itself originates in a place of moral knowledge that is independent of the Bible. And it is that intuitive moral judgment which leads us in the first place to look for biblical data to vindicate our intuition and to seek to explain scriptural texts that appear to be in conflict with it. Contrary to what Geisler would seem to suggest, you are not simply skeptical of Tom's belief because you've weighed all the relevant biblical texts and found the weight of evidence to support a denial of his claim. Rather, your very engagement with the biblical text itself is already informed by your belief that Tom's proposal constitutes a necessarily immoral action.

Okay, to be honest, I've been a bit presumptuous in assuming I know how you would reason in reaction to Tom's extraordinary claim. Perhaps I am wrong and you are even now shouting at this chapter your disagreement with me. Perhaps you think you actually would reason only with appeal to the weight of the biblical data. If that is the case who am I to say you'd reason otherwise?

Fair enough, but then I will say at the very least, that is not how *I* would reason. Nor do I believe that is how the vast majority of people would reason. As I noted above, people don't need a Bible on their shelf before they will recoil in moral horror at a parent killing their child as a devotional sacrifice. When presented with such unthinkable scenarios, people don't judiciously weigh the claim in light of the sum total of possibly relevant biblical evidence for and against the act before they draw a conclusion. Rather, they make an immediate, intuitive judgment and this judgment then informs how they assess the claim and read the biblical text. In short, they reason from their most basic moral intuitions. As a result, even if a person fails to respond to the many lines of evidence to which a particularly astute individual like Tom might appeal, this would not move them one step toward serious consideration of the claim that God really is calling Tom to hack apart his son as a devotional sacrifice. Rather, however strong their interlocutor's biblical case may seem to be, they will retain their skepticism. Surely, God *could not* be requiring such an action, they will insist. And how can they be so sure? The answer is as simple as it is powerful: because *they can just see that it is wrong.*

To sum up, I submit that it is clear that scripture is *not* our only basis for forming beliefs as to whether God has made a particular command or not. Indeed, it is far from clear that it is even the *primary* source. This is because one's conviction about whether God has in fact commanded Tom to sacrifice his child does not wax and wane depending on the strength of biblical precedent that can be provided for it. Rather, one's moral censure of the action is *independent* of the biblical case and indeed, that moral censure itself provides the impetus to *seek* biblical evidence that is consistent with one's intuitions that God made no such demand to Tom. That, in turn, establishes that our moral sense is not merely a matter of identifying and unpacking biblical texts. Rather, there is an extra-biblical source of moral reasoning that is operative here. But what, precisely, is it?

Moral Intuition and Rational Intuition

If our conviction that God surely did *not* command Tom to sacrifice his son is not derived from a close reading of the Bible, then from where does it derive? The source, it would seem, has to do with that belief-forming process which is sometimes colloquially referred to as *conscience* or a *moral compass*. It is by way of that doxastic (i.e. belief-forming) process that we form beliefs about moral facts including a basic grasp of good and evil and right and wrong. And by that moral perceptual faculty we are able to identify particular actions as *necessarily* morally right and others as *necessarily* morally wrong and still others as *possibly* morally right or wrong depending on additional factors. So, for example, while Tom believes that the act of devotionally killing one's child as an offering to God is *possibly* morally right (i.e. if God has commanded it), powerful moral intuitions support the conclusion that it is *necessarily* wrong (i.e. God could not command it).[54] For that reason, we believe that it could not possibly be a moral praiseworthy or laudatory (let alone *required*)

---

[54] Keep in mind that I am not expecting that you, the reader, will agree with me at this point that this is indeed necessarily wrong. I only hope that you can appreciate how one can form that belief based on a non-discursive intuition.

action, and so we conclude that God did not command it and that conclusion is independent of the results of any survey of biblical data.

But in that case, where precisely do these moral convictions come from? What exactly is this voice of conscience? What is this moral compass? Given that moral beliefs are playing a pivotal role in our interpretation of the Bible, it is important that we attempt to identify their source and justification. As a way into that analysis we will begin by drawing a comparison with another belief forming process, that which philosophers refer to as rational intuition. Rational intuition provides the way that we form basic beliefs about first principles of reasoning in mathematics and logic. Among the many axiomatic starting points of reason are Aristotle's three famous laws of thought:

- Law of Identity: everything is identical with itself.
- Law of Non-Contradiction: contradictory propositions cannot simultaneously be true.
- Law of Excluded Middle: for any proposition, either that proposition is true or its negation is true.

Rather than reasoning *to* these principles, we reason *from* them: they stand in the background of our rational reflection as intuitive starting points which guide us in the evaluation of all other claims.

Just as mathematical theorems are based on axioms—starting points of logic that we know immediately by rational intuition—so moral reasoning ultimately rests on *moral* intuitions, starting points of our moral perception. And just as rational intuition reflects an intuitive ability to grasp the necessary truth or falsity of particular logical axioms (e.g. the laws of thought), so *moral* intuition reflects the intuitive ability to grasp the truth/falsity of particular moral claims apart from any discursive reasoning process. As the Apostle Paul famously said, this basic moral knowledge is *written on the heart* (Romans 2:15). An example of a moral principle equivalent to the laws of thought is this formulation from Thomas Aquinas: "Good is to be done and evil is to be avoided." If you do not *begin* with the recognition of a basic moral intuition like this, you shall get no farther in moral reasoning than the man who denies the law of non-contradiction shall progress in logical reasoning.

While the starting points are intuitive, they are normatively identified and clarified on the occasion of experience. That is, it is by interacting with our environment that we come to understand precisely what the content of our moral intuitive knowledge is. Just as rational intuitions are clarified by way of the occasions that provide opportunity for rational reflection so moral intuitions are clarified by way of the occasions that provide opportunity for moral reflection. For example, I may never have thought about child sacrifice before, but on the occasion that Tom shares his intent to sacrifice his child, I come to perceive the intrinsic wrongness of this action. The experience provides the occasion by which I acquire that moral knowledge but the moral knowledge itself is immediate and carries a justificatory force that exceeds that specific experience thereby enabling me to judge not just the immorality of Tom's proposed child sacrifice but of *any possible child sacrifice*. In other words, I perceive not simply the wrongness of Tom's proposed action but the wrongness of *any* possible occasion of child sacrifice. The action is intrinsically wrong and I perceive that fact by way of moral intuition occasioned by the experience of hearing Tom's plan.

Moral perception emphasizes the complementary empirical sense that we often come to understand these moral truths on the occasion of some degree of reflective process or empirical interaction with the world. For example, you read a news report of a man raping a woman and torturing another man, and simply upon reading those reports, you form the immediate, intuitive belief that those actions are *always* morally wrong. You don't need to read further to know that rape and torture are wrong. In that way, you grasp the *necessity* of the wrongness of the actions.

The moral belief you now have in the wrongness of rape or torture is an immediate moral intuition. In other words, you do not form this belief by some discursive process of moving from premises to conclusions; rather, you come to form that belief automatically based upon your reflection of the type of actions under consideration. Simply by reflecting on those actions, you form an immediate belief that they are wrong.

This account provides a framework by which we may understand our trigger response to Tom. As with our immediate revulsion of actions like rape and torture, our response to Tom's proposal isn't a reasoned conclusion based upon an evaluation of biblical data. Rather, it is an immediate moral intuition. When Tom shares his plan to kill his young son in a devotional sacrifice, you do not reason through various steps to conclude that Tom is likely incorrect in this belief. Rather, your response is immediate, intuitive and independent of the biblical data.

I mentioned above that there is an analogy between moral intuition/moral perception and rational intuition/rational reflection and I invoked the mathematical equivalent of moving from axioms to mathematical theorems. In the case of moral perception, the process by which we clarify and articulate our moral thinking, a claim like "devotional child sacrifice is always wrong" would provide an equivalent for a moral axiomatic starting point for reason. As such, it could ground a formal moral argument such as the following:

1. If any action is always wrong then God would not command anyone to perform that action.
2. Devotional child sacrifice is always wrong.
3. Therefore, God would not command anyone to perform devotional child sacrifice.
4. Therefore, God did not command Tom to perform devotional child sacrifice.

The important thing to recognize is that as a regular course, we don't bother to articulate the implicit premises of our moral intuitions in an argument. Instead, it is typically sufficient to intuit the truth of premise 2. And so, we usually move automatically from powerful moral intuitions to the evaluation and censure of specific behaviors or actions such as Tom's proposed sacrifice. If we need to articulate a formal argument based on that intuition, we might attempt to do so if asked. But even if we struggle to translate our intuition into a winsome argument which would satisfy the logician, the fact remains that we have that knowledge by way of our own moral perception.

Sense Perception and Skepticism

People often use visual analogues to describe the non-discursive immediacy of their moral perception: "I can just *see* that this action is wrong." In this section, we will consider the weight and strength of sense perception in order to appreciate how it can provide a defeater to skeptical interpretations of sense perceptual data. As we consider how our immediate sense perceptual experience is able to overwhelm some standard skeptical objections, we will begin to understand how the weight of our moral intuition/perception is likewise sufficient to overcome or defeat skeptical challenges to those intuitions as with the claim that our moral intuitions are unreliable and that God may have commanded actions like child sacrifice and genocide.

We can begin by posing a skeptical philosophical question: *do you know* that there is a world external to the human mind? And if so, *how* do you know that? We can become oriented to this rather abstract discussion by way of an illustration from the popular sci-fi movie *The Matrix*. The big reveal in the film is that the reality we seem to experience is, in fact, an illusion: it turns out that all human beings are actually living in a computer-generated virtual reality. Within the world of the film, all the sensory experiences people believe that they have of the world around them are the product of a supercomputer matrix to which our inert bodies are connected. So, for example, I may think I am sitting in front of a computer typing on the keyboard, but it could turn out that I am in fact an inert body and my brain is being stimulated by a supercomputer to perceive these false images.

The haunting scenario posed by that memorable film brings us to a very common skeptical question which has been raised time and again in the history of philosophy, a question concerning how we know reality. Over the centuries, that perennial question has taken on various skeptical forms including the following:

- How do you know you're awake rather than asleep?
- How do you know you're not being deceived by an evil demon?
- How do you know you're not a brain in a vat?
- How do you know you're not a mind in a matrix?

All of these possible skeptical scenarios ultimately reduce to the same question: how do you know that there really is a world external to your mind, a world that you really do perceive through your sense perceptual experience?

Most people will provide a simple and straightforward answer to all these questions: "How do I know there is an external world? That's easy: *I experience it.*" They will then go on to describe that experience: they open their eyes and *see* the blue sky, they take a sniff and *smell* the flowers, they reach down and *touch* the grass, they listen and *hear* the chirping birds, they take a sip and *taste* their coffee. In short, the way they know there is a world external to the mind is because they have a basic sense perceptual experience of it.

Note that at this point our hypothetical respondent would be explaining their powerful conviction that an external world exists by appealing to basic perceptual experiences of that world. At first blush, that seems reasonable: as people encounter the world with the immediacy of their senses, they form the belief that they are seeing, smelling, feeling, hearing, and tasting reality external to the mind. And so, based on the occasions of this experience they believe that the real world exists. It is important to underscore that people do not typically undergo some kind of process of inferential reasoning from this welter of experience to an external world. People don't typically reason like this: "I seem to see blue sky. Therefore, I probably am seeing blue sky." Rather, their perceptual experience of seeing the blue sky provides the occasion to form the immediate belief "I am seeing blue sky", a sky that really does exist "out there" external to one's mind.

Most people live their lives never pausing to question their sense perceptual experience of an external world. And if they ever do come to question it, it is likely because they have encountered a philosopher who first posed the question. Regardless, now that *we've* posed the question, how satisfying is this response, a response that appeals to experience itself? Can you really sidestep all these skeptical scenarios raised by the philosophers, scenarios that question our beliefs about the external world? Can you set them all aside simply by reiterating that we do, in fact, see the blue sky and thereby sense perceive that world?

Let's start with the bad news. The doubtful philosophers who are keen to pose those skeptical scenarios in the first place will not likely be satisfied by an appeal to a simple, straightforward, *direct experience* of the world as evidence that it does, in fact, exist external to our minds. That will sound to them to be nothing more than begging the question. And so, they will likely retort that all that 'evidence' you are marshalling in favor of the external world is, in fact, perfectly consistent with the details of a dream, or the trickery of an evil demon, or the delusions of a brain in a vat or a computer-generated matrix. And so, as far as skeptical objections go, it would seem that we are back to square one. As the skeptics would have it, perhaps we don't know that there is an external world, after all.

For a famous exemplar of this kind of skeptical position, one could consider the great eighteenth century philosopher George Berkeley. He claimed that all these experiences that we take to be windows onto a world external to our minds really are just experiences *of* our minds. In a scenario something like an 18th century version of the matrix, Berkeley defended a position known as *idealism* according to which there is no world external to our minds. Rather, all that exists are minds and their ideas (i.e. sensory experiences and mental intentions). Berkeley also believed that God exists as the one Supreme Mind who sustains and unifies all these created minds, weaving together their ideas into one seamless, unified experience rather like a divinely orchestrated matrix. And so, that external world that we thought we were perceiving, for Berkeley, that external world really just is our mind experiencing its own ideas. For example, on Berkeley's view there is no sun out there shining down on you and warming your skin. Rather, there is just your mind, an immaterial substance, and the ideas that it experiences such as the sensation of physical warmth and the visual presentation of the sun in the sky. And God operates like the matrix as the one who correlates all these minds and their ideas into one seamlessly unified, interacting mental reality. There's just no need for a physical world 'out there' to explain everything we experience.

So as I said, the skeptical philosophers will not be persuaded by the average person's attempt to rebuff idealistic skepticism by appealing back to their direct experience of the world. Conversely, once the average person encounters the idealism of a skilled philosopher like Berkeley, they will probably find it well-nigh impossible to refute without begging the question by *assuming* the very external experiences that Berkeley and other skeptics question. The fact remains that you cannot refute Berkeley's view that the sun is an idea in your mind just by appealing to your experience of seeing the sun and feeling its warmth because, of course, the sum total of those sense perceptual experiences *could* just be the ideas in your mind as Berkeley claims.

Thus far, I've argued that you cannot refute the skepticism of the external world proposed by Berkeley and others like him simply by appealing to your direct experience of sense perceiving the world. But here's the really critical question: does it follow from this that *you are obliged to give up your belief that you are directly sense perceiving the external world?* No, in fact, that does not follow at all. The fact that you cannot *refute* Berkeley *does not* mean that you have to agree with him. Nor does it mean that you suddenly need to become agnostic about the whole question. You can still retain your convictions in the external world even if you cannot show Berkeley to be wrong.

How so? Consider an analogy from yet another type of belief: memory. Let's say you remember very clearly that you were at home alone all day yesterday working in your garden. So you are completely shocked when the police storm into your house and arrest you for a murder carried out at that exact same time. Later, when the detective is interrogating you, he outlines a motive for you to commit the crime, a motive which you cannot easily refute. In addition, you are dismayed to learn that two witnesses have identified you as the murderer and their confident testimony appears to be backed up by some surveillance footage which shows a car like yours arriving at the scene of the crime. Based upon that weight of evidence, the detective may be justified in believing that you are guilty of murder. However, it does not follow that *you* are obliged to believe that you are guilty. Nor would it require you to become agnostic as to your potential guilt. The motive, testimony, and surveillance footage notwithstanding, you could go right on trusting your very clear memory that you were, in fact, home working in your garden the whole time.

The contrast between you and the detective parallels the contrast between the world-realist who believes there is a world external to our mind that we perceive and the idealist or skeptic who rejects that claim. The skeptic may be persuaded by the evidence that there is no external world just like the detective is persuaded by the evidence of your guilt. But just as you have a private memory that grounds and thereby justifies your belief in your innocence so a person may have personal sense perceptual experiences every waking moment that ground and thereby justify their belief in an external world. Even if you cannot refute the detective, you are still justified in maintaining your belief in your innocence. And even if you cannot refute the idealist or skeptic, you are still justified in maintaining your belief in the external world. Thus, you would be perfectly within your rights to respond like this: "Look, I don't know how to refute Berkeley's 'idealism' or other skeptical scenarios. I concede that it is *possible* that I am wrong and that I really am asleep or in a matrix. Or maybe I'm a brain in a vat. But why should I be moved by the mere *possibility* that one of those scenarios could be true? What I *do* know is that my experiences *seem overwhelmingly* to be of a world external to my mind. And the power, the weight, the ineluctable *gravitas* of that experience, an experience that is clearly part of general common sense shared by most people, all that vastly outweighs the strength of your piddling skeptical claims that I am really just experiencing sensory 'ideas' in my head."

This practice of responding to skeptical challenges to sense perceptual experience by prioritizing the weight of one's common sense experience over skeptical philosophical challenges is not merely the last resort of the naïve layperson. In fact, such responses have a noble philosophical pedigree. For example, the great Scottish common sense philosopher Thomas Reid (a younger contemporary of Berkeley) offered a sharp riposte to the idealistic skepticism of people like Berkeley. On Reid's view, it is perfectly sensible that the weight of common sense immediate experience should be favored over the scenarios proposed by the skeptical objector. Indeed, as he suggests, we may not have much choice in the matter:

> My belief [in an external world] is carried along by perception, as irresistibly as my body by the earth. And the greatest

sceptic will find himself to be in the same condition. He may struggle hard to disbelieve the information of his senses, as a man does to swim against a torrent; but, ah! it is in vain. It is in vain that he strains every nerve, and wrestles with nature, and with every object that strikes upon his senses. For after all, when his strength is spent in the fruitless attempt, he will be carried down the torrent with the common herd of believers.[55]

Admittedly, Reid makes a particularly bold claim here as he suggests that, in fact, the skeptic's objections are offered in bad faith, for Reid supposes that the skeptic also believes deep down that the external world exists: he cannot help but to do so. Whether or not Reid is correct in that more ambitious claim, he is certainly right to note that for *many* of us, we really do have no choice in the matter. For us, at least, the sheer force of sense perceptual experience overwhelms any idealist attempts to question the existence of a world external to the mind. And for us 'simple' folk, we surely are justified in continuing to embrace the basic deliverances of our sense perception rather than vainly attempting to "swim against a torrent" of ineluctable experience that we cannot seriously deny.

Many other philosophers have joined Reid in exploring common sense rebuttals to idealism and skepticism. For example, more than a century after Reid, the British philosopher G.E. Moore offered his own famous refutation of Berkeley's kind of skepticism. In his essay "Proof of an External World," Moore provides the following deliciously straightforward rebuttal to idealistic skepticism about the external world: "Here's one hand and here's another."[56] In other words, Moore responds to the claim that we do not perceive anything outside of our minds by

---

55 Reid, *An Inquiry into the Human Mind on the Principles of Common Sense*, ed., Derek R. Brookes (Edinburgh: Edinburgh University Press, 1997), 169 (6.20).

56 Moore, "Proof of an External World," in G.E. Moore, *Selected Writings*, ed. Thomas Baldwin (Routledge, 1993), 169.

insisting that *he* perceives two hands outside his mind. The simple logic is that if Moore is actually now perceiving his hands "out there" in a world external to his mind, then it follows that there *is* a world out there external to our minds which we perceive.

To be sure, Moore is not claiming that he can provide a general proof to satisfy the skeptic just as one may not be able to establish to the satisfaction of the skeptic that we are *not* now in a matrix.[57] For that reason, Moore anticipates that the skeptic will retort like this: "If you cannot prove your premiss that here is one hand and here is another, then you do not know it."[58] Nonetheless, Moore flatly denies this conclusion. The fact that I cannot provide an argument to satisfy the skeptic does not prevent *me* from knowing that there is a hand external to my mind. Just as I don't need to be able to convince the detective before *I* can know that I didn't commit the murder, so I don't need to be able to provide a universally compelling disproof of skepticism to believe—and indeed, to know—that it is false. The key, as Moore observes, is that "I can know things, which I cannot prove; and among things which I certainly did know, even if (as I think) I could not prove them, were the premisses of my two proofs."[59] If Moore is right then it turns out that knowing depends less on being able to refute the skeptic to the skeptic's satisfaction and more on simply paying close attention to the quality and nature of one's own sense perceptual experience of the world, experience that simply overwhelms the skeptic's claim.

---

57 Recently, I dreamed that I was looking at my motorcycle when I noticed it had a different paint job. "This must be a dream," I reflected, "because that isn't the right paint job." But then I thought, "just to make sure this is a dream, I will pay close attention to my surroundings." So I stared closely at a picture on the wall, studying the details. And I listened closely and heard Muzak playing in the background. "Huh, the details are stable unlike a dream," I thought. "I guess this is reality after all." Then I woke up.

58 Moore, "Proof of an External World," 169.

59 Moore, "Proof of an External World," 170.

I think that Reid and Moore are both fundamentally correct in their replies to the skeptics. We are warranted, as Reid observes, in accepting the ineluctable deliverances of our sense perceptual experience. And as Moore adds, we can thereby treat that undeniable experience as providing a stronger 'proof' than the skeptic's alternative. Even if you cannot refute the detective's case, you are still justified in retaining your own belief in your innocence based on your powerful memory. And even if we cannot refute the idealist or skeptic's case, we are nonetheless fully warranted in believing in the external world based on our undeniable experience.[60]

Moral Perception, Fallibility, and Skepticism

One might agree with the idea that we can believe we reliably sense perceive a world external to the mind but still raise an objection to the extension of this argument to morality. After all, there are instances where moral intuition appears to fail us and such cases are not hard to find. For example, Cletus says that mixed race couples are an offense to God. You ask him why and he replies, "When I see a black fellow holding the hand of a proper southern belle, I can just *see* that it is wrong: it's an offense against nature. God made for each race to stay within its own kind."

I trust we will all agree that Cletus' belief is wrong, grievously wrong. And thus, his intuitive response to interracial dating reveals a deep fault in his moral intuition. But once we recognize

---

60 Within epistemology, the position I'm defending here is known as moderate foundationalism. I provide an academic defense of the position in *Theology in Search of Foundations* (Oxford University Press, 2009). Also see the popular exposition in my book *The Swedish Atheist, the Scuba Diver, and Other Apologetic Rabbit Trails* (InterVarsity Press, 2012).

that Cletus's moral intuition is faulty, we need to recognize that ours could be faulty as well. If Cletus's faulty moral intuition leads him astray when he condemns mixed race relationships then perhaps our faulty moral intuition is awry when it leads us to believe that devotional child sacrifice or genocide is necessarily wrong.

So should we conclude that our moral intuitive rejection of genocide as necessarily evil is just wrong? In order to answer this question, let's return to sense perception. Because, you see, moral intuition is not the only fallible doxastic process: errors may arise in our sense perception as well. I suspect that we all recognize that sense perception can mislead us for it is perfectly possible that we might experience either a hallucination (i.e. a perception in the absence of a corresponding sense perceptual stimulus) or an illusion (i.e. a misinterpretation of an actual sense perceptual stimulus). For example, you might perceive a voice calling you when none is there (auditory hallucination) or you might misperceive a white towel on the ground as your sleeping Maltese puppy (illusion). With the specter of errant perception looming on the horizon, a person might argue that the possibility of misperception by way of hallucination or illusion is sufficient to undercut the general reliability of sense perception.

But that's not the right response. If I may indulge at this point in a rather lowbrow illustration, I am reminded of the days when I used to watch the television program *Judge Judy*. After America's favorite judge would adjudicate a case, the plaintiff and defendant would be allowed a quick comment for posterity. On one occasion, I heard a female plaintiff, miffed that the male defendant had failed to repay a loan, offer this life-lesson: "Don't ever trust a man." But that is absurd: a single incident like that does not justify a general skepticism toward men. Rather, the correct lesson is to recognize that people (men included, clearly) can be dishonest. And so, you should be cautious when lending people money. By the same token, if you fall victim to an illusion, the lesson is not: Don't trust sense perception! It is still perfectly reasonable to trust sense perception generally. Instead, the lesson is that we should take care to look for clues that we may be misperceiving.

Needless to say, this same lesson applies to moral intuition. Yes, our moral intuition is fallible just like sense perception, memory, rational intuition, and every other doxastic process by which we form beliefs. But we should not assume that the possibility of error is itself sufficient to conclude that our moral intuition is generally unreliable. And so, the fact that Cletus is wrong about the morality of mixed-race dating does not constitute a reason for me to question my categorical intuitive censure of devotional child sacrifice or divinely commanded genocide. To be sure, it certainly is the case that people who have a different opinion about such matters may cause us to reflect on our intuitions. But if, after that reflection, we still find our moral intuitions to have an ineluctable power that overwhelms the dissenting voice, then we are justified in continuing to accept them.

In the same way that we find ourselves carried along by the basic deliverances of our sense perception, so we find ourselves carried along by the basic deliverances of our moral intuition/perception. In the same way that our experience of seeing the sun and feeling its warmth on our skin gives rise to the immediate and irresistible belief in an external world that we perceive, a world that includes a sun that shines and gives warmth, so our experience of contemplating particular instances of human moral action such as "God commanded Tom to hack apart his son in a devotional sacrifice" gives rise to an immediate perception regarding the moral status of the act: *No, this is wrong!* And just as the idealist's arguments for skepticism about the external world will be insufficient to overcome our conviction that the external world exists, so the moral skeptic's arguments that there is no objective moral value beyond our personal opinions may very well prove insufficient to overcome our immediate, intuitive sense that some actions like devotional child sacrifice are always wrong.

Christian philosopher J. Budziszewski describes this innate moral knowledge as follows: "St. Paul said that the knowledge of God's law is 'written on our hearts, our consciences also bearing witness.' The way natural law thinkers put this is to say that they constitute the deep structure of our minds. That means that so long as we have minds, we can't not know them."[61] In other words, our basic grasp of good and evil, right and wrong, is *innate*, it lies within us: we are *hard-wired* to have such knowledge. And as we encounter particular actions or states of affairs (e.g. Tom's claim about divinely commanded child sacrifice) either by way of hypothetical reflection or concrete experience, our moral perception provides immediate and undeniable deliverances as to the wrongness of the act.

Where sense perception is concerned, I have argued that we are justified in accepting the general deliverances of that perception, of granting those experiences the status of innocent until proven guilty. In addition, our most basic and ineluctable intuitive interpretations of that experience, such as the belief that our sense perceptual experiences do link us with an external world, are surely among the most secure deliverances of our sense perception and thus they are very well grounded over-against the incredulity of the would-be skeptic.

What about moral perception? What are the basic, bedrock convictions, the seemingly undeniable core deliverances of moral perceptual experience? As I have suggested, the intuition that it is always wrong to engage in the devotional sacrifice of another human being (and certainly of one's own child) is an excellent candidate for this kind of immediate moral knowledge. There are many others, as well. Budziszewski provides another starting point for reflection vis-à-vis the ethics of intentionally killing innocent human beings:

---

61 Budziszewski, *The Revenge of Conscience: Politics and the Fall of Man* (Spence, 1999), xv.

It is certainly one of the things we can't not know that no one may deliberately take innocent human life. The more particular doctrine of man as the created image of God seems unknown beyond the bible's sphere of influence; it is not one of the things we can't not know. Some intuition of the sacredness of human life is universal nonetheless, and this foothold in our nature is what makes the doctrine of the *imago Dei* so compelling once heard. In this sense it might be said that nature contains a premonition of biblical revelation. Unfortunately, the intuition of the sacredness of human life can easily be deflected into various forms of idolatry, in which we reverence *ourselves*—as God, partly-God, parts *of* God, gods, or on the way to becoming gods.[62]

Budziszewski argues three things here: first, there is a universal recognition of the intrinsic wrongness of deliberately taking innocent human life; second, this basic, universally recognized moral intuition or perception is further reified within the Judeo-Christian context in terms of the *imago Dei*; and third, it is possible to overcome the force of this direct moral perception by developing *ad hoc* rationalizations to justify various instances of deliberately taking innocent human life. For example, one might argue with an appeal to a utilitarian goal or one might invoke a divine command. But whatever the putative rationale given, Budziszewski insists that it is indeed a rationalization which is shown to be illegitimate because it violates our moral intuition. As Budziszewski succinctly puts it, "Deliberately blowing up a schoolbus full of children is wrong no matter what might be gained by it . . . ."[63] Thus, the mere fact that many people act contrary to that moral knowledge even as they purport to justify their actions is not, for us, evidence that they are right. Rather, it is evidence that they are rationalizing their refusal to recognize

---

[62] J. Budziszewski, *What We Can't Not Know: A Guide* (Spence, 2003), 35.
[63] Budziszewski, *What We Can't Not Know: A Guide*, 105.

and live in accord with the moral law within. And that applies equally to Tom who seems so convinced that God is calling him to the devotional killing of his precious child.

Budziszewski makes a similar point in his book *Written on the Heart* also with respect to the taking of innocent human life. Additionally, in the following passage he points out the extent to which human beings can rationalize their violation of their own moral knowledge proscribing such actions:

> the rule against the deliberate taking of innocent human life is an immediate precept—a general precept that follows so quickly on the heels of the primary precepts that it can hardly be distinguished from them. I cannot blot it completely out of my heart. But I can rationalize, can't I. "Yes, but that bastard I killed wasn't innocent! He took the job that should have gone to me!" In the same way, I can rationalize that the slave or unborn child whose blood I shed was not human or not alive or that I didn't really have a choice. I find a way to tell myself, "Yes, murder is evil, but this isn't murder"; "Yes, murder is evil but *this* murder isn't evil"; "Yes, this is murder and wrong, but I have to do it"; or "Yes, this is murder and wrong, but I'll make up for it later."[64]

As Budziszewski soberly observes, human beings have a long history of making excuses for running roughshod over their basic perception of the moral law: "the wide world over people also carved out excuses for themselves. I must not take innocent human life—but only my tribe is human. I must not sleep with my neighbor's wife—but I can make my neighbor's mine. I must

---

[64] J. Budziszewski, *Written on the Heart: The Case for Natural Law* (InterVarsity, 1997), 74. According to Budziszewski, we deduce the principle that we should not murder from the rule that we should not deliberately harm, 76. Conversely, it could be that we immediately intuit the wrongness of murder alongside the wrongness of harm simpliciter.

not mock deity—but I can ascribe deity to a created thing instead of the Creator."⁶⁵ The lesson, however, is that we need to recognize that our most basic moral perceptions, those immediate and ineluctable moral intuitions, those intuitions which we can't *not* know, this moral knowledge is more well established than any argument against it or any attempt to justify an exception to it. Consequently, those who reason carefully on their own moral knowledge must be ready and willing to call out attempts to persuade us that we do not know what we do, in fact, know.

Moral Perception and Theological Reasoning

If we have this moral intuition/perception that enables us to know with immediacy moral facts that we cannot *not* know, then we should ensure that this knowledge appropriately informs our theological reasoning. In short, our understanding of the nature of God and his revelation to us will be informed by our basic moral perception. Consider the famous words of Martin Luther at the Council of Worms: "Unless I am convicted by Scripture and plain reason—I do not accept the authority of popes and councils, for they have contradicted each other—my conscience is captive to the Word of God. I cannot and I will not recant anything, for to go against conscience is neither right nor safe. God help me. Amen."⁶⁶ Luther is right: it is a mistake to go against conscience. So we should not sacrifice on the altar of

---

65 Budziszewski, *What We Can't Not Know*, 4.

66 Cited in Roland Bainton, *Here I Stand: A Life of Martin Luther* (Nashville: Abingdon, 1978), 182. For a helpful discussion of Luther's view of conscience, see Robert K. Vischer, *Conscience and the Common Good: Reclaiming the Space Between Person and State* (Cambridge University Press, 2010), 56-58. Cf. George Forell, "Luther and Conscience," (2002), https://www.elca.org/JLE/Articles/991

any particular theology our conscience by denying that which we intuitively know cannot be true.

As important as this point is, it does require another caveat. As we noted above, moral intuition is (like all our other doxastic processes) fallible and thus vulnerable to error. In particular, one should be ready for the possibility that special revelation might offer a chastening critique of that which we believe to be true. If we don't keep this in mind, the danger is that we might end up rejecting some aspect of divine revelation because we chose to defer to the errant deliverances of our fallen moral intuition. As Charles Hodge memorably put it, "No man has a right to hang the millstone of his philosophy around the neck of the truth of God."[67] Needless to say, that fallibility is even more of a concern when considering our finite knowledge in contrast to the contents of an infinite mind. Should it not be expected that God's perfect grasp of the moral good and right would differ in significant respects from our terribly limited, finite, and fallible grasp? And if we recognize that fact then in those moments where we seem to have a divine command which appears to be evil, should we not conclude that the real lesson may be that God did speak and our moral beliefs are in error on this point? With that in mind, we will now explore further the tension which may arise between our current moral intuitions and putative revelation by surveying some differerent intuitions on some specific theological topics.

Let's begin with a consideration of how moral intuitions may differ as regards God and the problem of evil. Many Christians believe in meticulous providence, the view that God has intimate awareness of and control over every event that occurs in creation. This claim creates an obvious tension when heinous evils occur because one must consider that God allowed those evils for some specific reason. It is easy enough to say in principle that God allows evil as an abstract quantity for his sovereign purposes. But

---

67 Charles Hodge, *Systematic Theology*, vol. II (Hendrickson, 1999), 78.

it is an altogether different matter when you consider that 'evil' really is short-hand for an extraordinarily diverse list of events and states of affairs, some of which stagger the imagination and sear the soul with their horrendous depths of depravity.

At this point we will consider one of the most extraordinarily cruel and evil actions imaginable and then evaluate our intuitions regarding meticulous providence in light of that case. This real experience of evil was endured by a prisoner and his imprisoned family:

> I was given another choice: I rape my daugher or the guard does. I tried to reason with them, telling them that she was an innocent child . . . . They laughed and repeated the two choices. I looked at my daughter hoping that she would tell me what to do—our eyes met and I knew that I could not save her from those wretched men. I lowered my eyes in shame to keep from seeing my daughter abused. One guard held my face up, forcing me to watch this horrible scene. I watched, motionless, as she was raped before me and her little brother. When they were through, they forced me to do what they had done to her. My own daughter, my son forced to watch it all. How could anyone do that? What kind of men are they? What kind of father am I?[68]

How does this case interact with that which we can't not know? When one reads of such a horrific situation, it is natural to respond, as many do, that no perfectly loving, omnipotent and omniscient God could possibly have a morally sufficient reason to allow such a thing. Based on that intuition, one might conclude either that there is no god, or that God is not morally perfect, or that God was not sufficiently powerful to prevent this heinous evil.

---

68 Cited in Rachel Cooper, *Psychiatry and Philosophy of Science* (Routledge, 2014), 74.

But others disagree: while they agree that the act itself is an unimaginable evil, they believe that God could nonetheless have morally sufficient reasons to allow it, even if we don't know what those reasons are. So here, at least, is a very significant, substantive disagreement of intuitions.

It seems to me that those who reason against meticulous providence based on horrendous evils like this ground their conviction on the ineluctable intuition that these actions were horrifically evil, an intuition that all properly functioning human beings share. However, in my view, the person then reasons out from that secure point to the conclusion that God could not have a morally sufficient reason to allow this horrific evil. It seems to me that this extrapolation is significantly less secure than the initial intuition: the fact remains that there is significant disagreement over the legitimacy of that extrapolation.

Christians who find this extrapolation compelling must indeed revise their understanding of God. For example, theologian Thomas Jay Oord believes that such awful evils warrant the conclusion that God is not omnipotent and thus that meticulous providence is false. On Oord's view, God cannot prevent terrible evils and that's why they occur. They are not attributable to some grand plan.[69] I understand how Christians like Oord reason to that position. While they could be reasoning out from the initial intuition that the action is intrinsically evil to the conclusion that it would be intrinsically evil for God to allow it, they appear to be appealing to a discrete intuition: I call it the 'Good Samaritan Intuition' according to which it is intrinsically wrong to allow heinous evil to occur if you could have prevented it.

While I agree that the Good Samaritan Intuition constrains human action, I do not agree that it applies to God. The core issue here is an unwarranted extrapolation from human moral obligation to divine moral obligation. While it would be necessarily

---

69 Thomas Jay Oord, *The Uncontrolling Love of God: An Open and Relational Account of Providence* (IVP Academic, 2015).

wrong for human creatures to *allow these actions* if they could prevent them, it does not follow that it is necessarily wrong for God to do so. In my view, the proper response is to say that God is indeed omnipotent, and morally perfect and thus that he has morally sufficient reasons to allow every evil that occurs, even an evil as terrible as the moral horror endured by that poor father and his family. In my view, meticulous providence is more compelling than the claim that the Good Samaritan Intuition applies to God such that he is either not omnipotent or perfectly good.

To be sure, you don't have to agree with me. It seems to me that there is much room for reasonable people to disagree as they seek to reify particular moral intuitions and reason out from them in dialogue with their theological convictions. That's precisely why basic disagreements arise in fields like ethics and theology.

However, this kind of enduring disagreement does not provide a good reason to conclude that there is *no* bedrock of moral intuition available to us as individuals. Rather, it helps us to clarify precisely *what that bedrock is*. Even if we disagree on whether the Good Samaritan Intuition applies to God, I believe that properly functioning human beings who are truly attendant to the contents of their moral intuition are at least all in agreement that *the action of forcing a man to rape his own child is itself a necessary evil.* This belief, surely, is moral bedrock. And thus, any person who would claim that God commanded such an action must be repudiated with a conviction as secure and solid as any belief we should have about anything at all.

Let's consider one other example where moral intuitions can differ among reasonable persons: I'm thinking of the debate between Arminians and Calvinists on whether God loves all creatures equally or whether he has a special love for his elect creatures and thus only chooses those persons for salvation. In a debate over this question, Arminian theologian Thomas McCall raises his own moral objections to the Calvinist concept of God.[70] In response, his interlocutor, Calvinist John Piper, offered the following bit of advice: "Do not yet believe what I say. Your conscience forbids it. You dare not believe statements about God which, according to your own conscience, can only mean that God is what he is not."[71] It's important to appreciate the ground of Piper's caution. If we violate our most basic moral intuitions by denying our conscience, it will surely produce an even deeper distortion in our theology down the line.

I agree with Piper: that is sage advice. There are three things I think we should keep in mind: first, we are indeed responsible to our conscience when reasoning theologically (as in all other areas!). Second, it seems to me, at least, that the debate over Arminianism and Calvinism, like the debate over meticulous providence and God's allowance of evil, is a matter over which reasonable people disagree. In cases of such disagreement, we each must remain true to our own conscience. And finally, while there is room for that kind of reasonable disagreement, I do find myself compelled to conclude that other cases of moral intuition are such that they do *not* allow the same range of reasonable disagreement. In those cases, I am most confident to take the position that a careful acquaintance with our moral knowledge will allow any properly functioning human being to see the truth of the matter. The intrinsic wrongness of a man being forced to rape his own daughter is one such example. Every properly functioning human being should be able to see that this is intrinsically evil. I would submit that the wrongness of a man being commanded to sacrifice his son is surely another example. And the command to carry out the genocide of a people is still another.

---

70 To be sure, Calvinists do something similar when they seek to interpret passages like 1 Timothy 2:4 and 2 Peter 3:9 in a manner consistent with Calvinism. Everyone is guided by intuitions and control verses.

71 John Piper, "I believe in God's Self-Sufficiency: A Response to Thomas McCall," *Trinity Journal*, 29, no. 2 (2008), 234.

Needless to say, it is a great moral tragedy when people are coerced by theological pressure *to deny in word something that they can't not know with their heart.* The tragedy is compounded if that belief leads them to perform or verbally approve of actions that they really do know to be wrong. This leads us to an important and difficult question: *how does one know when to revise their theological conviction in light of their moral beliefs and when to revise their moral beliefs in light of their theological conviction?* How does one identify true moral bedrock and distinguish it from the fallible and possibly errant extrapolations? Unfortunately, there is no simple answer to that question. But the starting point for each one of us is that it must begin with careful reflection on what *we* believe to be the surest deliverances of our conscience, those moral intuitions that seem most secure to us, most deeply entrenched in bedrock. Like Luther, each one of us is responsible to our own conscience.

Moral Intuitions and Canaanites

At this point, we can return at long last to the question of biblical violence and moral intuitions. As I said at the outset in our contrasting responses to James and Tom, it is clear that our reasoning is not simply derived from scriptural texts but rather from these God-given moral intuitions which guide our reading of the text. We were designed so that our properly functioning moral faculties would inform and guide our reading of Scripture and the theologizing that flows from it. The question is, how should this affect the current topics at hand, namely genocide and the related topic of ethnic cleansing?

We can put the question like this: if one's conscience may justify one in rejecting Tom's claim of divinely commanded child sacrifice *a priori*, might it also justify one in rejecting the claim of a historic, divinely commanded genocide *a priori*? Can our intuitions bar the door to consideration of the claim that the perfect God of absolute love commanded the mass slaughter of an entire society: not just male combatants, but also women, children, infants, the mentally handicapped, and the elderly?

As I noted above, Christians will hopefully all concede that the most secure deliverances of our moral intuitions should inform our evaluation of theological claims and that they will, in at least some cases, warrant the acceptance of some specific claims and the revision or rejection of others. We also saw that not everyone will agree on precisely which claims to accept and which to revise or reject. However, that is not itself a problem. It simply means that judgments are, to some degree, person-relative. And so, after doing our due diligence and reflecting on the deliverances of our personal moral intuitions, each one of us will need to decide which theological doctrines we are compelled to reject or revise given our most deeply held intuitions always remembering that to go against conscience is neither right nor safe.

When it comes to the actual content of moral perception, we also saw above that Budziszewski identified among the basic moral deliverances the intrinsic wrongness of killing innocent human life. When it comes to explaining our categorical rejection of Tom's child sacrifice proposal, Budziszewski's innocence claim would seem a very plausible launching point for analysis: we recognize that God could not have commanded Tom to sacrifice his child because it is wrong to kill innocent human life. As I suggested, it is also possible that the actual intuition(s) that are operative here include the intuition that devotional sacrifice is wrong. At the very least, we can recognize that our intuitions do support the condemnation of Tom's proposal. And that is more important to me than identifying precisely which intuition(s) may be doing the heavy lifting in this case. In short, I am less interested in defining the precise set of intuitions that constitute our basic intuitive starting points of reason than in recognizing that our intuitive starting points, whatever they may be, have an overriding moral force to approve or censure particular actions.

If a moral intuition like Budziszewski's innocence claim would explain our *a priori* denial of Tom's child sacrifice plans it would equally explain a person's aversion to claims of historic divinely commanded genocide. Again, that seems very plausible to me. Indeed, to call it *plausible* hardly does it justice: it is *compelling*. Whatever the precise nature of the intuitions that flag the wrongness of the action, the *output* from them is that this proposed action of sacrificing a child appears to be intuitively wrong. And that is what is most important. Further, that same intuition against devotional child-killing can then scale up to apply to claims of devotional mass-killing and genocide.

And so, as I have reflected on these issues I find that for me it most certainly is the case that my conscience forbids consideration of the notion that God commanded the historic genocidal eradication of entire societies. From this it follows that whatever the biblical texts may mean to teach us, they cannot intend to teach us *that*. And insofar as your conscience likewise forbids the idea that God commanded such apparent moral atrocities, you ought not to believe it.

Of course, not all Christians will agree with that initial survey of intuitions regarding divinely commanded genocide. They will be inclined to place this issue into the same second-order category of reasoned disagreement as a debate over meticulous providence or Calvinist election. While I do believe that disagreement about something so fundamental as devotional child killing and genocide places our intuitive moral negations of those acts deep into the bedrock of our surest convictions, I wouldn't have bothered to write this book if all people already agreed with me! The obvious fact is that many people do disagree, even about claims that I consider so basic that I am inclined to think that no reasonable and morally properly functioning person should deny them. So how should we think of the fact that many do?

I could at this point adopt Thomas Reid's "bad faith" analysis to explain the disagreement: they don't *really* believe that. Rather, they are trying to convince themselves of that which they know cannot be true. While I see the lure of that interpretation (so eloquently stated by Budziszewski), I find it better to grant our interlocutor space to be faithful to their own moral convictions as they describe them even as we seek to present a reasoned case in support of *our* intuitions. And that is what I shall aim to do in the coming chapters. The fact remains that either there were historic divinely commanded genocides or there were not. Either it is *possible* that God could command genocide or it is not. These are important issues and where the question of biblical violence is concerned, we cannot afford *not* to address them. And while I shall seek to argue for the impossibility of divinely commanded mass killing or genocide by way of a close attention to moral intuitions that are clarified by way of careful reflection on paradigm cases, the fact remains that many Christians disagree with my conclusions.

In my experience, most Christians who continue to defend divinely commanded devotional mass-killing can at least sympathize with the intuitions to which I appeal in my own moral evaluation of the act. They too admit to feeling the pull of those intuitions, but they offer arguments to question or reject them. Among these responses are the following:

- God is the giver of life and he has the right to take the lives of the Canaanites.
- The Canaanites were exceedingly wicked and had no right to the land.
- The wickedness of the Canaanites would have corrupted the Israelites so it was necessary to protect the Israelites.
- This was a mercy killing for the Canaanite infants as they were saved from being raised in a corrupt culture by going straight to heaven.
- God's command determines what is right: *nuff said!*

These and countless other justifications have been offered to remove the cognitive dissonance between this theological belief and the deliverances of conscience *qua* the killing of innocent human life.

What should we who find our moral intuitions to be drilled deep into bedrock think of those kinds of defenses? While I don't find it helpful to invoke the charge of bad faith, I would be remiss not to admit that from my perspective such defenses do look like misguided rationalizations at best, the kind that Budziszewski provocatively claims constitute idolatrous rejections of the ineluctable deliverances of our moral intuition. To use his language, these kinds of apologetic defenses look to me like various instances of special pleading to defend an indefensible interpretation of the Bible: "Yes, murder is evil, but *this* isn't murder" or "Yes, this is murder, but they had to do it" or "Yes, this is murder and wrong, but they made up for it later".

Conclusion

So are these attempts to defend the Canaanite genocide legitimate rationales or, as I believe, are they pained rationalizations? What is the best way forward in seeking to settle this disagreement? In my estimation, the most important factor concerns the proper identification of our primal moral intuitions and so my argument shall be built on a close clarification of those intuitions with respect to the alleged divinely commanded actions.

To that end, the next chapter will lay out a methodology which will begin to explain how we can more effectively isolate the moral intuitions that are at issue so as to determine whether they really are drilled into the bedrock of ineluctable conviction. The method builds on careful reflection on paradigm cases of moral acts which can serve to isolate elements of the conscience, things we cannot *not* know, fixed points of secure moral insight like lighthouses which can then guide our theological reflection through turbulent waters.

For those like me who are already of the view that their conscience does not allow for historic divinely commanded genocide, this may be viewed as a salutary exercise to clarify their own moral thinking. However, for dogged advocates of historic divinely commanded genocide, I hope the next chapter will bring them to reconsider the nature, strength, and authority of their own moral intuitions in a way that invites a careful re-reading of the texts. And if not that, then my hope is that at least they will discover a new sympathy with those who say that they cannot believe God commanded such things for *their* conscience forbids it.

5

Moral Knowledge and Intimate Acquaintance

Tragically, the idea of a parent sacrificing their child in the belief that it is the divine will is not merely hypothetical. On November 23, 2004, Dena Schlosser, a suburban housewife from Plano, Texas, called 9-11 to report that she had offered her daughter to God. When the police arrived, they discovered "He Touched Me" playing loudly on the stereo while Schlosser stood in an ecstasy, gently swaying to the music, covered in blood and holding a large knife. The police frantically searched the home and soon found Schlosser's ten month old baby Margaret lying in her crib, her arms amputated.[72] "I want to give the baby to God," Schlosser had told her husband.[73] In later discussions with a court psychologist she explained that she believed God wanted

---

[72] "Texas Mother Who Killed Baby is Acquitted on Insanity Grounds," *The New York Times* (April 8, 2006), A11.

[73] See "Husband testifies in case of woman who cut off baby's arms," (Feb. 14, 2006), http://www.foxnews.com/story/0,2933,184731,00.html Cf. Alex Alvarez and Ronet Bachman, *Violence: The Enduring Problem* (Sage, 2008), 146.

her to offer her infant child to him as a sign of her devotion. And so, as with Abraham's willing offer of Isaac, Schlosser responded to the divine command.[74] She hewed Margaret into pieces much as Samuel had hewed King Agag.[75]

Whether the case is hypothetical or actual, concrete scenarios present us with a particularly vivid and illuminating window onto the moral evaluation of human action. In this chapter we will turn to the question of how we reflect on and isolate the contents of conscience, items of secure moral knowledge that will be important to guide our Bible reading and subsequent theological reflection. The core idea to which I will now appeal can be described as *the essential insight of intimate acquaintance*. These are instances where we subject hypothetical or actual cases to careful moral appraisal in order to gauge our intuitive moral response to them. The goal is to see whether these cases prompt a moral intuitive response at a deep, visceral level, a level which seems to bring us to the shuddering bedrock of secure moral knowledge. In the cases where this does occur, the moral deliverances of these illustrations provide fixed points, plumb lines for measuring moral claims. The role of these paradigm cases in moral reflection is described by Eleonore Stump:

---

[74] Schlosser believed God wanted her to sever her baby's arms as well as her own arms and head as divine offerings. "Mother Says God Told Her to Cut Baby," *Washington Post* (February 20, 2006), https://www.washingtonpost.com/archive/politics/2006/02/21/mother-says-god-told-her-to-cut-baby/77d4f25b-52a4-4884-8b74-634ead4b5adf/

[75] After her arrest Schlosser was diagnosed with post-partum psychosis and depression. Indeed, Schlosser had a history of postpartum depression. Alvarez and Bachman, *Violence: The Enduring Problem*, 146. During the trial it was also revealed that Schlosser had subsequently been discovered to suffer from a brain tumor. According to her defense attorneys the tumor could have precipitated hallucinations of the divine will. See "Texas Mother Who Killed Baby is Acquitted on Insanity Grounds."

It's true that our moral principles and our ethical theories rely on reason. But we build those principles and theories, at least in part, by beginning with strong intuitions about individual cases that exemplify wrongdoing, and we construct our ethical theories around those intuitions. We look for what the individual cases of wrongdoing have in common, and we try to codify their common characteristics into principles. Once the principles have been organized into a theory, we may also revise our original intuitions until we reach some point of reflective equilibrium, where our intuitions and theories are in harmony. But our original intuitions retain an essential primacy. If we found that our ethical theory countenanced those Nazi experiments on children, we'd throw away the theory as something evil itself.[76]

In the same way that we would reject any theory that countenanced Nazi experiments on children, so I would submit that we should reject any theory that countenances the genocidal slaughter of civilian populations. The challenge of the appeal to sustained moral reflection will be to bring others to that same conclusion.

Killing, Emotion, and Moral Intuition

It is important to appreciate that the *overt appeal to emotion* by way of paradigm cases of intimate acquaintance is not fallacious or manipulative. To think it is reflects a fundamental misunderstanding of the function of emotion in reasoning. The point is not that we seek to *manipulate* emotion in a gambit to bypass reasoning. The point, rather, is that we seek to bring the interlocutor into

---

[76] Stump, "The Mirror of Evil," *God and the Philosophers*, ed. Thomas Morris (Oxford University Press, 1994), 238.

closer understanding of the proper content of their own moral intuitions, intuitions that of their nature trigger an *emotional* reaction in the percipient and which provides the axiomatic ground or bedrock to sustain subsequent moral reasoning. The very nature of moral reasoning is such that it is grounded in intricate emotional responses of attraction and revulsion. To be sure, the emotional dimension of moral reasoning can be misused, but there is nothing problematic, in principle, with the appeal to emotion. Quite the opposite, in fact: the properly functioning moral agent contrasts at this point with the clinical psychopath who is unmoved emotionally as he is bereft of the ability to feel guilt for one's own actions or compassion and empathy for others.[77] To sum up, the powerful experience of emotions in cases of moral reflection on bedrock scenarios is *a sign of moral clarity not emotional manipulation.*

Next, we should note that personal acquaintance is important for moral assessment as it provides those occasions in which moral perception arises from our moral intuitions. Prolife advocates have long recognized this fact. When prochoice advocates of elective abortion employ language to describe abortion which seeks to maintain an emotional distance from the act (e.g. referring to the human fetus abstractly as 'uterine contents'), prolife advocates counter by employing language that intentionally seeks to personalize the fetus and appeal to the emotional connection between child and mother. From the perspective of the prolife advocate, the prochoice side seeks to deflect from our bedrock moral intuitions while the prolife side seeks to tap into them. And the manipulation comes not with appealing to our moral intuitions but rather with *suppressing* or *deflecting* them.

Consider the case of the one-time abortion rights crusader Bernard Nathanson who later experienced a high profile conversion to the prolife movement. In his book *The Hand of God*

---

[77] Robert D. Hare, *Without Conscience: The Disturbing World of the Psychopaths Among Us* (The Guilford Press, 1999), 40-46.

Nathanson recounts the experience that editing video footage of abortions recorded on ultrasound had on him and a colleague: "when he looked at the tapes with me in an editing studio, he was so affected that he never did another abortion. I, though I had not done an abortion in five years, was shaken to the very roots of my soul by what I saw."[78] This experience of *seeing* abortion from this perspective led Nathanson to produce *The Silent Scream* in 1984, a highly controversial short film which centered on depicting the dismemberment of a twelve-week old fetus in an abortion.[79] Nathanson observes that the pro-choice camp attempted to deflect from the emotional power of the film by raising the question of when the fetus gains sentient awareness, and thus the ability to feel pain. While the point at which the fetus gains sentience certainly *is* an important question, in Nathanson's view, raising the question in that context served as an attempt to deflect from the moral weight of the film, a response that could reasonably be interpreted as bearing a family resemblance to the *distraction* reading method.

To note another example of such paradigm reasoning, when considering the ethics of capital punishment, you may read abstract discussions of the practice within the context of various ethical theories. But it is quite another thing to *witness* an execution. Indeed, watching an actual case of capital punishment, like witnessing an abortion, may bring the individual into contact with strong intuitions regarding the act, intuitions that help one to clarify the conviction that capital punishment is intrinsically unethical. That would certainly seem to describe the experience of Leo Tolstoy on the dark occasion that he witnessed a public beheading:

---

[78] Nathanson, *The Hand of God: A Journey from Death to Life by the Abortion Doctor Who Changed His Mind* (Regnery, 2013), 146.

[79] You can read about the film here: https://www.imdb.com/title/tt1218041/?ref_=fn_al_tt_2

> When I saw the head divided from the body and heard the sound with which it fell separately into the box, I understood, not with my reason, but with my whole being, that no theory of the wisdom of all established things, nor of progress, could justify such an act; and that if all the men in the world from the day of creation, by whatever theory, had found this thing necessary, it was not so; it was a bad thing, and that therefore I must judge of what was right and necessary, not by what men said and did, not by progress, but what I felt to be true in my heart.[80]

Note first that Tolstoy's experience was *non-discursive*. He didn't *reason* to the wrongness of capital punishment. Rather, the experience of *seeing* a beheading provided the occasion in which he understood in a unique way what is entailed by execution. And his intuitive, visceral response was undeniable: *this is wrong*. The event provided the occasion for him to clarify his moral intuition in the intrinsic wrongness of capital punishment. That is the power and potential of intimate acquaintance to cultivate internal awareness of our moral intuitions.

Years before he became a renowned pacifist and dissident historian, Howard Zinn flew as a bombardier in WWII. The bombs Zinn dropped on the Nazi-occupied French countryside were laced with napalm (a highly volatile petrochemical and gelling agent which would cause objects to combust violently). Flying in sorties far above the landscape, Zinn would release his bombs into the silent rolling clouds and then return to base. Far up in the sky, he had extensive technical knowledge of these incendiaries and the kind of damage they could inflict. But as Zinn later reflected, that knowledge was abstracted from the concrete, real-world impact of the explosions on the terrorized civilian population far below:

---

80 Cited in Clarence Bauman, *The Sermon on the Mount: The Modern Quest for Its Meaning* (Mercer University Press, 1985), 13, n.

We had been trained to fly planes, fire guns, operate bombsights, and to take pride in doing the job well. And we had been trained to follow orders, which there was no reason to question, because everyone on our side was good, and on the other side, bad. Besides, we didn't have to watch a little girl's legs get blown off by our bombs; we were 30,000 feet high and no human being on the ground was visible, no scream could be heard.[81]

It was only when Zinn came down to ground level after the war and considered the actual implications of his actions up close—the decimated villages, the scarred, traumatized villagers, the smoking, charred corpses—that he could properly consider the full moral implications of his actions and assess them appropriately.

In the remainder of this chapter, we will consider concrete examples of paradigm cases to inform our moral reflection on two ethical questions. Launching off of Zinn's reflections, we shall initiate our own moral evaluation of these actions. The question is whether the Allied strategic bombing of civilian populations in WWII is consistent with the principles of just war. Our treatment of that question will focus on acquaintance descriptions of the impact/aftermath of the nuclear bombing of Hiroshima and the conventional firebombing of Hamburg. We shall conclude the chapter by returning to the related topic of state-sanctioned killing that was raised by Leo Tolstoy as we consider whether descriptions of actual cases of capital punishment in modern American society may illumine our assessment of the principled ethical status of state-sanctioned killing in general.

---

81 Howard Zinn, "Violence and Human Nature," in *Passionate Declarations: Essays on War and Justice* (HarperCollins, 2003), 42.

Melted Eyeballs, Melted Streets: The Moral Analysis of Allied Bombing in WWII

World War II is widely considered to be one of the clearest examples of a just war in history. However, even if we agree with the theoretical framework of just war analysis in general as well as the claim that this particular war satisfied the *jus ad bellum* (the just grounds for going to war), it doesn't follow that it also satisfied the *jus ad bello* (the just grounds for the conduct of war). In this section, I want to consider that latter issue more closely by giving attention to one important element in the Allied victory: the intentional and strategic targeting of civilian populations. The question is this: after we apply the essential insight of intimate acquaintance to the effects of the targeted bombing of civilians, can we say that such actions were just or should we offer a moral censure of them as a failure to satisfy the *jus ad bello*?

There has been no shortage of ethical defenses of the targeted bombing of civilians during WWII. One of the most famous is the 1981 essay "Thank God for the Atom Bomb" in which Paul Fussell employs a form of utilitarian calculation to argue that the bombing of Hiroshima and Nagasaki shortened the war and saved more lives than a protracted war that involved an Allied land invasion of Japan.[82] Based on this thesis, Fussell argues that the atomic bombing of the civilian populations of Hiroshima and Nagasaki was indeed justified.

Fussell makes a good case on utilitarian principles. But is there a way to step behind those principles and tap into some core ethical insights, some bedrock of moral intuition, which might undercut the viability of Fussell's premises from the outset? In short, can we secure the conclusion that it is wrong, *in principle*, to bomb civilians intentionally even if doing so could provide

---

82 See Paul Fussell, *Thank God for the Atom Bomb and Other Essays* (Summit, 1988).

a reasonable expectation of ultimately reducing the overall carnage of the war? Consider again the Nazi experiments on children to which Stump refers. A utilitarian like Fussell could argue in principle that carefully controlled experimentation on children could conceivably provide universal medical benefits to the human population that could far outweigh the suffering of the handful of children that were subject to these experiments. But would such reasoning be legitimate? Or does the bedrock of moral intuition instead support the conclusion that some actions are intrinsically wrong in themselves whatever the expected *outcome* may be? And if experimenting on children is always *verboten* irrespective of the anticipated goods that could come, might that not also be true of bombing civilian populations? And if that, what about genocide?

From the perspective of the essential insight of intimate acquaintance, if we truly want to evaluate the morality of the act and thus the legitimacy of the utilitarian approach, we cannot remain high up in the clouds in the cockpit of the Enola Gay placidly observing the expanding mushroom cloud billowing toward the heavens. Instead, we need to land the plane and walk into the midst of the smoking, radioactive carnage in order to consider up close what it actually means to nuke a civilian population. Only then can we truly have a good sense as to whether our moral intuitions will rise to vindicate or to condemn Fussell's reasoning.[83]

We will undertake this step of moral reflection by joining journalist John Hersey whose 1946 bestseller *Hiroshima*[84] provides a harrowing up-close account of the bomb and its aftermath. While the ground was still pulsing with radiation Hersey visited the bombed out city, weaving together the haunting recollections of six survivors of the bomb. Together, his account and

---

[83] One of the most powerful denunciations of the bombing is found in the haunting 1988 anime film *Grave of the Fireflies*.

[84] Hersey, *Hiroshima* (Knopf, 1946).

their words provide us with a powerful understanding of what it means to bomb a civilian population. And that in turn, will help to clarify and sharpen our moral intuitions to draw a final assessment of Fussell's reasoning.

To begin with, Hersey draws from the account of Dr. Sasaki:

> Before long, patients lay and crouched on the floors of the wards and the laboratories and all the other rooms, and in the corridors, and on the stairs, and in the front hall, and under the protecochere, and on the stone front steps, and in the driveway and courtyard, and for blocks each way in the streets outside. Wounded people supported maimed people; disfigured families leaned together. Many people were vomiting. A tremendous number of school girls—some of those who had been taken from their classrooms to work outdoors, clearing fire lanes—crept into the hospital. In a city of two hundred and forty-five thousand, nearly a hundred thousand people had been killed or doomed at one blow; a hundred thousand more were hurt.[85]

And then there are the haunting recollections of Mr. Tanimoto:

> he met hundreds and hundreds who were fleeing, and every one of them seemed to be hurt in some way. The eyebrows of some were burned off and skin hung from their faces and hands. Others, because of pain, held their arms up as if carrying something in both hands. Some were vomiting as they walked. Many were naked or in shreds of clothing. On some undressed bodies, the burns had made patterns—of undershirt straps and suspenders and, on the skin of some women (since white repelled the heat from the bomb and dark clothes absorbed it and conducted it to the skin), the shapes of flowers they had had on their kimonos.[86]

---

85 Hersey, *Hiroshima*, 34-5.
86 Hersey, *Hiroshima*, 39-40.

And now for the experience of Miss Sasaki:

> Miss Sasaki could not move, and she just waited in the rain. Then a man propped up a large sheet of corrugated iron as a kind of lean-to, and took her in his arms and carried her to it. She was grateful until he brought two horribly wounded people—a woman with a whole breast sheared off and a man whose face was all raw from a burn—to share the simple shed with her. No one came back.[87]

Here again is the hellish account of Mr. Tanimoto:

> Mr. Tanimoto found about twenty men and women on the sandspit. He drove the boat onto the bank and urged them to get aboard. They did not move and he realized that they were too weak to lift themselves. He reached down and took a woman by the hands, but her skin slipped off in huge, glove-like pieces.[88]

Finally, we turn to the nightmarish experience of a priest, Father Kleinsorge, who encountered the living dead gathered in a park:

> On his way back with the water, he got lost on a detour around a fallen tree, and as he looked for his way through the woods, he heard a voice ask from the underbush, 'Have you anything to drink?' He saw a uniform. Thinking there was just one soldier, he approached with the water. When he had penetrated the bushes, he saw there were about twenty men, and they were all in exactly the same nightmarish state: their faces were wholly burned, their eyesockets were hollow, the fluid from their melted eyes had run down their cheeks.[89]

---

[87] Hersey, *Hiroshima*, 44.
[88] Hersey, *Hiroshima*, 60.
[89] Hersey, *Hiroshima*, 68.

Before we conclude the ethical evaluation of Allied forces bombing civilian populations in WWII, we will consider one example from the European theater, the joint USAF and RAF bombing of Hamburg in 1943, aptly named "Operation Gomorrah". The bombing commenced on July 27 at 1 am and included over 10,000 pounds of bombs and explosives. In his 1997 Zurich Lectures W.G. Sebald provides a riveting description of the bombing and its aftermath:

> Within a few minutes, huge fires were burning all over the target area, which covered some twenty square kilometers, and they merged so rapidly that only a quarter of an hour after the first bombs had dropped the whole airspace was a sea of flames as far as the eye could see. Another five minutes later, at one-twenty A.M., a firestorm of an intensity that no one would ever before have thought possible arose. The fire, now rising two thousand meters into the sky, snatched oxygen to itself so violently that the air currents reached hurricane force, resonating like mighty organs with all their stops pulled out at once. The fire burned like this for three hours. At its height, the storm lifted gables and roofs from buildings, flung rafters and entire advertising billboards through the air, tore trees from the ground, and drove human beings before it like living torches. Behind collapsing facades, the flames shot up as high as houses, rolled like a tidal wave through the streets at a speed of over a hundred and fifty kilometers an hour, spun across open squares in strange rhythms like rolling cylinders of fire. The water in some of the canals was ablaze. The glass in the tram car windows melted; stocks of sugar boiled in the bakery cellars. Those who had fled from their air-raid shelters sank, with grotesque contortions, in the thick bubbles thrown up by the melting asphalt. No one knows for certain how many lost their lives that night, or how many went mad before they died.[90]

---

[90] Sebald, *On the Natural History of Destruction*, trans. Andrea Bell (Random

After reading these descriptions from Hersey and Sebald, and keeping in mind that there are tens of thousands more like them, you will have a better understanding of the ethics of bombing civilians, particularly in the theater of WWII. For me, such descriptions offer a powerful moral clarifying vision. Though I am sympathetic to Fussell's reasoning, the moral intuitions that I find to be triggered by these testimonial accounts are, in my view, driven into moral bedrock and as such they respond with an unequivocal voice of condemnation to the targeted bombing of civilian populations. I find that such actions belong in the same absolutely *verboten* category as those Nazi experiments on children. And consequently, I must conclude that any moral argument which would propose otherwise is itself an immoral framework which needs to be rejected. If I may borrow from Tolstoy, "no theory of the wisdom of all established things, nor of progress, could justify such an act; and that if all the men in the world from the day of creation, by whatever theory, had found this thing necessary, it was not so; it was a bad thing, and that therefore I must judge of what was right and necessary, not by what men said and did, not by progress, but what I felt to be true in my heart."

Perhaps you will disagree. Even after those descriptions, you may still find yourself siding with Fussell. If that is the case I would hope that at least you should be able better to understand the moral weight of the intuitions that drive those who disagree with you. And you may appreciate how each and all are responsible to their own moral intuitions.

House, 2003), 26-27.

The Foot of the Scaffold: The Moral Analysis of Execution

In the previous section we focused on the targeting of non-combatants in war. In this section, we will return to the same moral sphere as the event that appalled Tolstoy, namely, the ethics of state-based capital-punishment. Our launching point for concrete reflection on this topic will be a selection of case studies drawn from the book *Gruesome Spectacles: Botched Executions and America's Death Penalty*. This is a helpful volume because the author recognizes the central importance of thick narratival descriptions of specific occasions of state-based killing as a basis for careful reflection on the ethics and legality of various modes of capital punishment. Each chapter in the book is devoted to the history of a different method of capital punishment practiced in the United States. One thing that becomes clear is that they are *all* messy and none comes without some deeply troubling ethical implications.

Chapter 2 of the book is devoted to hanging, the predominant mode of execution in the nineteenth century. While hanging was common throughout the century, by the 1880s, public opinion began to build against this mode of execution due to several high-profile botched hangings. In 1882-83 the New York Times published ninety-one detailed accounts of hanging: "These stories related the sights and sounds of hangings in such a way as to bring their readers to the very foot of the scaffold. In all of their melodrama, the articles underscored one central, unavoidable truth about hangings: a huge percentage of them were botched."[91] With these accounts of intimate acquaintance, readers gradually became convinced that "the noose was outdated and gruesome".[92]

---

[91] Austin Sarat, *Gruesome Spectacles: Botched Executions and America's Death Penalty* (Stanford Law Books, 2014), 63.

[92] Sarat, *Gruesome Spectacles: Botched Executions and America's Death Penalty*, 63.

At the same time that public sentiment was turning against the noose, the technological application of electricity was being considered for a range of novel applications, and people began to view electrocution as promising a more efficient, reliable, and humane form of execution. However, despite the initial optimism, that promise was not borne out by the first state-based electrocution, that of William Kemmler on August 6, 1890. While a quick, clean death was promised, the result was anything but. After receiving the first shock, "Kemmler began to drool; his chest heaved, and he made strange noises. The warden again ordered the current turned on. But this time, as the electricity pulsed through Kemmler's body, white smoke appeared and a 'pungent and sickening odor' filled the death chamber. After seventy-three seconds the current was finally turned off. The execution lasted a total of eight minutes...."[93] Witnesses subsequently described the execution as "horrible" and "ghastly"[94] Nor did the process improve significantly in subsequent cases. And so, while electrocution would still be widely used for decades, gradually public sentiment began to build against the electric chair much as it had previously turned against the gallows.

By the late 1970s, another promising technology emerged which again provided the hope of a way out of the ethical and legal morass. Lethal injection was promoted as a more humane means of killing much as the grisly and unpredictable electric chair had a century before. On May 10, 1977, Oklahoma became the first state to adopt legislation directing use of lethal injection as a way "to find an alternative to the 'inhumanity, visceral brutality, and cost' of the electric chair."[95] Other jurisdictions soon began adopting lethal injection drawn by the fact that it "*appears* more humane and *visually* palatable relative to other

---

93 Sarat, *Gruesome Spectacles*, 69.

94 Sarat, *Gruesome Spectacles*, 68.

95 Sarat, *Gruesome Spectacles*, 117.

methods."⁹⁶ In other words, lethal injection promised to secure a visual experience for the observer that would be less likely to trigger powerful moral intuitions.

Thus, the primary appeal of lethal injection lay in the fact that it tends to shield the tortured brutality of killing from the observers. The standard form of execution is a three-drug protocol. The cocktail includes sodium thiopental which anesthetizes the victim and pancuronium bromide which paralyzes the victim in order to inhibit his ability to exhibit pain-behaviors. The pancuronium bromide was important to mask the process of killing from the ethically sensitive observer: "The condemned thus look peaceful before they die, and the spectacles of the severed head in a botched hanging or the smoke-filled death chamber after an electrocution gone wrong have all but disappeared."⁹⁷

The biggest ethical concern came with the fact that the final drug in the cocktail, potassium chloride, could potentially cause extraordinary pain to the victim. To be sure, given the paralyzing effect of pancuronium bromide that torturous agony would be shielded from observers. But "out of sight, out of mind" is hardly an ethical stance and consequently, many people have worried that lethal injection may, in many cases, simply shield the true agonizing brutality and inhumanity of the death from observers, thereby perpetuating a false sense of its ethical acceptability.

A further concern with this method is that at least 7% of planned lethal injection executions in the United States fail. The case of Rommell Broom illustrates the surprising difficulties that are associated with lethal injection. In Broom's case, the executioners spent two hours attempting to find a vein: "During the failed procedure, Broom winced and grimaced with pain. At one point, he covered his face with both hands and appeared to be sobbing, his stomach heaving."⁹⁸ By the time his execution was

---

96 Sarat, *Gruesome Spectacles,* 118, emphasis in original.

97 Sarat, *Gruesome Spectacles,* 120.

98 Sarat, *Gruesome Spectacles,* 136

postponed, Broom had over eighteen needle sticks in his body.[99] Ultimately, the state decided not to proceed with the execution and Broom remains on death row to this day. To sum up, lethal injection raises concerns both of the agony of the dying which may be hidden from the observer as well as the psychological distress of the prisoner when the process is extended or when it fails due to factors like the inability to secure a vein (a not uncommon occurrence).

In all these different types of execution, it is reasonable to conclude that increased direct acquaintance with each specific mode of killing (either through witnessing the event or hearing/reading detailed descriptions of it) leads to a growing awareness of the moral problems with the act. And in many cases, it may sustain the intuitive conclusion that one or more of these methods are wrong in principle.

As we have seen, the cases of failure are a major factor in evaluating capital punishment. However, if public revulsion to killing by hanging, electrocution, and lethal injection really is sourced simply in the fact that these methods are often botched so that they thereby increase suffering unnecessarily to the subject, then it may be time to make a return to the mode of execution that so appalled Tolstoy. That is precisely the surprising argument that John Kruzel makes in his article "Bring Back the Guillotine."[100] When you read the various methods of killing a human being described in *Gruesome Spectacles*, the case for the sharp blade of the guillotine does appear to be surprisingly strong: if our concern is to expedite the process and minimize

---

99 Sarat, *Gruesome Spectacles*, 140.

100 Kruzel also argues pragmatically that beheading is far better for organ donation "because the bodies of guillotined prisoners could be more quickly harvested for viable parts, unlike organs that may become unusable after lethal injection due to hypoxemia." "Bring Back the Guillotine," *Slate* (November 1, 2013), https://slate.com/news-and-politics/2013/11/guillotine-death-penalty-lethal-injection-is-cruel-and-unusual-punishment-slicing-off-the-head-is-the-better-way-to-go.html

the suffering and trauma of botched executions then it begins to look like a far superior and more humane mode of killing.

While the attractions of beheading as a mode of execution are significant, it does face one notable objection: beheading is one of the most overtly violent ways to execute a person and thus one that creates the greatest trauma for observers. As noted above, lethal injection, in particular, is designed to shield the horror of killing from spectators: paralyze a body and then slowly, 'gently,' destroy it from within. By contrast, the guillotine leaves nothing to the imagination: the gleaming metal blade drops with a whoosh and slices through the neck like a hot knife through butter, leaving the head to drop with a thud as blood pulses out in a fine spray from the stump of the neck.

Another way to look at it is that beheading is the most *honest* of the means of state-based killing, and thus the one that is most reliable at triggering our moral intuitions that *this is wrong*. Ironically, it could be that this *least un-ethical* means of killing provides the greatest moral clarity as to the general immorality of execution. And thus, we too may find ourselves being gripped with the same moral conclusion that so gripped Tolstoy. In that case, insofar as we might still prefer killing by lethal injection, it could be merely because that mode is fundamentally dishonest: it tells us a sweet little lie about the process of killing, shielding us from the true horror of the act, and so working to subvert the guiding light and fierce grip of our moral intuitions.

Conclusion

This chapter has focused on developing a method of moral reflection that can inform and guide our theological reflection. I have argued that we have innate moral knowledge, that which we may identify as moral intuitions, and these intuitions are clarified as we reflect on concrete hypothetical or actual cases of moral action. We explored the intimate acquaintance that informs our thinking with respect to descriptions of the effect of the targeted bombing of civilian non-combatants and of execution. In each case, at least some people will find contemplation of such cases triggering fundamental moral intuitions which justify them in concluding that those actions cannot possibly be moral. Those who may not be persuaded that these intuitions are indeed drilled into moral bedrock should at least be able to understand the weight they carry for others. The next step will be to consider how this fact may inform our thinking about biblical genocide. Genocide is an enormously complex phenomenon, so we will devote the following chapter to developing an account of it in its varied complexity as a basis for substantive acquaintance moral reflection.

6

On the Canaanites of Central Africa

The question before us is this: could God command a genocide? That is, could God command actions that seek to bring about the systematic destruction of an entire *genos*, an ethnic, cultural, and/or religious identity as such? Or is the moral indictment of this action drilled into moral bedrock equivalent to the evil of a man being forced to rape his daughter or a man engaging in the devotional killing of his son? Given the particularly violent natures of the genocidal directives in Deuteronomy 7 and 20 and the resulting actions of Joshua 1-12, the question before us is not only about genocide. It is more narrowly about a particular species of genocide, namely the most direct, overt, and cruel form, that which seeks the destruction of the ethnic, cultural, and/or religious identity by way of the mass targeted elimination of members of the group through close-contact killing. Thus, to secure the finest point on our moral analysis, it is this type of genocide on which we shall focus.

In order to apply our method of clarifying moral intuitions by intimate acquaintance to the evaluation of this type of action, we need to contemplate a detailed description of what this kind of genocide would look like. Based upon that data, we will then be in a better position of moral clarity to discern whether our intuitions are sufficient to compel us to conclude that we are indeed in moral bedrock such that God *could not* command such an action. As a basis for moral reflection, I have decided to focus on what is arguably the most infamous post-WWII genocide as a basis for moral reflection, one that unfolded in the small central African country of Rwanda between April and July 1994.[101] Over a few months, Hutus of the region butchered at least 800,000 Tutsis in a manner of killing that retains some deeply disturbing points of overlap with the genocide of Canaan.[102] Indeed, those many similarities would justify calling the Tutsi victims the Canaanites of central Africa.

Rwanda and Canaan: Differences and Similarities

Before I summarize several critical points of similarity that justify the Rwanda/Canaan comparison, I will briefly note one significant difference. While the Rwandan genocide involved Hutu genocidaires targeting some strangers it also involved multiple instances of genocidaires killing former friends, neighbors, and acquaintances. By contrast, the Israelite genocide of Canaan would have been restricted to the targeted elimination of strangers. Thus, the added sense of personal and social betrayal that

---

101 Tragically, Rwanda was the first genocide to be recognized by the United Nations. See United Nations Office on Genocide Prevention and the Responsibility to Protect, "When to Refer to a Situation as 'Genocide,'" United Nations https://www.un.org/en/genocideprevention/documents/publications-and-resources/GuidanceNote-When%20to%20refer%20to%20a%20situation%20as%20genocide.pdf

102 While the death toll is standardly listed as 800,000, some estimates range up to one million.

would have occurred in Rwandan killings would not have been a factor in Canaan. While this difference is worth noting, it is significantly outweighed by the many similarities which allow us to conclude that Rwanda is indeed a suitable analogue to model moral reflection on genocide in Canaan.

There are five primary reasons that I selected this specific genocide to facilitate a paradigm case for moral reflection on the events of Canaan.

First, the nature of the genocide. Rwanda is a clear and unambiguous genocide in which one ethic group (Hutus) acted with clear and predetermined intention to eradicate and displace another group (Tutsis), primarily through the most overt and direct of methods, that of mass killing.[103] This parallels the explicit directives to eradicate the Canaanites as outlined in Deuteronomy 7:1-3 and 20:16-18.

Second, the use of psychological terror. The Rwandan genocide was carried out with the perpetuation of psychological terror in the target Tutsi population. In some cases, that terror was so overwhelming that it manifested in behaviors of learned helplessness in the victims: "Many Tutsis no longer asked to be spared, that was how they greeted death, among themselves. They had stopped hoping, they knew they had no chance for mercy and went off without a single prayer. They knew they were abandoned by everything, even by God."[104]

While we do not have the benefit of the actual Canaanite perspective, we do find in the Israelite record references to their psychological terror and an impending sense of helplessness in the face of the inevitability of their destruction (e.g. Joshua 2:11). After the decimation of Jericho, the Canaanites begin to mount

---

103 In fact, there is significant question as to whether 'Hutu' and 'Tutsi' identify distinct ethnic groups. Ironically, the same ambiguity attends the actual distinction between ethnic 'Israelite' and 'Canaanite'.

104 Jean Hatzfeld, *Machete Season: The Killers in Rwanda Speak*, trans. Linda Coverdale (Picador, 2005), 143.

a defense (e.g. Joshua 7:4) and after the eradication of Ai there is a concerted effort to push back against the Israelites (9:2). Despite these increasingly desperate actions there appears to be a deep fear among the Canaanites as well as a haunting belief in the final inevitability of Israel's success (9:24). Thus, while the Canaanites do not necessarily demonstrate the behaviors of learned helplessness, they do exhibit evidence of psychological terror and a fatalism or hopelessness about their future.

Third, dependence upon close-contact low-tech killing. Rwanda was a 'low-tech' genocide, one that focused on achieving the end by way of close-contact killing via simple battle and agricultural implements, primarily the machete and secondarily the *masu* (a nail studded club) as well as other sharp agricultural implements and the limited use of firearms.[105]

The Bronze Age Israelite army obviously had no firearms, but they would have been equipped with swords (e.g. Joshua 6:2; 10:28) and spears (e.g. Numbers 25:7-8; Judges 5:8). As a result, the killing was close-contact and involved very similar intimate assaultive actions to Rwanda including the cutting, impaling, stabbing, slicing, bludgeoning, and hacking of victims.

Fourth, the promise of looting the victims as an inducement. This is certainly the case in Rwanda where, as Gourevitch writes, "As an added incentive to the killers, Tutsis' belongings were parceled out in advance—the radio, the couch, the goat, the opportunity to rape a young girl."[106] At first blush, this might seem to be a *contrast* to the Israelite conquest in Canaan. After all, the Israelites were initially commanded to turn everything over to the *herem* including all human beings and material goods. And of course, when Achan failed to do so, both he and his

---

105 Philip Verwimp, "Machetes and Firearms: The Organization of Massacres in Rwanda," *Journal of Peace Research,* vol. 43, no. 1 (2006), 5-22. Cf. Gourevitch, *We Wish to Inform You that Tomorrow We Will be Killed with Our Families,* 23.

106 Gourevitch, *We Wish to Inform You that Tomorrow We Will be Killed with Our Families,*115.

entire family were themselves turned over to the *herem* (Joshua 7). While that would appear to be an important difference, a closer look reveals substantial overlap on this point. To begin with, it is worth bearing in mind that from the outset the Israelites were allowed to acquire slaves and booty in the targeted neighboring tribes (Deuteronomy 20:10-15). What is more, beginning with the assault on Ai, Yahweh allows the Israelites to claim "plunder and livestock" (Joshua 8:2). Thus, looting *was* a part of the Canaanite genocide, even of the tribes within the land. Finally, it is also important to keep in mind that the entire genocide promised to the Israelites an idealized homeland, a land flowing with milk and honey (Exodus 3:17). Consequently, there was indeed a material *quid pro quo* underlying and motivating the Canaanite genocide: slaughter the indigenous population and you will receive their plunder, livestock, land, *and* God's blessing. In other words, the Israelites were indeed promised more than a material equivalent of the radio, couch, goat, and young girl.

Fifth, a shared background justifying religious context. Rwanda is the most Christianized country in Africa,[107] with approximately 90% of citizens identifying as Catholic, Protestant, or Adventist. So it is not surprising that Judeo-Christian beliefs formed a background ideological framework and justification for the genocide. In fact, Hutus explicitly invoked divine favor and guidance prior to and during the genocide. For example, a hill named Kibeho had become famous in this largely Catholic country during the 1980s as a place for receiving visions from the Virgin Mary. During this time, the hill attracted the attention of many pious Catholic Hutus including Madame Agathe, wife of Hutu President Habyarimana (whose later assassination would be the trigger for the genocide).[108] In the years and months before the violence, the Blessed Virgin allegedly predicted that "Rwanda would, before

---

[107] Gourevitch, *We Wish to Inform You that Tomorrow We Will be Killed with Our Families*, 79.

[108] Habyarimana's assassination by Hutus would be the flashpoint for the

long, be bathed in blood."[109] One way to read the prophecy was that God's impending judgment against Tutsis would finally be unleashed on the nation. Such 'prophecies' perpetuated a sense of providential inevitability to the coming genocide. And so, not long after the killing began it was no surprise when it was joyously reported that the Virgin Mary had now allegedly given tacit approval to the genocide.[110] What is more, several high profile Christian leaders were active participants in the genocide, the most infamous being Pastor Elizaphan Ntakirutimana who oversaw the Mugonero massacre which involved the slaughter of hundreds of his own Tutsi congregants.

To be sure, many Hutus struggled with deep cognitive dissonance over their role in the genocide. Some attempted to separate their faith from the killing[111] while others seemed to recognize at some level that God did not approve.[112] And a noble but all-too-small minority outright refused to participate in the carnage, boldly pointing out the direct contradiction that these massacres presented to their Christian faith.[113]

However, other Hutus seemed to experience no such tension as they embraced their roles as genocidaires with what can only

---

genocide but he led the ideological campaign against the Tutsis that prepared the way for genocide.

109 Gourevitch, *We Wish to Inform You that Tomorrow We Will be Killed with Our Families*, 79.

110 Gourevitch, *We Wish to Inform You that Tomorrow We Will be Killed with Our Families*, 136-7.

111 Alphonse: "I had been sincerely baptized Catholic, but I felt it preferable not to pray traditionally during the killings. There was nothing to be asked of God during that filthy business." Hatzfeld, *Machete Season: The Killers in Rwanda Speak*, 141. "God kept silent, and the churches stank from abandoned bodies. Religion could not find its place in our activities." Hatzfeld, *Machete Season*, 142.

112 "Deep down we knew that Christ was not on our side in this situation ..." Hatzfeld, *Machete Season*, 145, cf. 94-5.

113 Hatzfeld, *Machete Season*, 116.

be called religious fervor. As Timothy Longman has observed, many of the churches in this majority Christian country were active in the genocide: "numerous priests, pastors, nuns, brothers, catechists, and Catholic and Protestant lay leaders supported, participated in, or helped to organize the killings."[114] One Catholic named Adalbert recalls, "I was appointed killing boss because I gave orders intensely. Same thing in the Congolese camps. In prison I was appointed charismatic leader because I sang intensely. I enjoyed the alleluias. I gladly felt rocked by those joyous verses. I was steadfast in my love of God."[115] Hutus like Adalbert were fueled by a sense of divine purpose in the genocide.

A Catholic priest recalls "a woman who spent a whole day on the river bank killing other women who were handed over to her with a hammer. She was neither drunk nor under the effect of drugs. She was acting on her own free will, without any difficulty or remorse, without feelings; on the contrary, she was motivated by a great sense of morality."[116]

Another genocidaire named Alphonse recalls that after a day of killing Tutsis, they gathered the cows and "spent the evening slaughtering the cattle, singing, and chatting about the new days on the way. It was the most terrific celebration."[117]

To conclude, while many Hutu Christians experienced tensions with their beliefs and a minority rejected the genocide outright, the fact remains that the preparation for and conduct of the genocide was intimately tied to Christian beliefs, was

---

114 Longman, "Christian Churches and Genocide in Rwanda," *In God's Name: Genocide and Religion in the Twentieth Century*, ed. Omer Bartov and Phyllis Mack (Berghahn Books, 2001), 140. Cf. eds. Carol Rittner, John K. Roth, and Wendy Whitworth, *Genocide in Rwanda: Complicity of the Churches?* (Paragon House, 2004).

115 Hatzfeld, *Machete Season*, 140.

116 Ralph J. Hartley, "To Massacre: A Perspective on Demographic Competition," *Anthropological Quarterly*, 80, no. 1 (2007) : 244.

117 Hatzfeld, *Machete Season*, 93.

guided or encouraged by several recognized Christian leaders like Ntakirutimana, and was purportedly predicted and validated by alleged Marian revelations. In all these ways, the Rwandan genocide calls to mind the descriptions we read of the divine mandate for and conduct of the Israelite-led mass close-contact killing of Canaanites in Joshua.

To sum up, these five parallels make Rwanda a suitably close analogue to the Canaanite genocide on which to model careful ethical reflection. Not only was it a clear case of genocide, but it involved the perpetuation of psychological terror on the victims, was carried out by way of low-tech close-contact killing, offered the inducement of material looting, and depended on a justifying religious framework.

There is one additional factor that makes Rwanda a particularly useful thought-experiment for moral illumination and that is that it is a relatively recent event. One of the hurdles when thinking about the conquest of Canaan from an ethical perspective is that these events would have occurred more than three thousand years ago: put simply, a long time ago and far, far away. The effect of contemplating the ethics of an event in the distant past can be equivalent to contemplating the ethics of napalming a village from 30,000 feet: in each case, the distance can dim moral intuition and perception. By contrast, the comparative intimacy of a recent event overcomes this emotional distance by providing us with raw, contemporaneous reports of the carnage that allow us to experience the full emotional weight of genocide on the ground. Speaking personally, I myself have spoken to two survivors of the Rwandan genocide who later immigrated to Canada and their recollections of the terror and the uncertainty certainly helped me to understand aspects of the genocide with a greater emotional and ethical clarity. For all these reasons I believe that exploring the lot of Tutsis, the Canaanites in central Africa, provides a powerful way to clarify the ethics of exterminating Canaanites in the Promised Land. And that, in turn, will provide invaluable moral guidance when seeking how to read and understand the texts in Deuteronomy and Joshua.

The Atrocities

We can now turn to our case study proper. For decades preceding the genocide, Rwanda had struggled with deep social tensions between the Hutu majority and the Tutsi minority. These tensions had been fomented by the Belgian and French colonizers and their imposition of rigid ethnic identities upon the indigenous population (e.g. introducing an ethnic identity card system in the 1930s) as well as an ideological narrative touting Tutsi superiority as the natural ruling class. Factors like these were catalysts for fixing socially recognized ethnic identities and creating class conflict which erupted in the first widespread outbreak of Hutu violence against Tutsis in 1959. Tragically, that was just the beginning: the next thirty-five years bore witness to multiple isolated and sporadic Hutu-led attacks on Tutsis. This decades-long internecine violence finally reached a critical mass in April 1994 with the assassination of Hutu President Habyarimana, a man who had himself for years stoked violence and resentment against Tutsis. On April 6, his plane was shot down by Hutu militants who used the assassination as a pretext to unleash a final solution against the Tutsis.

At this point, I am going to recount some examples of the genocidal killing. In our survey of methods of state-based execution, we noted the messiness and moral ambiguity of acts like electrocution and lethal injection. As disturbing as those cases may be, it is important to keep in mind that those killings were carried out in controlled circumstances and were based on careful professional preparation. Despite that backdrop, many of the executions were still deeply morally ambiguous, botched or otherwise excessively extended exercises in inhumanity. The lesson is that killing people is a messy business even in the best of circumstances. With that as a backdrop, how efficient would you expect the killing to be when the context is a rolling genocide with a poorly trained army wielding machetes or swords against thousands of desperate, struggling victims in a frenzy of sporadic bloodlust? If the execution room of an American prison may witness morally horrific levels of suffering and a terrible number of botched executions, what would happen when the setting is a family living room, a backwoods swamp, and countless other impromptu ordinary settings where enraged executioners, former neighbors and friends, pursue their victims with masus and machetes?

We will begin with an account from Lieutenant-General Romeo Dallaire. As the genocide began, Dallaire was serving in Rwanda as head of the peace-keeping force UNAMIR (United Nations Assistance Mission for Rwanda). When the killing broke out in early April, Dallaire and his troops could do little more than chronicle the unfolding horror and plead with western nations to provide military intervention. In his book *Shake Hands with the Devil* Dallaire recounts arriving at Gikondo Parish Church with two colleagues, Brent and Stefan, in early April soon after the genocide began. Predictably, Tutsis had rushed to churches in this ostensibly Christian nation to seek safe sanctuary and this was one such case. However, the Hutus did not recognize sanctuary for 'cockroaches'. This is the scene from hell that Dallaire and his colleagues witnessed upon their arrival:

> Across the street from the mission, an entire alleyway was littered with the bodies of women and children near a hastily abandoned school. As Brent and Stefan were standing there trying to take in the number of bodies, a truck full of armed men roared by. Brent and Stefan decided to head for the church. Stefan went inside while Brent stood by the door to cover him and to keep the APC [armored personnel carrier] in sight. They confronted a scene of unbelievable horror–the first such scene

UNAMIR witnessed—evidence of the genocide, though we didn't yet know to call it that. In the aisles and on the pews were the bodies of hundreds of men, women and children. At least fifteen of them were still alive but in a terrible state. The priests were applying first aid to the survivors. A baby cried as it tried to feed on the breast of its dead mother . . . .[118]

The priests who survived the bloody assault recounted in agonizing detail how the terrible scene had unfolded. Dallaire recalls:

No one was spared. A pregnant woman was disembowelled and her fetus severed. Women suffered horrible mutilation. Men were struck on the head and died immediately or lingered in agony. Children begged for their lives and received the same treatment as their parents. Genitalia were a favourite target, the victims left to bleed to death. There was no mercy, no hesitation and no compassion.[119]

I am going to return to the topics of mutilation and torture later. Suffice it to say for now that these types of actions are a predictable by-product of mass close-contact killing.

In his book *We Wish to Inform You that Tomorrow We Will be Killed with Our Families*, journalist Philip Gourevitch recalls visiting Nyarubuye, a truly grisly memorial to the genocide which was centered on a complex with corpses in various states of decomposition littering the floor. While visiting the site, Gourevitch describes seeing decomposing severed heads, various bones and skulls with deep cuts, and even a Converse shoe jammed into a pelvis.[120]

---

[118] Dallaire, *Shake Hands with the Devil: The Failure of Humanity in Rwanda* (Da Capo Press, 2004), 279.

[119] Dallaire, *Shake Hands with the Devil: The Failure of Humanity in Rwanda*, 280.

[120] Gourevitch, *We Wish to Inform You that Tomorrow We Will be Killed with Our Families*, 16.

Dallaire's report at Gikondo Parish Church and Gourevitch's account of Nyarubuye are just two examples of what close-contact genocide looks like on the ground: indiscriminate slaughter resulting in a blood-soaked nightmarish landscape of decapitated heads, bowels spilled out in the dirt, amputated limbs, buzzing flies and the agonizing, desperate groans of the dying. Obviously, other genocides in other times and places will look different in various respects. But these *types* of events are a regular occurrence in close-contact killing genocides. When the genocidaires engage in acts of close-contact killing of the target group with various cutting tools like machetes or swords, when they aim to cause egregious bodily and/or mental harm to the target group, and when they attempt to inflict on the group conditions that bring about its destruction, we can surmise that the genocide will look in broad outline much like the horror that unfolded at Gikondo Parish Church and Nyarubuye. Thus, these eyewitness accounts of carnage provide essential on-the-ground content for our moral reflection on genocide generally, and the close-contact mass-killing of the Canaanites, in particular.

The Psychology of Genocide

As we saw above, torture and mutilation were common factors of the killing in Rwanda. It is important to recognize that these kinds of behaviors are not *incidental* to close-contact genocide. Rather, they are a predictable coping mechanism which aids killing like grease that aids the smooth running of an engine. To understand why this is the case we need to say something about human psychology and the overwhelming aversion to killing in properly functioning human beings.

Place yourself in the role of the genocidaire for a moment. What would that be like? What would the psychological and spiritual impact be upon your psyche? Daniel Goldhagen poses just this question as he asks us to imagine the brutality and cruelty of the close-contact killing of another human being:

> You cut him. Then cut him again. Then cut him again and again. Think of listening to the person you are about to murder begging, crying for mercy, for her life. Think of hearing your victim's screams as you hack at or "cut" her and then cut her again, and again, and again, or the screams of a boy as you hack at his eight-year-old body.[121]

How would those actions *not* have a devastating corrupting influence on your mind and your very soul? What would you need to do to overcome your enormous aversion to inflicting such atrocities on others?

In his landmark study *On Killing: The Psychological Cost of Learning to Kill in War and Society*, Dave Grossman studies this profound aversion that normal human beings have toward killing other human beings and how modern warfare has sought to overcome it in the training of soldiers. As he puts it, "The resistance to the close-range killing of one's own species is so great that it is often sufficient to overcome the cumulative influences of the instinct for self-protection, the coercive forces of leadership, the expectancy of peers, and the obligation to preserve the lives of comrades."[122] To put it bluntly, properly functioning human beings will do almost anything to avoid killing others, particularly when that killing requires intimate, close contact violent actions. And when people *do* end up engaging in acts of close-contact killing, it is almost always because they are *forced* to. Not surprisingly, the immediate and long-term psychological impact on those who cross the threshold is predictably devastating. As Grossman notes, "With very few exceptions, everyone associated

---

121 Cited in Livingstone Smith, *Less Than Human: Why We Demean, Enslave and Exterminate Others* (St. Martins Press, 2012), 132.

122 Dave Grossman, *On Killing* (Little, Brown and Co, 1995), 86.

with killing in combat reaps a bitter harvest of guilt."[123] And as Richard Prystowsky writes, "war never leaves the soldier. It infects his very being; it remains lodged in his psyche, disquieting his soul."[124]

It has been observed that "War is a mother lode of traumatic experiences and the chief source of the concept of PTSD."[125] Given the natural human aversion to violence, killing, and high stress situations, those who participate in the theater of war tend to experience severe psychological deterioration. Ironically, one common coping mechanism for addressing the trauma of killing is to double down on acts of dehumanizing violence and cruelty against the target group. By reinforcing the sense that this group is *less than human* or *worthy only of destruction,* one can seek to justify their actions. Consider the case of Jesse Spielman, an American soldier who was convicted of raping a fourteen year old Iraqi girl and then murdering both her and her family.[126] It would be more assuring to think that Spielman was a psychopath all along, one who revealed his true self on the battlefield. Far more disturbing is the prospect that the crucible of war can lead average people to commit such heinous acts. Nonetheless, the evidence supports the latter conclusion, at least in many cases: a well-adjusted, psychologically healthy individual who is forced to kill others will commonly experience significant psychological deterioration and the reaction to that deterioration may be to subject members of the target group to even more viciously cruel actions. One Vietnam vet describes the moral

---

123 Grossman, *On Killing,* 89.

124 Richard Prystowsky, "Bringing it All Back Home," *Encounter: Education for Meaning and Social Justice* (Summer 2005), 42.

125 "Rethinking Posttraumatic Stress Disorder," *Harvard Mental Health Letter,* 24, no. 2 (2007): 1.

126 Ryan Lenz, "Soldier Sentenced to 110 Years for Attack," *Washington Post* (August 5, 2007) http://www.washingtonpost.com/wp-dyn/content/article/2007/08/04/AR2007080401631.html

destruction of his own character as a result of participation in acts of killing on the battlefield as follows: "I was transformed from a simple island boy into a demon, a monster. That accounts for the second tour of duty. *Beginning to have fun, enjoy killing.*"[127]

As I said, this increased tendency to dehumanize and brutalize others is a rather ironic way to deal with the short-term trauma of close-contact killing. In that sense, it could be compared to the person with binge-eating disorder who addresses feelings of shame over body image by *increasing* their consumption of food. The effect that training to kill can have on the soldier was hauntingly portrayed by the psychological disintegration of Leonard Lawrence (aka 'Gomer Pyle') during basic training in the Stanley Kubrick film *Full Metal Jacket*. Lawrence enters boot camp as an amiable young fellow, but the brutality and othering he experiences from the drill sergeant and his fellow privates, methods that are themselves intended to lower his inhibitions to kill prior to entering the theater of war, have a devastating impact leading to his murder of the drill sergeant before he kills himself.

The vast majority of would-be genocidaires are not psychopaths.[128] As a result, these 'normal' individuals will eventually experience the devastating psychological deterioration wrought by close-contact killing. Nonetheless, in the short-term retaining a sharp ingroup/outgroup boundary buoyed by revulsion toward the outgroup provides an effective temporary means to overcome the aversion to killing. Needless to say, it is much easier

---

127 Chalsa M. Loo et. al., "Ethnic-Related Stressors in the War Zone: Case Studies of Asian American Vietnam Veterans," *Military Medicine*, 172 (2007), 970, emphasis added.

128 Estimates are that clinical psychopaths comprise less than one percent of the population, though subclinical psychopathy would be significantly more common. See James M. LeBreton, et. al, "Subclinical Psychopaths," *Comprehensive Handbook of Personality and* Psychopathology, vol. 1. *Personality and Everyday Functioning*, eds. Jay C. Thomas and Daniel L. Segal (Wiley, 2006), 389.

to maintain that dehumanizing boundary at a distance, while it is far more difficult to maintain it up close when the outgroup evinces all the signs of a common humanity with the ingroup. As a result, further coping mechanisms are necessary and that occurs when genocidaires double-down on the othering of the target group in the midst of close-contact killing. The ground of the othering can be ontological: i.e. this group is fundamentally *different* than us. Or it may be based on a contingent, historical grievance: i.e. this group has committed some corporate offense that needs to be redressed or which presents a threat to the well-being of the ingroup. Quite often, however, the ideological framing may drift between or blur these two distinct rationales without settling on one of them. This is hardly surprising given that the rationale typically serves as an *ad hoc* pragmatic defense of the indefensible.

One powerful tool is the dehumanizing rhetoric that describes the outgroup as a pestilence or disease.[129] For example, in Rwanda, the preferred rhetorical term to dehumanize Tutsis was *cockroach*. As one Rwandan genocidaire recalled, "Everyone was hired at the same level for a single job—to crush all the cockroaches."[130] Adolf Hitler infamously used dehumanizing disease rhetoric to justify the killing of Jews. In one letter he eschewed 'emotional' pogroms with their sporadic, unpredictable and messy nature in favor of a 'rational' program of eradication based on the claim that Jews are "breeding to depravity" and "like a racial tuberculosis of the nations."[131]

With that backdrop of rhetorical othering in mind, consider by way of comparison how biblical scholar Gleason Archer justifies the complete eradication of Canaanites:

---

129 See David Livingstone Smith, *Less Than Human: Why We Demean, Enslave and Exterminate Others*.

130 Hatzfeld, *Machete Season*, 15.

131 Cited in Frank McDonough, *Hitler and the Rise of the Nazi Party*, 2nd ed. (Routledge, 2014), 128.

The loss of innocent life in the demolition of Jericho was much to be regretted, but we must recognize that there are times when only radical surgery will save the life of a cancer-stricken body. The whole population of the antediluvian civilization had become hopelessly infected with the cancer of moral depravity (Gen. 6:5). Had any of them been permitted to live while still in rebellion against God, they might have infected Noah's family as well. The same was true of the detestable inhabitants of Sodom [. . .] So also it was with Jericho and Ai as well . . . .[132]

In every case the baneful infection of degenerate idolatry and moral depravity had to be removed before Israel could safely settle down in these regions and set upon a monotheistic, law-governed commonwealth as a testimony for the one true God. Much as we regret the terrible loss of life, we must remember that far greater mischief would have resulted if they had been permitted to live on in the midst of the Hebrew nation. These incorrigible degenerates of the Canaanite civilization were a sinister threat to the spiritual survival of Abraham's race.[133]

The language that Archer invokes to justify the genocide of Canaanites (and Sodomites, and in the case of the Flood narrative the *entire population of earth* save Noah's household) parallels Hitler's language against Jews in terms of "depravity" and "racial tuberculosis." For Archer, the Canaanites are a "cancer of moral depravity," a "baneful infection of degenerate idolatry and moral depravity," "incorrigible degenerates" who pose a "sinister threat" which must be cut from the body lest their moral depravity metastasize and threaten the spiritual purity of the Israelites. Note as well how Archer's language echoes the rationalizations called out by Budziszewski: "The loss of innocent life . . . was much to be regretted, but we must recognize that there are times when only radical surgery will save the life of

---

[132] Archer, *Encyclopedia of Bible Difficulties* (Zondervan, 1982), 158.
[133] Archer, *Encyclopedia of Bible Difficulties*, 158.

a cancer-stricken body." In Archer's moral calculus, Canaanite infants are like cancer cells.

Genocide that is carried out at a distance, as in the equivalent of dropping bombs from the clouds, may only require a sufficiently strong ideological justification. But as we have noted, close-contact slaughter requires additional psychological coping mechanisms to overcome the extreme aversion to killing. When you can look in the face of your victim, hear their screams and watch their tearful pleas for their children, it is increasingly difficult to maintain the psychological distance required of genocide. To be sure, the psychological distress would be significantly lessened in the case of genocides which are carried out through a more indirect means such as forced sterilization or the involuntary removal and reeducation of children. However, the events described in Deuteronomy 7, 20, and Joshua 1-12 entail genocide of the most extreme and direct sort: mass close-contact killing.

One key factor to overcome the aversion to killing is through coercion by pressuring others to participate in killing by way of threats of shame or retaliation. To return to Rwanda, Hutu Theodore Nyilinkwaya summarizes how the aversion to killing was overcome in specific individuals:

> So that guy comes with a stick. They tell him, 'No, get a *masu*.' So, OK, he does, and he runs along with the rest, but he doesn't kill. They say, 'Hey, he might denounce us later. He must kill. Everyone must help to kill at least one person.' So this person who is not a killer is made to do it. And the next day it's become a game for him. You don't need to keep pushing him.[134]

That is the initial challenge to get people to break that taboo against killing. Once they do this, they begin to create an ingroup

---

[134] Gourevitch, *We Wish to Inform You that Tomorrow We Will be Killed with Our Families*, 24.

bond, a band of brothers among the fellow genocidaires, a terrifying and yet powerful connection borne of shared experience and purpose as they undertake their grisly task together.[135]

However, crossing the initial threshold aversion to killing is just the beginning. As the genocide unfolds, there is an ongoing need to otherize and dehumanize the victims as one continually seeks to reinforce the message that this target group does not share a common humanity or that unique conditions warrant the eradication of the group despite a common humanity. As Hitler recognized with the pogroms, there is no cool, clinical killing in the conduct of a close-contact genocide. Instead, there are repeated acts of unpredictable cruelty, acts which, as I said, provide the grease for the gears in the engine of genocide. These include, but are not limited to, the actions of mockery, torture, mutilation, and rape. Not surprisingly, all these dehumanizing actions were predictably present in abundance in the accounts of Rwandan genocide:

- **Mockery**. Severed Tutsi heads were sold for a pittance during the genocide, a practice sarcastically referred to as "selling cabbages".[136] A genocidaire named Elie recalls, "They were praying and psalming among themselves. We made fun of them, we laughed at their *Amens*, we taunted them about the kindness of the Lord, we joked about the paradise awaiting them. That fired us up even more."[137] One of the cruelest of mockeries comes when the Hutus offer the Tutsis various morally perverse opportunities to have a stake in their own fate, calling to mind Sophie's choice. For example, a

---

135 For further discussion of the bonding experience in wartime which would be operative here, see Christopher Hitchens, *War is a Force that Gives Us Meaning* (PublicAffairs, 2002).

136 Gourevitch, *We Wish to Inform You that Tomorrow We Will be Killed with Our Families*, 115.

137 Hatzfeld, *Machete Season*, 143.

survivor of Rwanda's genocide named Edmond recalled that his brother-in-law begged that his children not be hacked into pieces. The Hutu genocidaires agreed but only on the condition that the father would throw his own children alive into a latrine well instead.[138]

- **Torture and Mutilation**. The killings regularly were extended to highlight the agony and dehumanization of the victims. Gourevitch recalls, "Inside the nave, empty and grand, where a dark powder of dried blood marked one's footprints, a single, representative corpse was left on the floor before the altar. He appeared to be crawling toward the confession booth. His feet had been chopped off, and his hands had been chopped off. This was a favorite torture for Tutsis during the genocide; the idea was to cut the tall people 'down to size,' and crowds would gather to taunt, laugh, and cheer as the victim writhed to death."[139]

- **Rape**: As Claudia Card observes, in cases of genocide the systematic rape of the women in the target population is so common that it could be referred to as an institution.[140] Though not as prevalent, defeated enemy combatants have also on occasion been victims of war rape as part of the final step of psychological warfare.[141] Rape is a common tool of dehumanization in genocide. One genocidaire in Rwanda named Leopord recalls: "We had sessions with girls who were

---

138 Gourevitch, *We Wish to Inform You that Tomorrow We Will be Killed with Our Families*, 240.

139 Gourevitch, *We Wish to Inform You that Tomorrow We Will be Killed with Our Families*, 202.

140 Claudia Card, *The Atrocity Paradigm: A Theory of Evil* (Oxford University Press, 2002), 128. For instance, during the spring of 1945 the Soviet soldiers advancing into Germany raped close to one million German women.See "Wartime Rape," in Merrill Smith, ed. *Encyclopedia of Rape* (Greenwood, 2004), 269.

141 See Diana Mililo, "Rape as a Tactic of War," *Affilia*, 21, no.2 (2006) : 196-205.

raped in the bush. Nobody dared protest that. Even those who were edgy about it, because they had received blessings in church for example, told themselves it would change nothing since the girl was marked for death anyway."[142] Leopord further recalls: "One day an official declared, 'A woman on her back has no ethnic group.' After those words, men would capture girls and take them to their fields for sex. Many others feared their wives' reproaches and raped the girls right in the middle of the killing in the marshes, without even hiding from their comrades behind the papyrus."[143] Some Tutsi women were raped and then killed while others were raped *multiple* times before they were finally executed.[144]

To be sure, the account in Joshua provides no such messy details of Israelite actions against the Canaanites. The narrative of chapter 6, for example, tells us only that the entire city of Jericho was devoted to the LORD and that every living thing was destroyed as a result. But we must remind ourselves that it is *de rigueur* for 'official' accounts of genocide throughout history to elide the grislier details. Humanizing the victims would threaten to devalorize the conduct of the genocidaires and that does not serve the propagandistic purposes of the official account.

With that in mind, we are right to be skeptical of any sanitized official account of genocide. In particular, the specific nature of the Canaanite genocide—extensive close-contact killing of a society by a rag-tag army wielding primitive implements like swords and spears and driven by a dehumanizing ideology—would lead us to expect the attendant processes of dehumanization: mockery, torture, mutilation, and rape. Torture and mutilation,

---

142 Hatzfeld, *Machete Season*, 96.

143 Hatzfeld, *Machete Season*, 134.

144 Larissa Peltola, "Rape and Sexual Violence Used as a Weapon of War and Genocide," Senior Thesis, Claremont McKenna College (2018); Viktoria Nicolaisen, "The systematic use of sexual violence in genocide," Gothenberg University (2019).

in particular, will be all-but essential concomitant effects given that the killing is not undertaken in controlled circumstances by the quick drop of a guillotine. Rather, it unfolds as a terribly messy, extended affair in which conflicted and zealous genocidaires hunt down desperate civilians in unpredictable conditions. Multiple non-lethal swings of the machete could elicit tremendous damage prior to the final mercy of death.

The suggestion that rape—that is, sexual acts undertaken against or without consent of the other party—could reasonably be expected to form a part of the Canaanite genocide will likely elicit the fiercest pushback from Christian defenders of the Canaanite genocide. I have long observed that Christians who seem to have little principled objection to the conduct of a 'biblical' genocide are fiercely opposed in principle to any notion that rape could have incidentally formed part of a divinely commanded genocide. However, it must be said that there is something deeply perplexing in this moral position given that the same intuitions which offer a categorical censure of rape would seem to offer an equally decisive censure of genocide.

Of course, those Christians who accept genocide while condemning rape frequently claim that they do so based on a biblical precedent for the former but not the latter. However, even setting aside the problems already noted with that biblicist approach to moral knowledge, we can say that biblically speaking, there are some notable problems with the confidence by which that denunciation is rendered. For example, we have already noted that in Numbers 31 we read that the Israelites slaughtered all the Midianite males and non-virgin females while taking the virginal females for their army. If Boko Haram invades a village in northern Nigeria and eradicates the entire village except for the virgin girls, does that sound like the right conditions to secure sexual consent? Imagine that soldiers in those circumstances then each take a girl who has just witnessed her family massacred: do you suppose that that traumatized girl is prepared to offer genuine consent to a matrimonial relationship and subsequent sexual contact with the genocidaire who massacred her family? The very suggestion is as offensive as it is absurd. Yet, that is the parallel situation of the Israelite soldiers who seize newly orphaned Midianite virginal teenagers and preteens for themselves. And it provides the ideological backdrop for the Israelite incursion into Canaan. Suffice it to say, as this was a society lacking modern notions of sexual consent, it is even more likely that some Israelite genocidaires would engage in non-consensual acts of sexual contact with persons from the target population. In other words, intermittent rape would likely be a byproduct of the genocide.

The Aftermath of Genocide

While genocide obviously devastates its victims, as I have sought to explain, the impact is also profoundly destructive of the participant genocidaires. The horror of genocide encompasses all: not just the immediate victims but also the butchers, the bystanders, and all others who remain behind.[145] It is impossible to calculate the impact of the horror of genocide on a country like Rwanda. One could turn to statistics to try and capture the long-term impact. For example, one 1996 study sought to measure the social/psychological impact of the genocide. The study revealed that 17.9 percent of respondents qualified as clinically depressed, far higher than the rates of 0.8-5.8 percent in African countries generally. In addition, 41.8 percent reported experiencing severe grief.[146] Not surprisingly, the high rates of

---

145 For the analysis of genocide by way of the categories of bully, bullied, and bystander, see Barbara Coloroso, *Extraordinary Evil: A Brief History of Genocide* (Viking, 2007).

146 Paul Bolton, "Assessing Depression Among Survivors of the Rwanda

depression and grief are directly correlated to the aftermath of the genocide.

But statistics, for all their objective value, nonetheless keep us six miles up in the clouds, as the destruction of individual lives disappears far below into the numbing abstraction of mere numbers on a page. Consequently, if we are to appreciate the full impact of this genocide, we need to return again to the killing fields. To that end, at this point I will recount some testimonies from Hutu genocidaires. One of these individuals, a man named Adalbert, chronicles the growing barbarism exhibited by the murderers as follows:

> There were some who brutalized a lot because they killed overmuch. Their killings were delicious to them. They needed intoxication, like someone who calls louder and louder for a bottle.
>
> Animal death no longer gave them satisfaction, they felt frustrated when they simply struck down a Tutsi. They wanted seething excitement. They felt cheated when a Tutsi died without a word. Which is why they no longer struck at the mortal parts, wishing to savor the blows and relish the screams.[147]

Another genocidaire, Pio, describes how "savagery took over the mind."[148] He goes on to explain: "Not only had we become criminals, we had become a ferocious species in a barbarous world. This truth is not believable to someone who has not lived it in his muscles. Our daily life was unnatural and bloody, *and that suited us*."[149]

It would seem that over time, the genocide gradually hived out

---

Genocide," in *The Psychological Impact of War Trauma on Civilians: An International Perspective*, eds. Stanley Krippner and Maria McIntyre (Praeger, 2003), 74.

147 Cited in Hatzfeld, *Machete Season*, 129.
148 Cited in Hatzfeld, *Machete Season*, 47.
149 Hatzfeld, *Machete Season*, 48, emphasis added.

the moral core of the participants as they increasingly descended into unimaginable viciousness and barbarism. Another genocidaire named Fulgence recalls:

> We became more and more cruel, more and more calm, more and more bloody. But we did not see that we were becoming more and more killers. The more we cut, the more cutting became child's play to us. For a few, it turned into a treat, if I may say so. In the evening you might meet a colleague who would call out, "You, my friend, buy me a Primus [beer] or I'll cut open your skull, because I have a taste for that now!"[150]

Examples like these could readily be multiplied.[151]

It is common to find genocidaires not only distancing themselves from their victims but also from their own heinous actions. In Pio's case, this phenomenon is evident as he describes his participation with a disconcerting degree of disconnectedness from his own actions: "This killer was indeed me, as to the offense he committed and the blood he shed, but he is a stranger to me in his ferocity. I admit and recognize my obedience at that time, my victims, my fault, but I fail to recognize the wickedness of the one who raced through the marshes on my legs, carrying my machete."[152] Pio provides a fascinating and profoundly disturbing example of the way that a genocidaire can emotionally distance himself from his own actions.

All these examples should serve to illustrate the absolutely brutal and dehumanizing impact of genocide on the perpetrators. To put it bluntly, genocide wreaks a terrible cost not only on the victims but on the genocidaires resulting in the corruption if not utter destruction of their moral character. So here is the obvious question before us: if the Hutu genocidaires "became

---

150 Hatzfeld, *Machete Season*, 50.

151 For some online resources see http://www.rwandanstories.org/

152 Hatzfeld, *Machete Season*, 48.

more and more cruel, more and more calm, more and more bloody" with their repeated killing, would the impact upon the Israelite genocidaires have been any different? If the Hutus found that "The more we cut, the more cutting became child's play to us," how would similar actions have impacted Joshua's soldiers? If some Hutus came to find killing was "a treat" then how many Israelites would have come to agree? And how are we to understand the alleged need to secure moral purity through the very actions that corrupt a national character so totally? As Seibert provocatively puts it, it is "logically incoherent" to command a moral atrocity in order to retain moral purity.[153]

Conclusion

In this chapter we have sought to apply our method of moral reflection on concrete instances of proposed actions to the conduct of close-contact killing genocide. The goal has been to acquaint ourselves with the moral status of these actions by clarifying our moral intuitions as we move from the view at 30,000 feet to an on-the-ground encounter with the intimate orgy of close-contact killing by way of primitive implements: e.g. machetes and masus in contemporary Rwanda and swords and spears in ancient Israel.

We have seen that properly functioning human beings (i.e. those who don't suffer from a personality defect like psychopathy) have a severe aversion to close-contact killing of other human persons. As a result, in order to carry out a close-contact genocide by way of killing individual members of the group, one must undertake several strategies to dehumanize and otherize the target group. This begins with rhetorical othering in which

---

153 Seibert, *Disturbing Divine Behavior: Troubling Old Testament Images of God* (Fortress Press, 2009), 79.

the outgroup is treated as ontologically inferior or as the proper target of a significant grievance. Here we noted, in particular, the disturbing overlap between the othering rhetoric of Adolf Hitler and that of contemporary Christian genocide apologist Gleason Archer. Finally, continued dehumanization also brings with it predictable consequences including further violence upon the target group such as mockery, torture, mutilation, and rape. While the book of Joshua is silent on such details in the Canaanite genocide, given the ubiquity of such behaviors in close-contact genocides, it is to be expected that they would be a predictable result of the systematic eradication of Canaanites. Torture and mutilation, for example, would be all-but-inevitable consequences of the sporadic slaughter of civilians. And mockery would be a predictable psychological coping mechanism to inure oneself against the psychological stress of hearing the cries and agony of the dying.

And so, it is reasonable to expect that the conduct of genocide in Canaan would not consist simply of the execution of Canaanites in a straightforward and clinical process like an antiseptic lethal injection in a state prison. Rather, there would be endless desperate and anguished struggles just like the messy, unpredictable pogroms that Hitler sought to eliminate: people would be horrifically wounded and mutilated, genocidaires would grow enraged while seeking to vent that rage in the cruelest acts of torture. In the midst of the melee, a significant number of women and young girls would likely be sexually assaulted as further acts of deprivation and dehumanization.

This leads us to the final point: the enduring impact that participation in genocide would have on the psychology of the genocidaires. (We will consider more fully the lingering impact on victims in chapter 9.) As we have noted, normal human beings have a powerful aversion to killing other human beings. That aversion will often prevent a soldier from killing an enemy combatant on the battlefield even when their own life is under threat. With that in mind, imagine the degree of moral aversion a normal human being would have to impaling a terrified mother and her crying infant child. If, as we should surely assume, the Israelites were normal human beings with healthy psychology rather than psychopaths able to kill with impunity, then the impact of this mass killing on the genocidaires and Israelite society more generally would have been *profoundly corrupting*. And that, surely, is the final irony, one which is worth highlighting: the mass killing of Canaanites was undertaken ostensibly to protect the Israelites from the very moral corruption they experience as they engage in close-contact mass killing of those very same Canaanites. If this is not an instance of the cure being worse than the 'disease' then what is?

7

Interpreting the Bible: Five Guiding Principles

In chapter 5, I outlined a method for theological reflection based on the clarification of moral intuitions/perception on the occasion of contemplating actual or hypothetical cases of moral action. Next, in chapter 6 we applied this method to the case of close-contact genocidal killing by considering an overview of the Rwandan genocide coupled with general observations about the common hallmarks of close-contact genocidal killing. That extended exercise provides us with a far better grasp of all that is being proposed by adopting a historical reading of the Canaanite conquest. In the remainder of the book we will consider more closely four main readings of the conquest passages in light of these moral challenges. But first, we need to complete our method by way of articulating a set of five hermeneutical principles to guide our interpretation of the Bible. Think of this as hermeneutics 101. I believe that these basic principles are justified by a Christian reading of the Bible and I shall seek to articulate and defend their internal logic from within that context. To be sure, these principles may not tell you how to interpret difficult passages like Deuteronomy 7 and 20 and Joshua 1-12. But I do believe that they provide a useful general guide for identifying the range of possible and plausible options available to the Christian reader.

Principle 1: Perfect God

There is an old saying: "Tell me about the God you don't believe in because I probably don't believe in him either." Time and again, I have seen the truth of that saying when I talk with people who profess to reject belief in God because God is a "cruel tyrant" or a "capricious bully" or an "inept landlord". To such people I must say that I don't believe in *that* God either. For starters, I believe that God is a perfect being, and that confession includes a range of assumptions about the nature of perfection which automatically negate the legitimacy of such polemical descriptions. Not surprisingly, the assumption of perfection also shapes how I interpret the depictions of God in the Bible which appear to be at odds with that ascription.

A Test Case: Perfect Knowledge

Let's consider a simple example of how this assumption of divine perfection shapes our reading of a particular depiction of God in the Bible. After Abraham faithfully seeks to carry out God's command to offer Isaac, God then intervenes, stopping Abraham from carrying out the action: "Do not do anything to him. Now I know that you fear God, because you have not withheld from me your son, your only son." (Genesis 22:12) The point I want to highlight here is not the moral conundrum presented by the *Akedah* itself but rather the underlying assumption that the event involved God's *testing* Abraham so that God could *learn* how his servant would react. While the text describes God as learning something about Abraham's character, I do not interpret that description literally precisely because my reading is informed by a prior theological assumption, one that I call the Perfect God Principle. In other words, I believe that God is a perfect being and that omniscience is one of the component attributes of divine perfection. Consequently, my interpretation should be guided by and consistent with that assumption.

But on what do I base this assumption of divine omniscience? Like a biblicist, I could limit my case to biblical passages which suggest that God has intimate foreknowledge of creaturely actions (e.g. Psalm 139:16; Isaiah 44:7) and treat those as control verses for interpreting passages like Genesis 22:12 where God is described as learning. But that method is insufficient because it simply puts the question back a step: what ultimately justifies privileging passages like Isaiah 44:7 as the interpretive control over passages like Genesis 22:12?[154] At this point, I would argue that we can justify a specific set of interpretive control texts by way of a prior theological *intuition*, an *a priori* commitment to the priority of a particular concept of perfection, a concept that includes perfect omniscience. It is because I believe that God is perfect and perfection includes comprehensive knowledge that I would prioritize Isaiah 44:7 as a control text for Genesis 22:12. For this reason, I *do not* believe that God lacked knowledge of how Abraham would act such that he needed to devise a test of Abraham's faithfulness. Rather, I believe that God surely *did* know in advance and thus Genesis 22:12 should be interpreted as anthropomorphic.[155]

The Importance of the Perfect God Principle

Christians will certainly disagree with one another on how precisely to understand the concept of divine perfection. But it is quite another thing to reject the concept altogether and claim that God is, in fact, far from perfect. The importance of the

---

154 This point has been effectively pressed by open theists.
155 See Randal Rauser, *Finding God in the Shack* (Biblica, 2009), 28-29.

Perfect God Principle can be illustrated by considering the radical repercussions that follow when a Christian explicitly rejects it.

In his book *Raw Revelation* biblical scholar Mark Roncace addresses (among other troubling topics) the morally problematic portrayals of God in the Bible.[156] Roncace doesn't mince words as he states that God "is portrayed as cruel, vindictive, childish, petulant, misogynistic, egotistical, genocidal, and maniacal."[157] Of course, the standard Christian response at this point is to explain how, despite these *appearances*, God is *not*, in fact, cruel, vindictive, childish, and the rest. And we know this not simply because we have a list of biblical texts that say otherwise but because we are committed *a priori* to the notion that God is perfect and this principle of perfection provides a key guide for how we interpret the text. That position, in turn, commits the Christian to seek some alternative explanation for this apparent contradiction such as exploring alternative readings of the troubling passages, revising our understanding of perfection, or (if all else fails) retreating to the mists of antinomy or paradox. But what the Christian *doesn't* do is surrender their commitment to the perfection of God. This principle should remain like a lighthouse guiding our biblical interpretation and theological reflection.

However, that is not Roncace's approach. Rather than affirm God's perfection and seek to reconcile it to these appearances to the contrary, he rejects the Perfect God Principle outright and thus concludes that sometimes God really is cruel, vindictive, childish, and the rest. The problem is not that God sometimes *appears* monstrous but rather that sometimes God *is* monstrous. This is how Roncace puts it within the context of the conquest of Canaan:

---

156 Mark Roncace, *Raw Revelation: The Bible They Never Tell You About* (CreateSpace, 2012).

157 Roncace, *Raw Revelation: The Bible They Never Tell You About* , 43.

> As honest Christians, we cannot say that we don't understand these troubling texts. No. We do understand them. We just don't find them palatable. How can we claim to comprehend the Bible when it says, 'God is love,' but then when God appears as deceptive, evil, and cruel, we say, 'No, God is not really those things.' Or we throw up our hands and say, 'There are some things we can never grasp.' Let's be real. Like Job says, we must take the good with the bad.[158]

Once again, on Roncace's view, it is not simply that on occasion God *appears* to be deceptive, evil and cruel but rather that God occasionally *is* these things. "For me," Roncace says, "the paradoxical God of Scripture—kind and cruel, good and genocidal, present and absent—*is the true nature of the God of the universe.*"[159]

As you can imagine, this approach offers a straightforward way to address biblical violence: sometimes God is just plain nasty, so get over it. As Roncace delicately puts it, "God is not perfect, and I can live with that. Why must God be perfect? Why can't we love a God who is in the process of growing and developing? We show genuine love for flawed people all the time."[160] Roncace is correct that we show love for flawed people. The problem, however, is that in the Christian tradition God is not simply another flawed being toward which we can show some love. Rather, God is a being we *worship*. And to be perfectly clear, 'worship' is not merely the extension of obeisance to a very powerful but terribly flawed being as if it were merely a pragmatic act of self-preservation. On the contrary, it involves recognition of the maximal greatness or unparalleled *worthship* of the being that is the object of worship, for he alone is *worthy*. As we read in the *Catechism of the Catholic Church*, "When we say 'God' we confess a constant, unchangeable being, always

---

158 Roncace, *Raw Revelation*, 77, cf. 78.
159 Roncace, *Raw Revelation*, 80, emphasis added.
160 Roncace, *Raw Revelation*, 83.

the same, faithful and just, without any evil. It follows that we must necessarily accept his words and have complete faith in him and acknowledge his authority. He is almighty, merciful, and infinitely beneficent. Who could not place all hope in him?"[161]

That is the kind of being that it makes sense both to love supremely *and* to worship absolutely: a being of maximal worthship, a being of unparalleled *perfection*. But this is not Roncace's understanding of God. He *doesn't* believe that God is constant, faithful, just, good, *perfect*. Instead, he views God as flawed. Indeed, 'flawed' would seem to be a gross understatement, for Roncace baldly declares on the back cover of his book that "God can be a misogynistic, genocidal maniac". Whoa, a misogynistic, genocidal *maniac*?! Let's put that into some perspective. Imagine that your friend admits that her new boyfriend is, um, flawed. You press her for clarification. "Well," she admits, "sometimes he's a misogynistic, genocidal maniac . . . but other times he's like real sweet!" After that 'revelation,' would you advise her to stay with him? Of course not! You'd tell her to run for the hills. Needless to say, it makes no sense to *worship* any being that fits that description. As for *loving* such an individual, you can choose to do so if you wish, just like your friend can choose to stick with her new boyfriend. But surely such a decision would be foolhardy, self-destructive, and doomed to heartbreak.

The starting point is to recognize that the concept of perfection is essential to the Christian concept of God. But what precisely are the attributes that constitute perfection? For the purposes of my argument, I have no need to offer a comprehensive theoretical proposal. Instead, it is sufficient to affirm that perfection includes omniscience (as noted above) as well as omnipotence and moral perfection.[162] These attributes are

---

161 *Catechism of the Catholic Church*, http://www.vatican.va/archive/ENG0015/_P7C.HTM

162 For an introduction to Perfect Being Theology and the operation of perfection intuitions in theological reflection, see Katherin A. Rogers, *Perfect Being*

sufficient for our study because they collectively secure that God is maximally capable of producing an inspired biblical text which is consistent with his perfect ends. While I will not be offering a specific theory of inspiration here, my own view is best described by way of the middle knowledge model endorsed by William Lane Craig.[163] Because God omnisciently possesses perfect middle knowledge (i.e. knowledge of counterfactual possibilities) he can orchestrate the conditions in which human creatures will freely write the precise words that he desires in his canon. Once those words have been written, God appropriates them into his canon by making *their* words *his* words.[164] While that is a quick summary of my view, for the purposes of this discussion I need only assume the *plenary inspiration* of the totality of Scripture, a point that will be unpacked under my third principle pertaining to canon. To conclude, when we approach the Bible we do so under the commitment that it was produced by a perfect divine author consistent with his ends.

On Reading a Perfect Author

As I have said, I am limiting my analysis of divine perfection to the claim that God is a maximally worthy object of worship who is omniscient, omnipotent and morally perfect. Thus, as with the example of cruelty cited above, when we encounter any biblical text which appears to be inconsistent with God's moral perfection, we have the following options: 1. *The text is in error;* 2. *My understanding of the text is in error;* 3. *My understanding*

Theology (Edinburgh University Press, 2000). Cf. Yujin Nagasawa, *Maximal God: A New Defence of Perfect Being Theism* (Oxford University Press, 2017).

[163] William Lane Craig, "'Men Moved by the Holy Spirit Spoke from God,' A Middle Knowledge Perspective on Biblical Inspiration," *Philosophia Christi*, 1 (1999), 45-82.

[164] For more on a model of biblical inspiration in terms of the divine appropriation of human words, see Nicholas Wolterstorff, *Divine Discourse: Philosophical Reflections on the Claim that God Speaks* (Cambridge University Press, 1995).

of moral perfection is in error. You might wonder, however, how we can consider the possibility of error vis-à-vis option 1. That is an important question and we shall return to address it in Principle 2. But first we need to consider what it means to read a text with a commitment to the perfection of the (divine) author.

Once we commit ourselves to the idea that God is a perfect author, we are also committed to making sense of the biblical text in accord with that assumption, even when it doesn't appear to make sense. In other words, when there *appear* to be errors in the text, the belief that the author is perfect will predispose the reader to seeking an interpretation which is nonetheless consistent with authorial perfection. Only when it becomes overwhelmingly clear that there is no plausible or possible alternative interpretation available will one become obliged to surrender their prior commitment to the perfection of the author.[165]

We can unpack the logic here by considering a cinematic illustration courtesy of the film *The Shining*. This revered 1980 horror movie is based on the Stephen King novel of the same name. It was directed by famed auteur Stanley Kubrick and is widely considered one of the greatest horror films ever made. Despite its stellar reputation and famed director, the film appears to have some rather glaring continuity errors. (A continuity error involves a lapse in the self-consistency of a scene.) In fact, a continuity error is evident in what is perhaps the most iconic

---

165 In *Theology in the Age of Scientific Reasoning* (Cornell University Press, 1990), chapter 3, Nancey Murphy defends a theological model based on the philosophy of science of Imre Lakatos which rejects the category of falsification in favor of a more nuanced model of holistic engagement where core theoretical claims in a theory are connected to data-points by way of revisable secondary theses. With this model, a theory is in principle open to endless adaptation in the secondary theses to avoid falsification. However, in reality, theories are not retained forever. Rather, they are eventually abandoned when they are simply no longer worth retaining. That basic approach under-girds my view of the Bible as the product of a perfect author.

scene in the entire film. In the famous 'Here's Johnny' segment, Jack (Jack Nicholson) takes an axe and hacks open one of the panels in the door to the bathroom where Wendy (Shelly Duvall) is hiding. But when we see the door again a moment later, *both top door panels are missing*. This is one of several notable continuity errors,[166] and at the industry standard website, Internet Movie Database, it is listed as one of the 'goofs' (i.e. filmmaker errors) in the film.[167]

However, should we really think of these apparent continuity errors as unintentional 'goofs'? That seems to me like a highly dubious assumption given that Kubrick is widely recognized to be one of the most brilliant and meticulously detailed filmmakers of all time. Elsa Colombani describes him as "a ruthless perfectionist who would require hundreds of takes from his actors, Kubrick is today considered one of the greatest visionaries of filmmaking . . . ."[168] As Colombani observes, *The Shining* is one of Kubrick's greatest achievements and it "truly seems to haunt American culture . . . ."[169] As an example of his relentless quest for perfection, Kubrick famously reshot the scene of Jack typing his novel for various different language markets, even going to the trouble of translating and reshooting the infamous sentence "All work and no play makes Jack a dull boy" that Jack repeatedly types into the colloquial equivalents in French, German, Italian, and Spanish.[170] And consider this: *The Shining* holds the world

---

166 See Dan Peeke, "10 Continuity Errors in Stephen King's The Shining," *Screen Rant* (March 1, 2020), https://screenrant.com/stephen-king-shining-continuity-errors/

167 https://www.imdb.com/title/tt0081505/goofs

168 Elsa Colombani, "Introduction," *A Critical Companion to Stanley Kubrick*, ed. Elsa Colombani (Lexington Books, 2020), 1.

169 Colombani, "Introduction," 2.

170 Meg Honigmann, "Stanley Kubrick showed that perfectionism pays off," *1843 Magazine* (May 2, 2019), https://www.economist.com/1843/2019/05/02/stanley-kubrick-showed-that-perfectionism-pays-off

record for the most reshoots of a single scene: 127 times.[171] Film aficionados give endless attention to the details of *The Shining* and have developed multiple interpretations of the film including the theory that it is a metaphor for the destruction of the American Indian or even that it is Kubrick's cryptic admission that he conspired with the U.S. government to fake the 1969 moon landing.[172]

Given the fact that Kubrick is famed for giving relentless attention to detail, the most reasonable and charitable response to apparent continuity errors like the missing door panel is that they are not errors in the conventional sense at all. Rather, we should instead conclude that those so-called 'errors' were included by the filmmaker for a reason. The challenge of the viewer is to figure out what that reason might be. To note another example, it would be foolhardy to attribute the infamously confused and contradictory nature of the floorplan of the Overlook Hotel to a lack of attention to detail; rather, it is best explained as a carefully wrought visual illustration of the unpredictable and illogical labyrinth nature of the hotel itself (a phenomenon which is mirrored by the infamous hedge maze outside).[173] Suffice it to say, the careful viewer of the film will insist that if you haven't yet explained some particular 'error' or 'goof' in *The Shining*, you better keep thinking because *Kubrick surely knew what he was doing even if you don't.*

If we should properly have that degree of deference to a great filmmaker like Kubrick, how much more should we defer to the expertise of an artist that we believe to be, quite literally, *perfect?*

---

171 Kieran McMahon, "23.7 Facts About Stanley Kubrick's 'The Shining,'" *IndieWire* (March 26, 2013), https://www.indiewire.com/2013/03/23-7-facts-about-stanley-kubricks-the-shining-100294/

172 For a survey of these and other theories, see the documentary *Room 237*.

173 To note one of many examples, the office for the manager, Stuart Ullman, has a window to the outside, but that is *impossible* for the floorplan has Ullman's office in the bowels of the hotel.

And of course, that which applies to cinema applies equally to literary expression. Consequently, a Christian who believes they have encountered within the biblical text the literary equivalent of a cinematographic goof had better look closer because God surely knew what he was doing even if you don't.

In his book *Inspired Imperfection* Greg Boyd offers a brilliant metaphor for thinking about these apparent errors. He appeals to the Japanese art and craft of Kintsugi in which broken pottery is reassembled by placing the shards together with a bright gold lacquer. Rather than hide the cracks, this lacquer *highlights them* so that they become part of the final work. In that manner, would-be flaws in the pottery are transformed into qualities of beauty and value. In a similar way, apparent errors within the biblical text may be viewed as providential to the integrity of the whole in a process that Boyd calls *inspired imperfection*. He argues that this process culminates in Christ crucified, the ultimate 'error' that becomes an essential revelatory insight to the whole:

> we wouldn't say that the cross fully reveals God *in spite of* the humanity, the sin, and the God-forsaken curse that Jesus bore. To the contrary, the cross fully reveals God *precisely because* it reveals a God who, out of unfathomable love, was willing to stoop to an unsurpassable distance to enter into solidarity with our humanity, our sin, and our God-forsaken curse.[174]

It should be noted that Boyd is an open theist and as such, he believes that God does not exercise meticulous control over events; nor does God know the future contingent actions of free creatures. Boyd's Kintsugi analogy works best within that context as the artist doesn't know which way a pot will break; they simply respond once it has broken by reassembling and lacing the cracks with gold. But I am not an open theist: rather, as I

---

[174] Boyd, *Inspired Imperfection: How the Bible's problems enhance its authority* (Fortress, 2020), 95.

said above, I believe that God providentially planned for every jot and tittle that composes the text via his middle knowledge. For this reason, Kintsugi is not a perfect fit with my view of inspiration. Nonetheless, it does offer a useful heuristic insofar as it highlights the main point that alleged flaws in fact serve the overall integrity of the work.

If we begin with this commitment to God as the Perfect Author, it will not tell us how to address apparent flaws, errors, or 'goofs' within the text. But it will give us confidence that God knows what he is doing even when we do not. In my 2009 paper "'Let Nothing that Breathes Remain Alive,' On the Problem of Divinely Commanded Genocide," I present an argument against particular readings of the violence in the Bible. The first premise of my argument is foundational to the Perfect God Principle: "God is the most perfect being there could be".[175] From that starting premise, I argue ultimately that God did not command genocide because a perfect being would not command a moral atrocity and genocide is a moral atrocity. I end the article as follows: "While this may not yet tell us how we should respond to biblical narratives of divinely sanctioned violence, at the very least it will save Christians from the sorry spectacle of attempting to convince ourselves and others of that which everybody knows cannot be true."[176]

You may or may not agree with me at this point, but I hope you can at least appreciate the reasoning. Much as the Kubrick fan reasons "That extra missing panel in the bathroom door *cannot* be a goof, so Kubrick must be doing something else in that scene" so I believe the Christian should reason, "God cannot command an actual genocide, so he must be doing something else in the texts which seem to say that he does." From that starting point,

---

175 Rauser, "'Let Nothing that Breathes Remain Alive,' On the Problem of Divinely Commanded Genocide," *Philosophia Christi*, 11 (2009), 28-29.

176 Rauser, "'Let Nothing that Breathes Remain Alive,' On the Problem of Divinely Commanded Genocide,"41.

this approach then commits the reader to exploring re-readings of the problematic texts that seek to vindicate the intentions of the artist in light of these background beliefs.

I would add that while a doctrine of biblical inerrancy is not explicitly endorsed here, it is a tacit implication of the principle. As I said above, every jot and tittle is in the text because God planned it to be so. To be sure, the skeptic might reply like this: "Yeah, but we don't have the autographs; we only have copies of the autographs, and while they are very reliable overall, there are various variant readings between them. What is more, we don't have universal agreement in the Christian church about the very nature of canon. So how does that work with your concept of inerrancy, Mr. Theologian?"

To begin with, it is of course standard to limit the property of inerrancy to the *autographs* to the extent where there are distinct autographs. (However, that is a far more complicated proposition when the current form of the text is a product of a gradual evolution over years or decades by multiple authors/redactors.) I would submit we should affirm that the *process* should be viewed as part of God's providential and inerrant intention in the formation of the book. We can put it like this: could a capable author have reasons to allow for the destruction of his original manuscript, leaving behind only imperfect copies? Sure, she could have many reasons to do that. Could she have reasons to bring it about that in the future particular communities of readers could have canon disputes about which exact writings constitute her oeuvre? Certainly, there are all sorts of conceivable reasons why an artist/author could allow for such nuance and complexity to enter into their literary legacy as received by a reading community. How much more in the case of a perfect author who could be operating at levels of nuance and sophistication that finite readers can hardly imagine? It could be that the loss of autographs is itself part of the inerrant extended performance of the author. With that in mind, we should be very careful about presuming that such details as the loss of autographs or the existence of disagreement on canon somehow constitute a problem for the Christian: on the contrary, it is possible that such phenomena constitute a *feature* rather than a bug.

While I accept a concept of biblical inerrancy, the inerrancy of which I speak is *not* the view common among Christian conservatives that ascribes inerrancy to every speech act of the human author. Rather, I identify inerrancy with the intentions of the perfect God who oversees the composition and compilation of the entire text: if God is the perfect author then at least with respect to God's intentions there will be no errors or goofs present in the text. God, after all, knows perfectly well what *he* wants to say. But that divine intention may not always be available to the human author.

Principle 2: Two Authors

The final paragraph of the last section introduced a distinction between human and divine authors in the text while restricting inerrancy to the divine author. That brings us to our Two Authors Principle, for now we are in a place to revisit the first of our three options when reading problematic moral content. Once again, the options are as follows: 1. *The text is in error;* 2. *My understanding of the text is in error;* 3. *My understanding of moral perfection is in error.*

In the example of Kubrick the Meticulous Filmmaker, I pointed out that we should interpret alleged errors such as the apparent continuity error of the missing door panel as in fact not being errors at all in the conventional sense. Rather, we should conclude that they were purposefully included by our uniquely skilled filmmaker and it is the task of the viewer to figure out what the motivations of the filmmaker are in including that discontinuity. If we apply that logic to the Bible, then we would likewise assume that there are, in fact, no errors in the Bible. But in that case, it would seem that 1. *The text is in error* is not an option. So how can we reconcile the existence of error with a perfect author?

One Text, Two Authors

The way out of this dilemma is to recognize that our authorial model parts ways with the Kubrick illustration at just this point: in the illustration, *The Shining* is explained simply in terms of the intentions of the director. But our understanding of the Bible is more complicated than that given that, as we have seen, each text is attributable both to a divine author *and* a human author and these two authors can have distinct intentions. From this perspective, in one respect, it may be more helpful to think of God as a divine *editor* rather than *author*, for an editor can take the words of an author and appropriate them in a new collection which imbues them with novel meaning beyond the intention of the original author. Thus, the human author writes their texts and God appropriates those texts into his canonical collection. And as God does so, he may use the speech acts of those human authors in ways that they did not themselves originally intend.[177]

According to the Two Authors Principle, every biblical text has both a divine author and a human author and the meaning of the divine author may diverge from that of the human author.[178] Theologians have often made a crucial distinction at this point between the literal sense (*sensus literalis historicus*) and the plenary sense (*sensus plenior*). While these terms have

---

177 For further discussion of an appropriation model, see Wolterstorff, *Divine Discourse: Philosophical Reflections on the Claim that God Speaks*.

178 See Gregory A. Boyd's discussion of prosopological exegesis: *The Crucifixion of the Warrior God: Interpreting the Old Testament's Violent Portraits of God in Light of the Cross*. Volume 1: *The Cruciform Hermeneutic*, 504-7.

been defined in various ways,[179] I will be defining them for my purposes as follows:

- Literal sense: The human author's intent. (Note, this does not entail *literal meaning* for the human author's original intent may have been idiomatic.)
- Plenary sense: The divine author's intent, an intent *which may be distinct from the human author's intent.*

Insofar as errors appear, they will be of necessity limited to the intents of the human author since the perfect divine author by definition cannot make an error relative to his intentions. To put it another way, if there *is* an error in the literal sense, it follows that it was *inerrantly included* by the divine author. And thus, from this perspective, it would be possible to recognize, as per 1., that there are literary 'goofs' within the text. But as with Kubrick's continuity errors, these 'errors' would be limited to the human authorial intent even as they are inerrantly included relative to the divine authorial intent.

As we explore this idea further, we can begin by considering a few clear examples where the divine plenary sense of a text has been commonly understood to diverge from the human literal sense. Straightforward examples of this phenomenon which appears very close to the tradition of pesharim (distinguishing surface and deeper meaning) can be found in the way that Old Testament texts are appropriated in the New Testament to be specific messianic prophecies:

- Isaiah 7:14: "Therefore the Lord himself will give you a sign: The virgin will conceive and give birth to a son, and will call him Immanuel."

    The literal sense: Isaiah proclaims that God will provide

---

179 For a classic study, see Raymond E. Brown, *The Sensus Plenior of Sacred Scripture* (St. Mary's University, 1955).

a sign that King Ahaz will destroy his enemies in virtue of a young woman conceiving and bearing a son.

The plenary sense: God will provide a sign of the incarnation of his Son in virtue of a young virgin conceiving.

- Hosea 11:1: "When Israel was a child, I loved him, and out of Egypt I called my son."
  The literal sense: God called Israel out of Egypt.
  The plenary sense: God called Jesus out of Egypt as the New Israel.

And just to complicate things a bit more, it is worth noting that when the author of Matthew quotes Hosea 11:1 in Matthew 2:15 he thereby expresses his own literal sense which is shown to be the plenary sense of Hosea 11:1. Thus, it is possible that the same text may simultaneously be the literal human sense of one biblical passage (Matthew 2:15) and the divine plenary sense of another passage (Hosea 11:1).

Another example where the literal sense may diverge from the plenary sense is the so-called *vestigia trinitatis*, anticipations of the Trinity in the Old Testament. In this case, the idea is that God intended to reveal glimpses of the triune divine nature in texts where the human author was likely unaware of any such revelation. Some examples of texts that have been interpreted as *vestigia trinitatis* include the following:

- Genesis 1:26: "Therefore the Lord himself will give you a sign: The virgin will conceive and give birth to a son, and will call him Immanuel."
  The literal sense: God deliberates about the creation of human beings, perhaps in conjunction with a heavenly council of spiritual beings.
  The plenary sense: God the Father deliberates about the creation of human beings by addressing the Son and Spirit.

- Psalm 33:6: "By the word of the Lord the heavens were made; their starry host by the breath of his mouth.

    The literal sense: A description of creation in terms of poetic Hebraic parallelism.

    The plenary sense: A metaphorical description of God the Father creating through his Son (the Word) and Spirit (the Breath).

These days, many biblical scholars are very critical of the search for the *vestigia trinitatis*, believing that it constitutes an eisegetical projection onto the text. While that is a legitimate caution, it is certainly possible in principle that the text may have meanings placed there by the divine author which were not anticipated by the original human author. And that is my only point here.[180]

There are countless additional examples one may identify where the divine plenary meaning may differ from the human literal meaning. And as we continue we will be appealing to this critical distinction as offering an important framework for understanding morally problematic content. My intent here is not to argue for any of these particular readings *qua* the plenary sense. Rather my concern is simply to illustrate that the *concept* of two authors and the possible divergence between human and divine authorial meanings is well established in the Christian tradition.[181]

---

180 For a helpful discussion of the place of the *vestigia trinitatis* in contemporary theology, see David Cunningham, *These Three Are One: The Practice of Trinitarian Theology* (Blackwell, 1998), 90-107.

181 We can actually illustrate this idea in the case of filmmaking as well. Let's say that a director sets up a scene in such a way that he surprises an actress, leading the actress to forget her line and instead cry out in terror. While the actress made an error relative to her intentions for the scene, the filmmaker set up the situation precisely to achieve that response which fits perfectly with *his* intentions for the scene. In this way, you can have an actress' acting error which is inerrantly planned and used by the director. A similar concept is at play in

And so, while I am committed to a concept of biblical inerrancy, as I said above, that concept is limited to the plenary sense of the divine author. At this point, we can return to the issue of alleged goofs in the final product, although in this case I will switch from the cinematic analogue (*The Shining*) to a literary one: *Ulysses* by James Joyce. One of the most notable facts about *Ulysses'* publication history is that it includes many apparent typographical errors, 'errors' which were 'corrected' by well-meaning but deeply misguided copy editors. The scandal is that Joyce included many of these so-called errors for good reason much as Kubrick is believed to have intentionally included the alleged continuity errors in *The Shining*. In Joyce's case, it would appear that he was often working at an extraordinarily subtle and detailed meta-level completely lost on many a hapless copy-editor.[182] There is a rather charming irony about it all since, as Patrick McCarthy writes, "*Ulysses* is, among other things, a novel about the inevitability of error."[183] The lesson is this: even if the text seems to commit an error, it doesn't follow that Joyce the author thereby committed an error. He knew what he was doing.

Since I believe God is not merely a great author but the one perfect author, I am committed to the reading assumption that

---

an edited volume. An editor may gather a collection of writings from human authors and some of those writings may contain errors on the part of those human authors. But if the editor intentionally gathers those writings with the purposes that those human authorial errors will be illustrative in some manner and thereby serve the overall purpose of the work, then that editor may inerrantly include human errors within his collected volume.

182 For a great example, see Stan Carey, "When is a typo not a typo? In the wor(l)d of Ulysses," *Sentence First,* https://stancarey.wordpress.com/2017/06/06/when-is-a-typo-not-a-typo-in-the-world-of-ulysses/

183 Patrick A. McCarthy, "'Ulysses': Book of Many Errors," *European Joyce Studies,* vol. 22 (2013), 195.

God did not commit any errors in the plenary sense even if God inerrantly included human errors in the literal sense.

Once again, we must recognize that the principle goes further. The claim is not only that the divine author's meaning can add to or supplement the human author's meaning. Potentially, it could actually *subvert* or *contradict* the original human author's meaning. For example, the divine author could adopt an ironic attitude toward the perspective of the human author.[184] The lesson is that we cannot decide *a priori* the limits as to what God's divine authorial intentions may be in appropriating various human authorial voices into his canon of Scripture. Instead, we need to draw upon all our resources—including our moral intuition and other guiding hermeneutical principles—as we consider various possible readings.

The Two Authors Principle provides us with an essential insight for approaching biblical texts. Even if the *literal sense* endorses a particular view that we believe to be imprudent or flatly immoral, it does not follow that the *divine sense* does so as well. We may not know what the plenary meaning of the text is, but insofar as we believe God to be a perfect author, we would reasonably believe that there is such a meaning to be discovered.

Prophetic Texts and Two Voices

The Two Authors Principle may apply to many biblical texts, but there are some texts which appear to collapse the two voices in the sense that these texts were inspired not by indirect divinely providential appropriation of human texts but rather by a direct divine speech act through the human agent. This would seem to be the case in prophetic texts which are commonly understood to involve the voice of God speaking directly through the prophet to the audience. As we read in 2 Peter 1:21: "For prophecy never had its origin in the human will, but prophets,

---

[184] In later chapters we will explore Psalm 137 from this perspective.

though human, spoke from God as they were carried along by the Holy Spirit."

While the texts we are focusing on in this book do not include the prophetic writings (Nevi'im), as such, it is helpful to understand how the Two Authors Principle can be applied even in this context. This is not least because the biblical prophets also include some content that is morally problematic.[185] To that end, I will take a moment to map out one possible way of thinking about the prophetic texts which maintains a principled distinction between the plenary and literal sense that continues to allow for possible human error with respect to the inerrant plenary divine purposes even in these cases. However, I should be clear that I am not committed to this view: I merely include it for the sake of discussion.

In his book *The Philosophy of Hebrew Scripture,* Yoram Hazony challenges the assumption that texts which describe God as directly speaking to the reader should be classed as revelation rather than works of reason. As he observes, "if that were the case, then we would long ago have ruled out as works of reason some of the most famous works of philosophy ever written—works that are today unchallenged as works of reason, and, indeed, regarded as the basis for the tradition of Western philosophy."[186] As an example, Hazony cites the great Greek philosopher Parmenides who "writes philosophy as though it were—revealed to him by a god."[187] Parmenides was not an exception: the inspiration of the gods provided a familiar literary motif for sharing one's philosophical views in ancient Greece. Nor need one think of it as a *facon de parler* as such, but rather as a literary form reflecting the actual process of reasoning aided by divine illumination as understood by the philosopher.

---

185 See, for example, Ezekiel 9 and 16.

186 Hazony, *The Philosophy of Hebrew Scripture* (Cambridge University Press, 2012), 6.

187 Hazony, *The Philosophy of Hebrew Scripture,* 6.

Hazony cites additional examples like Empedocles and even Socrates who also framed their philosophical ruminations in a revelatory context.[188] Examples like these reveal that there was a rich Greek tradition at this time of viewing philosophical reasoning in accord with "revelation or some other form of assistance from a god."[189]

With this backdrop, Hazony then argues that we can approach the biblical prophets in like manner as authors speaking within a literary motif of divine speech which reflects their understanding of their own sophisticated reasoning and reflection. The proof is in the pudding, of course: the best way to defend this thesis is by a close analysis of a text that will demonstrate how it exhibits the same rich philosophical desiderata indicative of a carefully reasoned work in the great traditions of philosophy. And that is what Hazony provides with a careful reading of Jeremiah, illuminating the epistemological themes of the book and, in my view, establishing that this great prophet was indeed an ancient philosopher of the first order.[190]

It is important to recognize that Hazony is not denying the category of revelation within Scripture. Rather, he is arguing that philosopher and prophet are *not* mutually exclusive categories and thus, reason may be exercised conjointly with revelation: the two may exist together in the same philosophical, literary work as the human thinker works to expound the divine mind by way of his philosophical reflection. Consequently, when a prophet like Isaiah or Jeremiah speaks with the voice of God, one need not think simply of the divine author taking control of the human author like an automaton. Rather, one could interpret this process as constituting a human person carefully reasoning through some particular issue by way of a literary motif of divine revelation and that this work of ancient philosophical thinking

---

188 Hazony, *The Philosophy of Hebrew Scripture*, 8.

189 Hazony, *The Philosophy of Hebrew Scripture*, 9.

190 Hazony, *The Philosophy of Hebrew Scripture*, Chapter 6.

was subsequently appropriated by God into his canon. At that point, the work additionally assumes a plenary sense with respect to the intentions and aims of the divine author.[191]

Principle 3: Canon

A poorly made film or book may include characters or scenes that do not serve the whole work. For example, a character walking down the street suddenly pauses, picks up a note, reads it, and looks nervously around before continuing on his way. In a poorly edited film or a poorly written book, that suggestive scene might never be explained. By contrast, you can be assured that an expert director or master author will ensure that each scene is only included if it serves the overall purpose of the whole story.

The same principle applies to the Bible. The Canon Principle concerns the importance of reading and interpreting the part of a work in light of the whole canon given that the whole provides the context for ultimately understanding the part and each part serves the whole. Think of any portion of a work from a master artist such as a scene from Kubrick's *The Shining* or Joyce's *Ulysses*. Given the skill of the director or the author, you should always assume that the part is meaningfully related to the whole and thus the whole can illumine the significance of the part.

---

[191] The Two Authors Principle may very well have universal application in Scripture such that there are *always* two authors, the human author of the literal sense and the divine author of the plenary sense. However, it is beyond the scope of the present work to opine dogmatically on such general questions. My concern here is limited to articulating a framework of inspiration, inerrancy, and hermeneutics sufficient to address the interpretation of Deuteronomy 7 and 20 and Joshua 1-12.

A case in point: in one of the infamously strange scenes of *The Shining*, a quirk so subtle that you could easily miss it, Jack Torrance is waiting for his interview to be the caretaker of the Overlook Hotel when the manager, Stuart Ullman, comes out to meet him. As Ullman walks toward him, Jack looks up from a magazine, puts the periodical down, and rises to greet Ullman. Fair enough, but if you look closely, you will see that the magazine Jack was reading is a copy of the pornographic publication *Playgirl*. This makes little sense at first blush, of course, as most hotels don't leave pornographic magazines lying around the lobby. But given that we know Kubrick only includes details with a specific reason we have excellent grounds to believe that there must be some explanation for the choice to include *that* magazine. Like what? Here's one theory: that edition of the magazine includes a story on incest and many interpreters believe that one of the themes of *The Shining* is that Jack molested his son, Danny. Consequently, on this interpretation, the magazine is a subtle clue pointing back to the incest theme that is woven through the whole film.[192] Regardless of what theory we consider, however, the main point is that the interpreter will assume that there is *some* reason for the inclusion of the magazine and thus that this individual anomaly should be interpreted in light of the overall film and its themes.

The same principle applies to the Bible. My approach to the work embodies a commitment to the belief that this entire collection of diverse and disparate writings is intended as a single revelation to the reader. In that case, every passage of the Bible should be interpreted in light of the whole as surely as with any other unified work by an exceedingly competent artist. If there

---

192 Meredith Danko, "25 Facts About Stanley Kubrick's *The Shining* for its 40th Anniversary," *Mental Floss* (May 23, 2020), https://www.mentalfloss.com/article/55893/25-things-you-might-not-know-about-shining#:~:text=So%20when%20Jack%20Torrance%20is,may%20have%20experienced%20sexual%20abuse.

is some strange detail that doesn't seem to fit in its immediate context, we should seek to interpret it in light of the whole.

Now here's an objection: "Yeah, fair enough, that might work with a 'strange detail'. But the genocidal conquests of Joshua aren't an incidental detail you might miss like a cryptic glimpse of a magazine in a movie scene. These are *major* events in the Bible. Indeed, violence is woven throughout the work." True enough, but the Canon Principle is not limited to the interpretation of minor events or details: it also applies to major events and motifs. Imagine, for example, that you're watching a war film which consists of a barrage of violent battle scenes that seem to romanticize war. However, near the end of the film, the main character has a single conversation with a fellow soldier which reframes all the previous battle scenes ironically as pointless and harmful. One scene could change the meaning of the whole by revealing a major theme or motif. Thus, the Canon Principle applies to all aspects of the work ranging from incidental details to major events and motifs: in a coherent and self-consistent work by a skilled artist, *all* the elements will contribute to and be interpreted properly in light of the whole. And one character or event can change our interpretation of the entire work.

This is an important principle to keep in mind with biblical violence in particular given the long history of people who have proposed excising portions of canon (either literally or practically by way of neglect or *de facto* censorship) due to the violence in the text. Of course, the first and most infamous critical editor in this regard was Marcion, a teacher who came to Rome in the 140s. His significant wealth and charisma gained him a hearing in the church for a time, but Marcion rejected the Hebrew Scriptures altogether as false writings which told the story of an inept god who created the world as a failed experiment and then who aligned himself with Israel as an exemplar of petty partisanship and violence. When the full implications of his teaching became clear, Marcion was banished from the orthodox Church. Today, it is common to find Christians denouncing fellow Christians like myself who question established readings of biblical violence as "Marcionites."[193] That charge is simply inappropriate polemic run amok, a bald case of attempting to poison the well: Christians like myself are not rejecting the Old Testament at all, but simply seeking an alternative reading of violent texts within the total canon.[194] And that is indeed the point: I affirm the critical importance of accepting the entire canon as plenarily inspired and I remain committed always to read each part in light of the whole.

According to the Canon Principle, the reader should carefully seek to identify control texts which serve as guides for identifying and interpreting themes and understanding particular passages. For example, I mentioned earlier the conflict between Calvinists and Arminians. As I noted, Calvinists treat a passage like Romans 9 as an important control text which outlines that God is sovereign in salvation and determines whom he will save and whom he will not save. By contrast, the Arminian identifies as control texts passages such as Ezekiel 18:23, 1 Timothy 2:4 and 2 Peter 3:9 which refer to the divine will to save all. Whatever your control texts may be, canonical reading emphasizes the unity of the canonical whole and thus directs us to seek a resolution of these apparently incompatible witnesses. It does not, however, help us to identify which principle(s) we should follow to identify our control texts. Thus far, I have invoked an essential principle of moral intuition and a commitment to

---

193 Unfortunately, Boyd incorrectly classes me as a sort of neo-Marcionite, albeit with some caveats. See *The Crucifixion of the Warrior God: Interpreting the Old Testament's Violent Portraits of God in Light of the Cross*. Volume 1: *The Cruciform Hermeneutic*, 343.

194 By contrast, Marcion's canon was a truncated version of Luke and ten Pauline epistles: a far cry from the 39 Old Testament books and 27 New Testament books of the Christian canon. The development and exact boundaries of canon are beyond the purview of this study. For a good introduction see F.F. Bruce, *The Canon of Scripture* (IVP Academic, 2018).

divine perfection. But in the next two principles we will see two additional guides to aid our reading of biblical violence.

Principle 4: Jesus

In the previous section, I discussed a hypothetical war movie full of violent battle scenes. As one watches the film, those scenes are presented in a way that could be interpreted as valorizing battle. However, a critical conversation near the end of the film by one particular character reframes all those scenes in an ironic light which questions the impulses that lead to war in the first place. That character and that particular scene provide an essential heuristic, an interpretive key to unlock the whole.

For the Christian, Jesus is the key to unlock the whole of Scripture. The Jesus Principle is predicated on the assumption that Jesus is the final and ultimately authoritative locus of divine revelation. He is the one in whom the fullness of deity dwells in bodily form (Colossians 2:9). He is the power and wisdom of God (1 Corinthians 1:24). As Jesus said, "Anyone who has seen me has seen the Father." (John 14:9) As a result, Jesus is the guide for understanding who God is and what Scripture demands of us. On the Road to Emmaus he famously opened the scriptures, showing how those texts should all be read in light of him: "And beginning with Moses and all the Prophets, he explained to them what was said in all the Scriptures concerning himself." (Luke 24:27) And so, when he met with the disciples, "he opened their minds so they could understand the Scriptures." (Luke 24:45) The entirety of the Law is fulfilled in him (Matthew 5:17).

What this means for the Christian is that the life and teachings of Jesus provide the final guide for all interpretation and application. He is our guide through the hermeneutical labyrinth of the Bible. Paul Copan states the point well:

if we stop with the Old Testament, we won't see the entire story line as it's brought to completion in Jesus. The Old Testament was in many ways anticipatory of something far greater. So if Jesus truly brought a new covenant for the true Israel and has begun to renew the creation as the second Adam, then we ought to concern ourselves with how his incarnation, ministry, atoning death, and resurrection shed light backward on the Old Testament, with all its messiness.[195]

The question is how does Jesus shed light backward on the 'messiness' of divinely commanded genocide? We can put the question simply in terms of *continuity* or *discontinuity*, *completion* or *correction*. In other words, do the life and teachings of Jesus exist in *continuity* with the murderous violence of the first Joshua and as a *completion* of Israel's battlefield work? Or, more radically, does Jesus' coming represent an important *discontinuity* in the story like that soldier whose speech critiques, deconstructs, and/or ironizes by way of reframing the battle scenes that came before?

Christians that take the continuity-completion response are keen to point out that in their view Jesus never condemns the violence of divine genocide. Indeed, he speaks harsh imprecations against his critics and warns of coming judgment. On this view, the Jesus Principle does not justify a radical critique of the biblical genocide passages.

But other Christians take a more radical view.[196] Ironically, while Paul Copan takes the continuity-completion view, he concludes his book *Is God a Moral Monster?* with the following quote from Timothy Keller:

---

195 Copan, *Is God a Moral Monster? Making Sense of the Old Testament God* (Baker, 2011), 221, ff.

196 See Boyd, *The Crucifixion of the Warrior God: Interpreting the Old Testament's Violent Portraits of God in Light of the Cross*. Volume 1: *The Cruciform Hermeneutic*, 209-223, Appendix 2.

> If your fundamental is a man dying on the cross for his enemies, if the very heart of your self-image and your religion is a man praying for his enemies as he died for them, sacrificing for them, loving them—if that sinks into your heart of hearts, it's going to produce the kind of life that the early Christians produced. The most inclusive life out of the most exclusive possible claim—and that is that this is the truth. But what is the truth? The truth is a God become weak, loving, and dying for the people who opposed him, dying forgiving them.[197]

I say this is ironic because it seems to me that Keller eloquently summarizes the case for the radical-discontinuity view. Once the Christian begins to contemplate the extraordinary implications of the life and teachings of Jesus, that provides a unique perspective on rethinking biblical violence from Jesus' own warnings about posthumous judgment straight on back to the violence of the Canaanite conquest. This changes everything.

Specific teachings of Jesus provide a particularly powerful capsule summary of his view. Consider, for example, the justly famous Parable of the Good Samaritan. I began this book with a slightly amended version of that parable, one in which the word 'Samaritan' was replaced with the word 'Canaanite'. That simple act is meant to stress that Jesus' teaching radiates out as truly universal so that it encompasses every alienated party, every individual from an outgroup. If we want to understand what it means to love our neighbor, we will need to think in terms of those people we are *least* inclined to love, the Canaanite no less than the Samaritan. The Jesus Principle compels me to read the entirety of Scripture in light of the life and teaching of Jesus.

When we encounter difficult moral content in Scripture, the proper response is to return to the idea of control texts. According to the Jesus Principle, the primary set of control

---

197 Cited in Copan, *Is God a Moral Monster? Making Sense of the Old Testament God*, 222.

texts for understanding the canonical whole of Scripture are found in the life and teachings of Jesus. This commitment is *not* as some have erroneously claimed, tantamount to proposing a canon within a canon. Rather, it is a commitment to the belief that the sum total, fullness and completion of God's revelation comes in Jesus Christ such that the whole of scripture should be read in light of him.[198]

In his book *Changing Our Mind* David Gushee provides an interesting example of the practical way that this commitment shapes the Christian mind. Gushee recalls the German Christians who rejected the vociferous anti-Semitism of the Nazis. And he asks, why was it that these Christians utterly repudiated the Nazification of the church when so many other nominal Christians unwittingly embraced it? The difference, he says, is that their approach to the Bible wasn't simply based on interpretations of a list of isolated Bible verses, verses which under the right circumstances could be distorted by a new framework to justify anti-Semitism. Rather, these Christians had rooted their entire engagement with Scripture in a holistic saturation in the life and teaching of Jesus, and this formation simply made it *unthinkable* to consider Nazism:

> The righteous minority of Christians who rescued Jews, right in the teeth of unchristlike anti-Jewish Christian traditions, cited motivating texts like the Golden Rule, the Double Love Command, the Good Samaritan, and the saying about being our brother's keepers. They highlighted broader biblical themes like the sacred worth of every person, and our obligation as Christians to be compassionate, merciful, and just.[199]

Based on this example, Gushee advises that

---

[198] One popular expression of this principle is found in the movement known as "Red Letter Christians": https://www.redletterchristians.org/

[199] Gushee, *Changing Our Mind,* 3rd ed. (Read the Spirit Books, 2017), 140.

We must cling to Jesus' example and the way he conducted his ministry. We must spend a lot of time in the gospels. If we do we might notice his warnings about religious self-righteousness and contempt for others deemed to be sinners; his embrace of outcasts and marginalized people; his attacks on those religious leader types who block access to God's grace; his elevating as examples those who simply and humbly pray for God's mercy; his teachings about God's prodigious grace . . . .[200]

One might speak at this point of the familiar example of how a bank-teller learns to identify real currency over-against the counterfeit. That skill is acquired not simply by learning about a list of discrete facts in a checklist which identify real currency. Rather, it comes by developing an intimate *feel* for the real stuff through regular handling of and interaction with it in a variety of circumstances. As your familiarity grows, you can intuitively recognize the real thing and as you do, you also become more adept at identifying the counterfeit. The same may be said of Christian discipleship: the more we spend time with God as revealed in Jesus Christ the more we are equipped to identify genuine vs. counterfeit interpretations of Scripture.

Principle 5: Love

The final principle is built squarely on the life and teaching of Jesus. It recognizes that the proper reading of Scripture should always bring us into conformity with God as revealed in Jesus. And that means a growing love of God and neighbor. Many Christians have posited a hermeneutical principle to capture this essential congruence between Scripture and spiritual and ethical formation. For example, Charles H. Cosgrove proposes

---

[200] Gushee, *Changing Our Mind,* 140.

the following principle: "*Moral-theological considerations should guide hermeneutical choices between conflicting plausible interpretations.*"[201] On Cosgrove's account, the principle functions *ceteris paribus:* in other words, all other things being equal, the positive moral/spiritual formative interpretation is the preferred one. But I believe we are justified to endorse the principle in a stronger form as follows: even when other independent biblical or theological considerations may favor interpretation A, if acceptance of interpretation A would inhibit the increased love of God and/or neighbor, then I would take that as *an overriding reason to reject interpretation A.*

In my view, the heart of the Love Principle is ultimately found in Paul's familiar statement on the purpose of Scripture in 2 Timothy 3:14-17:

> [14] But as for you, continue in what you have learned and have become convinced of, because you know those from whom you learned it, [15] and how from infancy you have known the Holy Scriptures, which are able to make you wise for salvation through faith in Christ Jesus. [16] All Scripture is God-breathed and is useful for teaching, rebuking, correcting and training in righteousness, [17] so that the servant of God may be thoroughly equipped for every good work.

This passage is often cited as evidence for the concept of all Scripture being *God-breathed* or inspired. While that is certainly true, we cannot miss the equally important point Paul is making concerning the *end* for which these texts are God-breathed. According to Paul, that end is to make us wise for salvation through faith in Christ Jesus by way of teaching, rebuking, correcting, and training in righteousness. Thus, it follows that

---

201 Cosgrove, *Appealing to Scripture in Moral Debate: Five Hermeneutical Rules* (Eerdmans, 2002), 154, emphasis in original.

when interpreting Scripture we should seek and favor those interpretations consistent with this end.[202]

Can we say more about what it means to be wise for salvation through faith in Christ Jesus? Jesus himself provides us with the answer in a famous exchange with the rich young ruler. In this memorable encounter, this young man asks Jesus what one must do to inherit eternal life. Jesus replies by turning the question back on the young man who promptly answers, "'Love the Lord your God with all your heart and with all your soul and with all your strength and with all your mind'; and, 'Love your neighbor as yourself.' 'You have answered correctly,' Jesus replied. 'Do this and you will live.'" (Luke 10:27-28) However, the Rich Young Ruler is not satisfied with this answer because he wanted to justify himself and so he then poses a famous follow-up question: "Who is my neighbor?" (v. 29) At that point, Jesus replies with his timeless parable that places the hated Samaritan as the hero of the story. The lesson: if you want to be like Jesus and find his Kingdom, then you must love others the way that man loved his injured neighbor, and remember that means loving people from the outgroup, from your equivalent of the Samaritans, as readily as you love anyone else.

So how does this all fit into interpretation of the Bible? We can put the pieces together like this. To begin with, the purpose of the Bible—its *raison d'etre*—is not merely to give us a divine doctrinal information dump, but rather to make us wise for salvation through faith in Christ Jesus. And *that* means creating people who love God with all their heart, soul, mind, and strength and who love their neighbors as themselves. And 'neighbor' means not simply some select people from your

---

202 It can be rather shocking to realize how this most influential of all passages on Scriptural inspiration defines the term not with respect to the production of a repository of facts—the obsession of so many conservative evangelical inerrantists—but rather with a text aimed at the holistic transformation of the person into a disciple of Jesus.

ingroup—family, friends, acquaintances—but also the people from various outgroups: the wayfarer, the stranger, and yes, the *enemy*. While this message is clearly seeded in the Old Testament (see for example, Leviticus 19:18 and 19:34), it has often been missed. And if ever it has been missed, it is surely so in the case of interpreters who demonize a people group as cancer deserving of total annihilation.

If that is what scripture is for, if it is for the end of conforming us into the image of Jesus so that we may love all people, including outsiders, the others, the outgroup, the wayfarer, stranger and enemy, if it reaches out to and encompasses both Samaritans *as well as* Canaanites, and if it calls us to love all these people as we love ourselves, then any reading which is inconsistent with that ethical, spiritual goal *cannot* be correct and *it needs to be rejected*. As the Perfect Author Principle reminds us, God cannot fail to write a book that is perfectly adept at achieving the purposes for which he created it. So if our current way of reading portions of Scripture is not creating greater lovers of God and/or neighbor, if it instead leads us to objectify and dehumanize our neighbor as when theologians like Archer demonize Canaanites as a "cancer of moral depravity" and "baneful infection," then we need to return to the texts and seek a new interpretation because that reading *cannot* be right. No reading that reduces our neighbor to being a *disease* can be a correct reading.

St. Augustine defended this principle by succinctly observing that we ought always to read so as to increase one's love of God and neighbor.[203] And keep in mind that love of neighbor means wishing shalom (well-being; flourishing) for people you would not choose as a neighbor, people with whom you are not natural allies, people which you might otherwise be inclined to dehumanize or objectify. Eric Seibert proposes the thesis like

---

203 Cf. Jerome Creach, *Violence in Scripture*, Interpretation: Resources for the Use of Scripture in the Church (Westminster John Knox Press, 2013), 4.

this: "the Bible should never be used to inspire, promote, or justify acts of violence. This means, among other things, that the Bible should not be read in ways that oppress or otherwise harm people."[204]

The Love Principle will not tell us how a difficult text should be interpreted: indeed, none of these principles will do that. But what this principle, and all five principles collectively, will do is provide a warning system to begin to identify errant interpretations and guide us toward a better and more Christ-like reading.

I mentioned above that Yoram Hazony offers an astute philosophical analysis of the prophet Jeremiah's epistemology. At one point in his analysis, Hazony points out that Jeremiah believed that the wisdom of the Torah "gradually forces itself upon the mind of the individual by trial and error."[205] In other words, the Law is shown over time to be a proper guide to illumine human experience: by your fruits you discern its practical wisdom for human flourishing. I would commend that a practical criterion like that may be applied here. If a reading of Scripture is correct it will be vindicated by the resulting evidence of the reader's growth in love for God and neighbor. So that is our final principle: we are reading well when our reading increases love of God and neighbor. We are not reading well when our reading does not increase love of God and neighbor.

Conclusion

As we go forward in surveying interpretive options, we should be guided by these five principles. We should always interpret with a commitment to God as the perfect primary divine author

---

[204] Eric Seibert, *The Violence of Scripture: Overcoming the Old Testament's Troubling Legacy* (Fortress Press, 2012), 2.

[205] Hazony, *The Philosophy of Hebrew Scripture*, 174.

who makes no mistakes relative to his ends in composing this work. Second, for every passage there is both the primary author and the secondary human author, their voices may differ, and if they conflict then the divine author takes priority over the human author. Further, any errors of the human author were inerrantly included by the divine author/editor. All Scripture is plenarily inspired and can properly be interpreted within a canonical text as the work of one primary divine author. The guide for interpreting this text is the life and teachings of Jesus. The end goal of correct interpretation is the cultivation of love of God and neighbor. And we must remember ever and always that 'neighbor' includes those from the outgroups, the margins, the wrong side of the tracks. As we proceed, we will allow these five principles to join our overt appeal to moral intuitions as we vet different interpretations of Scripture in pursuit of the proper way to understand the Canaanite conquest.

8

The Genocide Apologists

In this chapter we will consider the first of our four interpretive approaches, a viewpoint that I have dubbed the 'Genocide Apologists'. Some people may find this label to be an overly polemical description or even an attempt to poison the well against the position. For example, Walton and Walton insist that the term 'genocide' is simply inappropriate when speaking of the Canaanite conquest (or those who defend it) since the Israelites would not have agreed to the term:

> When we translate the event as holy war or jihad or genocide, or even conquest, we are not translating the event properly, because those words and ideas do not mean the same thing to us that the logic and imagery used to describe the conquest would have meant to the original audience, either in terms of their connotations or their objectives. When we hear words such as *genocide* we interpret them as 'a thing that should never be done.' But the text does not depict the conquest event in terms of a thing that should never be done.[206]

---

[206] John H. Walton and J. Harvey Walton, *The Lost World of the Israelite Conquest*

Walton and Walton are partially right here. There clearly is a possibility that we can misread what is being described in the text. However, it is spurious to say that the text is non-genocidal because the Israelites believed their actions were permissible. As we saw in chapter 2, genocide is defined as the attempt to eradicate a genos, i.e. an ethnic, cultural, and/or religious identity as such. And whether or not a genocidaire agrees with the appositeness of the term to describe their actions has precisely *no* relevance to the question of whether those actions themselves qualify as genocidal.

The truth is that I have chosen that label not to get a polemical leg up on my opponent, still less to poison the well. Rather, I have done so because I believe it is the most accurate description of the position under consideration. The Genocide Apologist's position is under-girded by two central claims. First, God did in fact issue commands in history which meet the legal definition of genocide and the Israelites subsequently carried out those commands on the Canaanite population. Second, given that God is morally perfect and that God's commands to human beings constitute moral obligations for those human beings, it follows not only that actions which meet the legal definition of genocide may be *morally permissible*, but that in at least some cases (i.e. when God commands it) such actions are *morally obligatory*.

The position of the Genocide Apologists rests on what is seen by adherents of the view as a straightforward, literal reading of Deuteronomy 7 and 20 and Joshua 1-12. Yes, these passages do appear to describe God commanding the eradication of Canaanites as well as the driving out of any survivors from the land. And yes, the Israelites then acted on that command resulting both in the mass killing of Canaanites and in the forcible expulsion of all survivors from the land. And yes, these actions would qualify as genocide and ethnic cleansing by modern definition.

(InterVarsity Press, 2017), 257.

In my experience, many evangelical Protestant Christians are *de facto* genocide apologists whether or not they would accept the label, as such, to describe themselves. To be sure, few have more than the most rudimentary familiarity with the formal legal definition of genocide. Thus, it is another question as to whether they would recognize (let alone appreciate!) the label. But it is common to find evangelicals assuming straightforward readings of the passages in Deuteronomy and Joshua as accurate depictions of past historical events in which the Israelites eradicated Canaanites by divine command. While this view may be common among evangelicals, it is not limited to them. The truth is that it is a well-established position in Christian history. Indeed, as a nod to those historical roots, we will begin our survey of selected opinions with the great sixteenth century theologian John Calvin.

John Calvin on Canaanite Genocide

Calvin, of course, knew nothing of the term 'genocide'. Regardless, his views can retroactively be properly described as genocidal relative to the modern definition. He candidly discusses these issues in his *Commentary on Joshua*. Calvin first considers the key Hebrew concept of *herem*, an act that represents an absolute turning over to God of possessions (material objects, animals, or people) that are set apart "as completely as if they were annihilated." The Greek equivalent term, Calvin notes, is *anathema*:

> Hence the exhortation to beware of what was under anathema, inasmuch as that which had been set apart for God alone had perished, in so far as men were concerned. It is used in a different sense in the following verse, where caution is given not to place the camp of Israel in anathema. Here its simple meaning is, excision, perdition, or death. Moreover, God

destined vessels made of metals for the use of the sanctuary; all other things he ordered to be consumed by fire, or destroyed in other manners.[207]

With that background, we then turn to the act of committing the entire city of Jericho to the *herem* or cutting them off as *anathema* and thereby consigned to destruction. At this point, Calvin offers a candid discussion of the theological and ethical issues at play. He begins,

> The indiscriminate and promiscuous slaughter, making no distinction of age or sex, but including alike women and children, the aged and decrepit, might seem an inhuman massacre, had it not been executed by the command of God. But as he, in whose hands are life and death, had justly doomed those nations to destruction, this puts an end to all discussion.[208]

The phrase "an end to all discussion" appears to echo the familiar reprimand, "Who are you, O Man?" (Romans 9:20) as an attempt to kibosh all further critical enquiry. However, Calvin is not simply telling us that we creatures have no right to be concerned, end of discussion. He is also offering an argument. The fact is that God has a *right* over creation that no other creature has because God is the source of life and death. Further, it follows that God can delegate this authority to others (e.g. the Israelite soldiers) so that they may carry out actions that in any other instance would be immoral. If God issues a command to human creatures to end the life of other human creatures by the way of a machete or sword, then those human creatures now have a moral obligation to carry out that command by massacring their fellow humans. And consequently, the same actions which

---

207 Calvin, "Commentary on Joshua," trans. Henry Beveridge, Christian Classics Ethereal Library, https://ccel.org/ccel/calvin/calcom07/calcom07.ix.i.html

208 Calvin, "Commentary on Joshua."

would, in other circumstances, constitute "indiscriminate and promiscuous slaughter," are within this context a pious manifestation of God's good and praiseworthy will.

To consider an analogy, imagine that you're driving when a police officer flags you down. He places an injured person in the backseat of your car and instructs you to drive to the nearest hospital: "And you can exceed the speed limit" he says. "We need to save this person's life!" This unique circumstance coupled with the authority of the police officer could provide an exceptional case where exceeding the posted speed limit could be morally, and perhaps legally, justified. Calvin is simply applying the same logic to the present case: under God's authority Israel undertakes actions of mass killing and forcible expulsion of another group, actions which would be immoral and illegal in other contexts but which are permissible and even obligatory under the divine authority and command. And if you object that committing genocide is far more extreme than exceeding the speed limit, Calvin can reply that God's power and authority are far greater than any police officer.

Calvin also takes note of a further justification for the act related to God's longsuffering nature: "We may add, that they had been borne with for four hundred years, until their iniquity was complete. Who will now presume to complain of excessive rigor, after God had so long delayed to execute judgment?"[209] Here Calvin is adding to his *Sovereign God* defense a *Longsuffering God* defense. For a pale point of comparison, imagine some obnoxious neighbors who repeatedly ignore the city bylaws by refusing to cut their lawn. When the bylaw officer finally tickets them, the city has the right to issue the ticket. But in addition, the bylaw officer could point out he waited fully *four weeks* to issue the ticket, thereby giving the neighbors ample time to comply with the bylaw. In like manner, God delayed judgment against wicked Canaan and he did so for four hundred years all

---

209 Calvin, "Commentary on Joshua."

while his people, the rightful occupants of the land, were kept in bondage in Egypt. Consequently, when God finally comes and justly expels the squatters they surely have no ground for complaint. If anything, we should recognize that God was merciful in delaying judgment for *centuries*.

While Calvin makes some important points, the act of seeking to eradicate an entire population still appears to be extremely harsh, excessive, and cruel. Even if we conceded that some members of the population were morally culpable to the point of deserving execution, surely that cannot justly be extended to *children*, can it? Calvin offers this response:

> If any one object that children, at least, were still free from fault, it is easy to answer, that they perished justly, as the race was accursed and reprobated. Here then it ought always to be remembered, that it would have been barbarous and atrocious cruelty had the Israelites gratified their own lust and rage, in slaughtering mothers and their children, but that they are justly praised for their active piety and holy zeal, in executing the command of God, who was pleased in this way to purge the land of Canaan of the foul and loathsome defilements by which it had long been polluted.[210]

Here's the basic idea: while it is *usually* the case that hacking children into pieces is wrong, this occasion is an exception because the children in question were *Canaanites*, a group that was uniquely corrupt, loathsome, cursed by God, and thus like a disesed forest worthy only to be ground up in a cosmic wood-chipper. Indeed, one might argue at this point, as many Genocide Apologists indeed have, that the real problem is that we fail to appreciate just how completely corrupt and reprobated this race was such that even its devilish spawn would need to be subjected to the edge of a sword.

---

210 Calvin, "Commentary on Joshua."

We can sum up Calvin's main points as follows:

- God is Lord over all, and thus he grants life to all things every moment; consequently, God can choose both when he will withdraw life or if he commands a human being to act as his proxy in ending the life of another human being; if God does command this, it becomes the moral obligation of the human being so-commanded to act;
- God showed mercy to the Canaanites by allowing them to exist as usurpers in the land for as long as they did (400 years!);
- The Canaanites were exceedingly and uniquely wicked as a people and as a result they were deserving of total eradication, even their children and infants.

Contemporary Genocide Apologetics

Many contemporary Christians follow Calvin's uncompromising embrace of biblical genocide. For example, three of the four essayists in the book *Show Them No Mercy: Four Views on God and the Canaanite Genocide*, defend the historical and ethical dimensions of the Canaanite eradication. One of those essayists is Eugene Merrill. In his essay on "The Case for Moderate Discontinuity," he begins by summarizing Yahweh war: "Nowhere in the modern reading of Old Testament texts is the theodicic problem more acute than in coming to grips with so-called 'holy war' more commonly correctly described now as 'Yahweh war.' Common in this concept was genocide, the wholesale slaughter of men, women, and children."[211] Merrill openly admits that "Yahweh war and its use of *herem* was also genocide, by both design and

---

[211] Merrill, "The Case for Moderate Discontinuity," in *Show Them No Mercy: Four Views on God and Canaanite Genocide,* ed. Stanley N. Gundry (Zondervan, 2003), 64-5.

practice."[212] However, given that God's commands are perfect and morally obligatory upon creatures, Merrill concludes that in *this case* genocide was warranted: "The issue, then, cannot be whether or not genocide is intrinsically good or evil—its sanction by a holy God settles that question."[213] And so, God willed to empower a chosen agent, Israel, to carry out the genocide.

Merrill advises that the best way to understand the nature and ethics of what he terms "Old Testament genocide" is to examine the main texts that authorize it.[214] While expositing Deuteronomy 13, he observes that

> Yahweh war . . . is essentially war against the imaginary gods of the world who challenge the sovereignty of Yahweh. In this sense, Yahweh war can perhaps more properly be termed deicide rather than homicide. Only by Yahweh's swift and complete defeat of false gods can his sovereignty be guarded and celebrated. It follows, then, that those who promote and practice the worship of other gods—Israelites included—must expect the fate of those gods, that is, total eradication.[215]

It turns out that Merrill's definition is, in fact, surprisingly apt. By opting to describe the real goal of the conquest as 'deicide', that is, the eradication of Canaanite gods and thus Canaanite religion, Merrill identifies *religious identity* as the unique *genos* that is targeted for extinction in the conquest. This makes it clear that "the utter destruction (*ḥrm*) of man and beast (6:21) and the burning (*srp*) of the city itself (6:24)"[216] was indeed an intentional genocide, a concerted attempt to eradicate Canaanite religious identity in its entirety.

---

212 Merrill, "The Case for Moderate Discontinuity," 93.

213 Merrill, "The Case for Moderate Discontinuity," 93.

214 Merrill, "The Case for Moderate Discontinuity," 70.

215 Merrill, "The Case for Moderate Discontinuity," 71.

216 Merrill, "The Case for Moderate Discontinuity," 72.

Norman Geisler also addresses the moral question of genocide in an article in his *Big Book of Christian Apologetics*. According to Geisler, the complete eradication of the Canaanite people was a moral necessity to protect the purity of the Israelites from the corrupting influence of this degenerate people: "In the case of the Canaanites, it was necessary in establishing a holy nation and priesthood to exterminate the godlessness of the city and its people. If anything had remained, except that which was taken into the treasure house of the Lord, there would have always been the threat of heathen influence to pull the people away from the pure worship of the Lord."[217] Needless to say, if Israel had drifted off course from their call to be a blessing to all the nations of earth (Genesis 12:2-3), then collectively the people of earth would've suffered immense loss. In that way we can see that the limited suffering of the Canaanites was necessary to prevent much greater suffering later.

We find another striking example of genocide apologetics in a 2009 essay by Christian philosopher Clay Jones. In "We Don't Hate Sin So We Don't Understand What Happened to the Canaanites: An Addendum to 'Divine Genocide' Arguments,"[218] Jones defends the genocidal slaughter of Canaanites due to the deep wickedness of their society. Interestingly, Jones' method in defending the genocide echoes my method in this book in one key respect: he agrees that proper moral appraisal depends on a carefully constructed and emotionally moving understanding of the situation. The one monumental difference is that his method is restricted to a thick description of the *sins of the Canaanites* rather than the remedy provided by the Israelites. Thus, Jones believes that we won't understand the ethics of Israelite actions until we first understand the depth of Canaanite sin:

---

217 Geisler, *The Big Book of Christian Apologetics*, 67.

218 Jones, "We Don't Hate Sin So We Don't Understand What Happened to the Canaanites," *Philosophia Christi*, 11, (2009), 53-72.

> What I am suggesting is not merely vibrant language usage that better captures the brazen experience of evil. Although it is interesting to note that when language becomes diluted, morally, it can help tame and pacify our outrage toward evil. I have come to discern that as a matter of attitude or outlook, we need to look much more frankly at human evil than we customarily do, especially when we are engaged in philosophical reflection on the problem of evil.[219]

Thus, Jones argues that the Canaanites were deserving of complete eradication due to their deep well of depravity. He writes, "most of our problems regarding God's ordering the destruction of the Canaanites come from the fact that God hates sin but we do not."[220]

Jones then sets about cataloguing the varied sins of the Canaanites with this warning: "much of what follows is admittedly disturbing. And if it is not disturbing to us, perhaps there is something more disturbing about our lack of being rightly disturbed?"[221] Jones' summary includes six categories of sinfulness which he believes are collectively sufficient to warrant the slaughter of an entire society. These include "idolatry, incest, adultery, child sacrifice, homosexuality, and bestiality."[222] Jones is unsparing in recounting the depth of Canaanite depravity. For example, regarding bestiality, he baldly observes, "If they were

---

219 Jones, "We Don't Hate Sin So We Don't Understand What Happened to the Canaanites," 54.

220 Jones, "We Don't Hate Sin So We Don't Understand What Happened to the Canaanites," 53.

221 Jones, "We Don't Hate Sin So We Don't Understand What Happened to the Canaanites," 54-55.

222 Jones, "We Don't Hate Sin So We Don't Understand What Happened to the Canaanites," 55.

having sex with just about every living thing they could get their hand on, and they were, then all had to die."[223]

To be sure, Jones provides no evidence that bestiality was widely (let alone universally) practiced in Canaan. Instead, all he gives us are some literary references to sex with animals. By way of pushback, even in the most licentious societies not *every* adult is a sexual libertine. And this is to say nothing of small children, infants, or the severally mentally and physically handicapped. So what justifies Jones in baldly claiming that *every* Canaanite was seeking to have sexual intercourse with "just about every living thing they could get their hand on"? Frankly, the claim is absurd: indeed, to be blunt, it sounds very much like the reckless hyperbole of a genocidaire attempting to justify crimes against humanity. Be that as it may, Jones insists that the sexually licentious nature of the society was sufficiently excessive to warrant killing every member of that society. This same basic point is carried through for the other key hallmarks of depravity.

Even as he defends the justice of completely eradicating this people, Jones attempts to preempt the predictable rebuttals by noting that "what God commanded Israel to do to the Canaanites was not genocide—it was capital punishment."[224] Thus, Jones appears to believe that attributing the actions to the divine will justifies an exemption from the legal category of genocide. However, that is mistaken. Every genocidaire appeals to unique exceptions and offers particular justifications for their actions, and the claims that the act is a just punishment and that it has been commanded by God are go-to rationalizations from time immemorial. But the fact that a genocide apologist attributes the act to the divine will simply isn't relevant: genocide is, first and foremost, a legal designation which is fixed by the definition

---

[223] Jones, "We Don't Hate Sin So We Don't Understand What Happened to the Canaanites," 66,

[224] Jones, "We Don't Hate Sin So We Don't Understand What Happened to the Canaanites," 68.

of the 1948 Convention on the Prevention and Punishment of the Crime of Genocide. Any act which meets that standard is, by definition, genocide whether or not Jones or anyone else claims it was God's will.

What about the claim that the Canaanites were uniquely sinful? In their book *The Lost World of the Israelite Conquest*, Walton and Walton rebut apologetic attempts to justify the genocide by appeal to the unique sinfulness of the Canaanites. They challenge the assumption of the unparalleled depravity of this people.[225] And they point out that the Joshua narrative provides a literary depiction of the Canaanites which conforms to a familiar ancient literary trope of "invincible barbarians destined to be destroyed by the gods."[226] In this trope, the barbarians do not *become* savage through depraved actions: rather, it is part of their nature as "destructive, subhuman monsters."[227] (Similarly, Michael Heiser argues that the *herem* applies to the elimination of the bloodlines of the *Nephilim*. In other words, it is a genocide sourced in *ontological* inferiority.[228]) Walton and Walton thus argue that it is misguided to attempt to impugn the Canaanites as uniquely wicked; instead, we need to recognize that they provide a "negative example and a foil of the ideal of the covenant order."[229] From this perspective, Jones' entire approach to the Canaanites appears to be a deeply misguided attempt to demonize an ancient people as uniquely worthy of destruction due to sin. And that is the same kind of dehumanizing rhetoric that has been invoked by countless genocide apologists before him.

Jones concludes his essay by turning from the distant past to the present as he engages in a blushingly cherry-picked survey of contemporary American culture and society, one which

---

[225] Walton and Walton, *The Lost World of the Israelite Conquest*, part 2.

[226] Walton and Walton, *The Lost World of the Israelite Conquest*, 144.

[227] Walton and Walton, *The Lost World of the Israelite Conquest*, 147.

[228] *The Unseen Realm: Recovering the Supernatural* (Lexham Press, 2015), 204.

[229] Walton and Walton, *The Lost World of the Israelite Conquest*, 156.

parallels his blushingly cherry-picked survey of ancient Canaanite society. (At least the man is a consistent cherry-picker.) His shocking intent here is to justify the conclusion that the United States as a society allegedly embraces the very same sins and exhibits the very same debauchery that warranted the complete destruction of Canaan: idolatry, incest, adultery, child sacrifice (cf. abortion), homosexuality, and bestiality.[230] As Jones soberly observes, "A cursory read of at least the idea currents in American culture often reads like a sequel to Canaanite practices."[231] And so, while Jones doesn't explicitly say it, the implication is very clear: if God justly commanded the Israelites to slaughter the Canaanites *en masse* for their collective sins, and if America's sins are equivalent to Canaanite sins, then it follows that God could likewise justly command the collective slaughter of all 320,000,000 Americans (presumably with the exception of a few Rahabs and their families).

Evaluation

The Genocide Apologists are to be commended for their consistency and forthrightness: for the most part, they do not obfuscate about their position; they see the implications of their reading and they willingly embrace it. While some of them attempt to distance themselves from the *term* genocide, they all willingly accept that God commanded an unmitigated slaughter of the Canaanite population due to their sins and/or their ontological inferiority. And thus, in their view the slaughter was

---

230 Incredibly, Jones' evidence that America collectively is culpable for bestiality to a degree sufficient to warrant genocide consists of a reference to an arthouse movie and excerpts from the lyrics of a Metallica song.

231 Jones, "We Don't Hate Sin So We Don't Understand What Happened to the Canaanites," 68.

a morally laudatory action on behalf of the Israelites. Genocide is not merely justifiable: when God commands it, it is *morally obligatory*.[232]

The Genocide Apologists offer a sober challenge, one that we should not be *too* quick to dismiss, a challenge that our contemporary moral thinking may be flawed and in need of a radical retooling based on the witness of Scripture. Perhaps the lesson is that we need to allow the Bible to correct our fallible moral intuitions. Eric Seibert describes the reasoning as follows:

> some people assume that these concerns largely reflect *modern* sensibilities. They believe people today struggle with the more demanding portraits of God in the Old Testament because these portraits conflict with contemporary beliefs about God as tolerant, loving, and nonjudgmental. In this context, any critique of God's behavior in the Old Testament becomes suspect and is regarded as nothing more than an attempt to make God in one's own image.[233]

It would be foolhardy not to pause at least for a moment to recognize that there may be a legitimate caution here. As we have noted, our moral intuitions are fallible and prone to error just like every other source of belief. For example, a century ago, so-called enlightened liberal progressives enthusiastically embraced the concept of eugenics, confident in the ability of modern society to build a better and brighter future for all. Fifty years ago, many Christian conservatives assumed that interracial marriage was somehow against God's law. They were sure of it.

---

[232] Notably, on this approach moral permissibility need not be limited to the range of cases that are *commanded* by God as the *herem* is sometimes voluntarily undertaken by the Israelites independent of any divine command to do so (e.g. Leviticus 27). That allows for a significantly broader range of instances independent of divine command where genocide could, on this view, be morally licit.

[233] Seibert, *Disturbing Divine Behavior: Troubling Old Testament Images of God*, 68.

One does not need to look far to find other examples of profound moral error. And as these two examples illustrate, moral error can equally imperil the *progressive* and the *conservative*. Given that we're *all* prone to error, could it be that the unequivocal condemnation of genocide which is popular in our day is but one more error? Could it be that we will come to recognize that error in the future no less than the error of approving eugenics or censuring interracial marriage?

While there will never be a completely error free human perspective on moral value and obligation, we need not secure infallibility to defend our most secure convictions. And we do have a methodology in place, a method that takes our own limited perspective and fallibility into consideration and yet can still justify the conclusion that we may retain our core convictions after careful consideration of the dissenting opinions. That is, once I face a challenge to my belief in the wrongness of genocide I turn to reflect carefully on my most basic moral intuitions and if they still seem indisputably correct then I am justified in retaining them and continuing to reason from them as the plumb line of moral action, even as I concede that I still *could* be wrong. Eleonore Stump *could* be wrong about categorically rejecting Nazi child experimentation as inherently evil just as I *could* be wrong about categorically rejecting devotional child sacrifice, devotional rape, and genocide as inherently evil. Nonetheless, we are justified in treating those basic intuitive deliverances as the starting points of moral reason until we are given some sufficiently weighty counter evidence, and as I see it, the Genocide Apologist has yet to give us any.

But is that too hasty? What might be the counter evidence and how strong is it? Let's return to our model of intuitive reflection and consider further the Canaanite genocide in light of the Rwandan genocide. The simple question we shall need to consider is whether it is remotely plausible that we are in this kind of deep moral error in our thinking about the intrinsic evil of events like the Rwandan genocide.

For starters, it is disconcerting to note how the Genocide Apologists develop a rhetorical framing of Israel's actions in Canaan which has such clear and disturbing parallels with the justifications for other historic genocides. For example, Archer's insistence that the Canaanites are a "cancer of depravity," which itself is rooted in biblical precedent (e.g. Deuteronomy 9:5; 20:18) bears a haunting echo with Hitler's description of Jews as a racial tuberculosis and the Hutus decrying Tutsis as a pestilence of cockroaches. If the Jews really are a racial tuberculosis and if the Tutsis really are a pestilence of cockroaches, then it is appropriate to call them such and to act to limit the threat. And if, as Jones claims, every single Canaanite really was attempting to have sex with every living thing they could "get their hand on" then that might indeed require radical measures to protect the Israelites and their livestock from the craven sexual assaults of this race of inexplicably sex-obsessed libertines.

But, of course, we don't seriously countenance such scenarios as live options. Rather, we need to call out such language as baldly dehumanizing rhetoric that imputes disease and sub-humanity to an entire collective group in order to rationalize bringing about their destruction. Once we are equipped to flag justifications for genocide as morally abhorrent rhetorical othering, it becomes grossly implausible to think that in *this* particular instance of the Canaanites the imputation of collective shared ethnic/religious/national disease or subhumanity is an *accurate* characterization that would truly warrant the mass slaughter of an entire society, men and women, elderly and infants, wealthy and destitute, intelligentsia and mentally and physically handicapped.

The dehumanizing rhetoric merely sets the stage for the actual genocide. The final moral evaluation comes as we resolve to consider in detail what is being proposed by the Genocide Apologists as informed by our best understanding of contemporary close-contact mass killing genocide (i.e. Rwanda). It is important at the outset to call out the *special pleading* which is endemic to these treatments, an informal fallacy according to which one makes unjustified exceptions to a general principle. For example, if close-contact genocidal mass killing by way of cutting, bludgeoning, and stabbing implements (e.g. the Hutu machete and masu) predictably begets the brutal dehumanizing acts of mutilation and torture, then it is special pleading to claim it somehow did not have those consequences when the genoicidaires were ancient Israelites and their implements were swords and spears. And it is special pleading to claim that, as Calvin imagines, the killing in this one instance would have somehow been driven solely by "active piety and holy zeal, in executing the command of God". If close-contact genocides like that of Rwanda pressure the genocidaires to dehumanize victims by actions like mutilation, torture, and rape in order to overcome the overwhelming aversion to killing, then it is special pleading to insist that such extreme psychological coping mechanisms would not be operative in the case of the Israelites.

The fact is that contrary to Calvin's pious imaginings, we have excellent reason to believe the Israelites would have been driven by *fury* against the enemy. Consider the infamous story we discussed earlier, that of Phineas, son of Eleazar, son of Aaron, who in righteous zeal pursued an Israelite man and his foreign wife into his tent and plunged a spear through their stomachs (Numbers 25:7-8).[234] Now shift to the context of modern Rwanda. Whether it is Phineas furiously plunging his spear into the stomach of a wide-eyed Midianite woman or Leopord angrily burying his machete into the forehead of a wide-eyed Tutsi woman, these exceedingly violent acts would not plausibly be driven simply by Calvin's "active piety and holy zeal". Such actions would inevitably be carried to some significant degree by blinding hatred for the target victims. And the resulting genocide would not be 'clean' as in a dispassionate,

---

[234] For an important discussion of biblical violence that begins with this disturbing story, see Collins, "The Zeal of Phineas: the Bible and the legitimation of violence."

quick, and 'merciful' eradication of the 'enemy' by the flash and slice of a finely sharpened guillotine. Rather, it would be the messy pogrom that Hitler warned against, a painfully uncontrolled process that would spill out in "lust and rage" as victims are egregiously injured, mercilessly mocked, cruelly mutilated, tortured, and raped. In the language of state-based execution methods, this mode of societal execution is the equivalent of dropping a dull and rusty guillotine with a sickening thunk a mere third of the way into the victim's neck, and then knocking it free and slowly raising it again for another go while the poor bloke squirms in agony. That is the brutal messiness of the type of killing undertaken in close-contact genocide. That is the sentence that the Genocide Apologists embrace for untold numbers of the men, women, and children of Canaan, a society that they insist is so irredeemably wicked that it must be extirpated, cut out like a cancer, burned like a pestilence.

With that in mind, I return to my moral intuitions. As I reflect on that thick narratival description of what close-contact genocidal killing actually looks like, I don't find myself inclined at all to chasten or question those intuitions. On the contrary, such careful reflection leaves me even *more* resolved to recognize the profound error of the Genocide Apologists. To suggest that one ethnic, religious, or national group of people really is a cancer that needs to be eradicated *in toto* faces overwhelming skeptical opposition, an incredulity that wells up from the core of my being and swamps the terribly flimsy, *ad hoc* special pleading of the Genocide Apologists: "They wanted to have sex with everything!" "They were the children of Nephilim and so not really human!" "They were a cancer, a racial tuberculosis!" "They all had to die!" My skeptical revulsion toward such bald rationalizations is borne of powerful intuitions that are triggered by a contemplation of actual close-contact mass genocidal killing. It is only intensified by the uncountable number of times that human beings in the past have appealed erroneously to such claims to justify horrific crimes against fellow human beings.

We don't give a moment's consideration to the apologists for the genocides of Armenia, Nazi German, or Rwanda. So why do we do so in this one exception, that of ancient Canaan?

Needless to say, these skeptical conclusions are supported by the Perfect God Principle which seeks to interpret the Bible as the product of a perfect divine author. This certainly applies to the concept of moral perfection, but it is also worth highlighting the extent to which it is affirmed by the omnipotence of that perfect being. The Genocide Apologists commonly claim that genocide was required as a radical means to protect the Israelites from the sin of the Canaanites. But that would entail that the only way an omnipotent God could protect the Israelites from the sin of the Canaanites was by way of slaughtering the whole society or something worse. Really? As Stephen Chapman puts it, "apparently—this is the hard part—God was not able, given the violence of the world, to preserve Israel purely nonviolently although, even so, Israel's history witnesses to and moves toward nonviolence as it moves toward Christ."[235] To call that claim, as Chapman does, merely the "hard part" is to win the Palme d'Or of understatement. To suggest that this was the least grisly avenue open to an omnipotent being who wished to secure the moral purity of the Israelites is to strain credulity well past the breaking point.

This brings us to the Jesus Principle: the extraordinary proposal of the Genocide Apologists is also in profound tension with the life and teaching of Jesus. Is it at all plausible to believe that the Jesus who scandalized many in his audience by stressing one's obligation to love all, including those from the most hated and mistrusted outgroups like Samaritans, tax collectors, lepers, and adulterers, is it plausible to think that he would add, "But *not*

---

235 Chapman, "Martial Memory, Peaceable Vision," in *Holy War in the Bible: Christian Morality and an Old Testament Problem,* eds. Heath A. Thomas, Jeremy Evans, and Paul Copan (IVP Academic, 2013), 64.

the Canaanites. They are truly beyond redemption and should be slaughtered totally"? I don't think so.

And this leads us to consider the Love Principle. As we have seen, participation in genocide is profoundly destructive of Christian character and has a brutalizing effect on the participants. The overwhelming urge not to kill other human beings is overcome by dehumanizing the victims ("They are cancer!" "The children of Nephilim!" "Racial tuberculosis!") and inflicting atrocities on them like mutilation, torture, and rape, all buoyed by the cruelest acts of hatred and mockery. All I can say is that it seems to me that such actions *obviously* have no place in the central call to love one's neighbor as oneself. Cultivating hatred of outgroups in order to secure their extermination is as beneficial to being a disciple of Jesus as serial adultery is beneficial to a healthy marriage.

While the commission of genocide is horrific, it is important to recognize that the apologist's *defense* of genocide is also deeply counter-productive to the Christian's call to love one's neighbor. That apologetic requires, at minimum, the imposition of a disintegrating cognitive dissonance in which one loves and humanizes outgroups over here but mercilessly dehumanizes and otherizes outgroups over there. And that, in turn, requires one to cauterize their emotions of compassion and love toward some groups (such as the Canaanites) by resolving to treat these individuals as damnable, irredeemable wretches so that even their children, their infants, their elderly, their mentally and physically handicapped, their destitute, must all collectively be butchered in orgies of close-contact slaughter. When considered against the call of Jesus to love our enemies, this is a recipe for cognitive dissonance if ever there was one.

As we have seen, Genocide Apologists regularly employ profoundly dehumanizing language of the Canaanites in order to justify their eradication. Such crude and vulgar othering rhetoric is utterly inconsistent with the Christian's call to humanize and love outgroups rather than devise perverse new rationales to justify their destruction. As I noted above, Gleason Archer's description of the Canaanites as a disease (i.e. "cancer of moral depravity") is one such example and it closely parallels the disturbing othering rhetoric of other genocidaires like Hitler's description of Jews as racial tuberculosis. The Christian who is being conformed to the love of neighbor should be pursuing ways to *humanize* outgroups, not *dehumanize them*. They should be seeking ways to reach out to and understand the outgroup, not new ways to describe them as an irredeemable disease which make it easier to justify their eradication.

For a particularly disturbing illustration of the way that genocide apologetics corrupts the Christian's witness, consider how Clay Jones moves seamlessly from the genocide of ancient Canaan to the warrant for genocide in contemporary America. He writes: "A cursory read of at least the idea currents in American culture often reads like a sequel to Canaanite practices." By taking that extraordinary step, Jones demonstrates the perverse and profoundly corrosive impact that Genocide Apologetics has on Christian thinking. His survey of American depravity is extraordinarily limited, arbitrary and cherry-picked. He invokes such isolated cultural citations as a bestial theme in an arthouse film and an excerpted lyric from a Metallica song as evidence for a general societal corruption so absolute that it would *warrant a punitive mass slaughter of the entire American population!* Here I must be blunt: anyone who flirts with such an absurd and profoundly offensive bit of reasoning as this has on this point abdicated the most basic commitments and expectations of Christian discipleship. It is disturbing enough when the rationale for mass slaughter is limited to a forgotten people of the ancient Near East: it is quite another thing when it is boldly applied to the present society in which one lives. While Christians are called to love most radically, as Jenkins sadly notes, the attempt to justify genocide "leaves believers recycling genocidal statements that are discredited in the secular realm."[236]

For a very practical illustration of the corrosive effect this kind of apologetic has, consider the position that Jones stakes out with respect to gay people. There may be no more Canaanites today, but there are millions of gay people and many of them have suffered greatly and experienced painful social ostracization by the church and their own families. While persecution of and prejudice against gay people can still be found in North America, it is orders worse in many other countries around the world such as Iran, Russia, and Uganda, a country that has been considering for several years the adoption of legislation that would punish participation in consensual same-sex acts with death.[237] Tragically, Christians have often been at the vanguard of oppressing gay people rather than loving them as Jesus calls us to do.

With that in mind, when Jones provides his cumulative case for the principled justification of a mass extermination of Americans, he devotes significant energy toward outlining the presence of each one of his chosen five sins in American life. The one exception is same-sex relationships: in this case, Jones believes it is sufficient only to provide a single sentence: "Nothing more needs be said about homosexuality."[238] The flippancy of that statement is chilling. Jones is suggesting that it is just *obvious* that the widespread American acceptance of the legal and moral status of monogamous same-sex relationships provides powerful evidence in support of a cumulative case to warrant the mass extermination of the American population. This is an excellent illustration of how Jones' attempt to otherize the

---

236 Jenkins, *Laying Down the Sword*, 231.

237 "Uganda: Brutal Killing of Gay Activist," *Human Rights Watch*, https://www.hrw.org/news/2019/10/15/uganda-brutal-killing-gay-activist

238 Jones, "We Don't Hate Sin So We Don't Understand What Happened to the Canaanites," 70.

Canaanites bleeds into his Christian interaction with outgroups in our own day. And with such reasoning we need to ask: would Jones support the implementation of contemporary legislation to kill gay people? Does he think that a society that kills gay people is, all things being equal, a more just and holy society? He certainly seems to suggest as much.

Here is the lesson: when you begin to defend the genocide of ancient peoples through the methods of dehumanization and othering, that effort will affect how you think about outgroups in our own day. We have enough warnings from church history about the extent to which Genocide apologetics corrupts Christian witness.[239] In real time, we can see in Jones' terrifying rhetoric the extent to which a genocide apologetic subverts the Gospel with profoundly disturbing dehumanizing language which is utterly inconsistent with Jesus' call to love our neighbor. Seibert is right to warn that "This kind of rhetoric, which emphasizes the need to eliminate one group of people to preserve the 'purity' of another, is extraordinarily dangerous."[240]

---

239 See Jenkins, *Laying Down the Sword*, part 2.
240 Seibert, *Disturbing Divine Behavior*, 78.

9

The Just War Interpreters

The Genocide Apologists believe that God really did issue the directives of Deuteronomy 7 and 20 such that these constituted moral obligations for the Israelites to eradicate the Canaanite population, obligations which the Israelites subsequently carried out in Joshua 1-12; further, the directives that the Genocide Apologists attribute to God and the subsequent actions that they credit to the Israelites meet the modern legal definition of genocide. There are many Christians who agree with the Genocide Apologists that God issued these commands as recorded and also that the Israelites faithfully carried them out as moral obligations, but they disagree with the claim that these commands and the kind of actions described qualify as genocide. Instead, they seek to reframe the incursion into the land as a justified military conflict, one that might be interpreted and explained within the broader confines of the conventional boundaries of just war theorization.

Just as I began the previous chapter with a stipulation about the use of the term 'Genocide Apologists' so I shall begin here with a clarification and disclaimer pertaining to the use of the term 'Just War Interpreters'. It is important to recognize at the outset that the defenders of this position do not necessarily seek to describe the incursion into Canaan as a just war in the conventional sense. For one thing, defenders of this position commonly emphasize the *sui generis* nature of these events as unique commands for a particular time and place in Israel's history. The battle is uniquely God's as Heath A. Thomas explains: "Emphasis lay not upon human beings with swords and spears but rather upon God himself, who fights for his people, who receives the spoils of war (as opposed to random looting or personal benefit from the warriors) and (oddly, to our minds) even receives *worship* through the process of warfare."[241] Consequently, it does not follow that this kind of event could occur today. The unique circumstances of God commanding and then carrying out this eradication of Canaanites through human agents should be seen as unique and unrepeatable.

While those are important caveats, nonetheless these interpreters do believe that when the actions described in these biblical passages are understood properly, they are seen to be non-genocidal and instead to conform more closely to the basic logic of just war theory. As Copan and Flannagan put it, "sometimes divine 'wrath' is carried out by the state."[242] Thus, under certain conditions, the follower of God may properly participate in a war that delivers divine wrath to another people: "the disciple may faithfully serve in the God-ordained state, which may require the use of force to oppose evildoers."[243] In the

---

241 Thomas, "A Neglected Witness to 'Holy War' in the Writings," in *Holy War in the Bible: Christian Morality and an Old Testament Problem*, 69-70.

242 Copan and Flannagan, *Did God Really Command Genocide? Coming to Terms with the Justice of God* (Baker, 2014), 302. In this chapter of their book, Copan and Flannagan defend just war theory in which force can justifiably be used to stop or prevent evil. This provides the broader framework in which the unique circumstances of Israel's invasion of Canaan can then be understood.

243 Copan and Flannagan, *Did God Really Command Genocide? Coming to Terms with the Justice of God*, 302.

view of Just War Interpreters like Copan and Flannagan, these conditions were met in the case of Israel's conquest of Canaan. Once again, the claim is not simply that the invasion of Canaan *is a just war*. Rather, the claim is that as we identify the unique circumstances that obtained in this case, we can recognize that Israelite actions should not be classed as genocidal but rather as broadly *consistent with the principles of just war*.

Just war theorists standardly identify two sets of criteria that would be required for just war: the right to undertake a war (*jus ad bellum*) and the right conduct of war (*jus in bello*). When properly understood the claim is that the divine directives can be seen to be just ground for war given these unique circumstances including the divine authority, the threat of the Canaanites, and the central importance of Israel retaining purity in order to bless the nations. And further, the Israelites faithfully carried out the battle in terms of the principles of proportionality, discrimination, and responsibility.

While the Just War Interpreters agree that God commanded the actions described in Deuteronomy 7 and 20 and that the Israelites subsequently carried out these directives, they disagree with the Genocide Apologists over just what those actions are and how they should be categorized. The gist of their reading of the texts is that God never, in fact, commanded the complete eradication of a people. Rather, they claim that this sweeping language of destruction (e.g. Deuteronomy 20:16-17: "do not leave alive anything that breathes. Completely destroy them") should be interpreted as hyperbolic war rhetoric, while the primary literal directive was to expulse the Canaanites from the land as illegitimate squatters: in short, a forced resettlement. Further, they insist that God did not target Canaanites arbitrarily because of some racial or ethnic identity marker but rather because of the unique sinfulness and the corruption of their collective character. Given the divine command and the focused intent of the Israelite actions, it is claimed that these events simply do not meet the standard definition of genocide or ethnic cleansing.

While the Just War approach is becoming increasingly popular in recent years, the most influential and formidable defenders of this view are Paul Copan and Matthew Flannagan with their important book *Did God Really Command Genocide?* For that reason, I will focus my critique of the position in dialogue with their work while also critically engaging additional defenders including Justin Taylor and Joshua Ryan Butler.

Neither Genocide nor Ethnic Cleansing

While the Genocide Apologists understand that the biblical texts depict acts which meet the legal definition of genocide, the Just War Interpreters flatly deny the appropriateness of this categorization. To begin with, they recognize that the moral baggage associated with the term provides a powerful impetus to deny it if at all possible. As Copan and Flannagan observe, the concept of genocide "carries a heavy rhetorical punch, which often calls forth echoes of Rwanda or the Holocaust."[244] Copan also notes, "Terms like *genocide* and *ethnic cleansing* evoke negative emotions in all of us."[245] Indeed. Given these factors, it is hardly surprising that there would be a strong predisposition to motivated reasoning to demonstrate that the divine directives of Deuteronomy 7 and 20 and the resulting Israelite actions described in Joshua 1-12 do not meet the legal definition of genocide or ethnic cleansing.

Given their recognition of the moral baggage that comes with the genocide and ethnic cleansing labels, Just War Interpreters are keen to pre-empt any association with these morally-loaded concepts. To that end, they attempt to argue that the (divine)

---

244 Copan and Flannagan, *Did God Really Command Genocide?*, 130.
245 Copan, *Is God a Moral Monster?*, 163.

directives against Canaanites and resulting battles lack essential features of genocide or ethnic cleansing.

Before we consider the stronger arguments for the Just War Interpreters, we will evaluate some less than compelling claims. The first claim is that the events of Deuteronomy and Joshua should be exempted from the category of genocide because these actions were uniquely commanded by God. As you can imagine, the critic will point out that *Deus Vult (God wills it!)* is a common justification of war crimes throughout history. So the mere fact that a genocidaire insists that their actions are one unique instance of God actually commanding the eradication of a people will be unlikely to persuade many who are not already convinced by the claim. However, as I pointed out earlier, even if we grant that God *did* command this particular instance of complete societal eradication, that bit of information is simply not germane to the legal definition of genocide. To put it simply, the legal definition of genocide makes no exemption for divinely commanded actions. So it is just irrelevant from the perspective of international law whether God commanded the act. To put the point in a contemporary legal framework, while God may not be accountable to the International Criminal Court in The Hague, those who carry out God's commands to eradicate entire civilian populations most certainly are.

Second, it is also often claimed that the Israelites' actions should not be considered genocidal because they were not driven by hatred of the Canaanites. Rather, they were simply committed to carrying out the divine will in the manner imagined by John Calvin, with a pious God-intoxication carrying forward every swing of the sword and thrust of the spear. And if that image of God-intoxicated butchers sounds unsettling on its own terms, we may think, perhaps, less in terms of pious zeal and more in terms of the gritty determination to complete an unpleasant job. Consider, for example, a man who works in a slaughterhouse and has no personal animus against the cows he must kill: terminating bovines with a captive bolt pistol is simply part of his vocational obligations. *Mutatis mutandis* for the Israelites called to kill Canaanites: it need not be something they relish; it is simply part of their vocational obligations. As Paul Copan puts it, "Ethnic cleansing is fueled by racial hatred. The alleged ingroup pronounces a pox on the outgroup and then proceeds to destroy them."[246] But Copan insists that such "xenophobic attitudes didn't prompt the Israelites to kill Canaanites."[247]

In addition, Just War Interpreters claim that the killing was also not motivated by the intent to eliminate a particular ethnic group. As the argument goes, the Israelites were simply carrying out the ugly business of eradicating a threat to their moral purity in pursuit of their singular goal to bless all nations. Yes, counterintuitive though it may seem, the idea is that *Israel needed to eradicate the Canaanite nation to ensure that they would remain faithful in their call to bless* all *nations* (though *not* the Canaanite nation, presumably). Further, the claim that the attack was not borne by a personal vendetta against the Canaanites is underscored by the fact that a few fortunate members of the community (i.e. Rahab and her family; the Gibeonites) were spared from the onslaught due to their own resourcefulness in making self-servng alliances. Justin Taylor makes the claim in his article "How Could God Command Genocide in the Old Testament?":

> Even though the destruction is commanded in terms of totality, there seems to have been an exception for those who repented,

---

[246] Copan, *Is God a Moral Monster?*, 163.

[247] Copan, *Is God a Moral Monster?*, 163. Similarly, Barton Priebe writes, "If this [the invasion of Canaan] is an act of divine justice, then it would be inaccurate to call it 'genocide,' . . . . Genocide is fueled by racial hatred, but the Bible never asserts, or even hints, that the Canaanites were destroyed because of their ethnicity. God did not order the destruction of the Canaanites because of their race; he destroyed them because of their sin." "Why is the Old Testament So Violent?" in *Everyday Apologetics,* eds. Paul Chamberlain and Chris Price (Lexham Press, 2020), 86.

turning to the one true and living God (e.g., Rahab and her family [Josh. 2:9], and the Gibeonites [Josh. 11:19]). What this means is that the reason for the destruction of God's wicked enemies was precisely because of their rebellion and according to God's special purposes—not because of their ethnicity. "Ethnic cleansing" and genocide refer to destruction of a people due to their ethnicity, and therefore this would be an inappropriate category for the destruction of the Canaanites.[248]

Taylor invokes the familiar apologetic that the Canaanites were targeted not because of ethnic, religious or nationalist concerns *simpliciter* but because of their sin. And based on this fact he concludes, the actions do not meet the legal definition of genocide or ethnic cleansing.

So what should we think of these arguments? Let's begin with the idea that the Israelites' actions should be exempted from the category of genocide insofar as they were not motivated by fear, anger and/or other 'xenophobic attitudes'. The claim that such distinctions are somehow relevant to the categorization of genocide is fallacious: the legal definition of genocide does not require a specific emotional attitude of hatred, hostility or fear in the would-be genocidaire. So even if we concede that the Israelites somehow managed to carry out these horrific actions with dispassionate detachment from the victims, it simply does not follow that the actions would thereby be classed as non-genocidal. What is more, I would add, ironically enough, that the genocide which can be carried out as a cool, dispassionate calculation without the fuel of personal animus toward the target group is, if anything, a *more* terrifying phenomenon, for that type of clinical detachment from moral horror is not properly *human*. That said, the image of genocidaires driven

---

248 Taylor, "How Could God Command Genocide in the Old Testament?" Gospel Coalition (February 13, 2013), https://www.thegospelcoalition.org/blogs/justin-taylor/how-could-god-command-genocide-in-the-old-testament-2/

forward by Calvin's God-intoxicated zeal is arguably even worse yet. The devout slaughter of infants and children in God's name is, in my view, among the most blasphemous of actions. Better to be carried forward by your own bald prejudice alone than to project those hatreds onto the God who loves and desires the shalom of all creatures.

It should also be noted that the claim in passages like Deuteronomy 20:18 that the mere *existence* of Canaanites constitutes a corrupting threat against Israelites certainly looks xenophobic under any reasonable construal of the term. Imagine, by analogy, if a man said that the United States should close their borders to immigration from Latin America because Latino immigrants threaten to undermine the "American way of life". Such a categorical, sweeping indictment of Latinos would certainly exhibit xenophobic attitudes. To be sure, the Christian Just War Interpreter will insist that this is an unfair comparison and that in the case of Joshua the Canaanites really did pose a unique and imminent threat that needed to be eliminated by these harshest of measures. Perhaps, but the fact remains that such claims will inevitably appear to the person not already persuaded by this reading as yet more bald special pleading.

There is also a fundamental tension between this "corruption defense" and the claim that many Canaanites survived the Israelite mass killings and ethnic cleansing. While Just War theorists claim that since the killing wasn't completed this somehow warrants us in exempting Israelite actions from the genocide label, *what it actually does is call into question the whole legitimacy of the corruption defense*. After all, if Israel ultimately *could* continue to fulfill God's purpose for them to bless all nations *alongside* the surviving Canaanites then perhaps this group was not such a uniquely dangerous corrupting influence after all. To borrow Archer's language, one cannot allow cancer to continue growing within the body. So if one can leave a condition untreated, we must consider that perhaps that condition was never cancerous to begin with.

As for Taylor's claim that the actions were driven not by ethnic hostility but rather by a need to redress egregious sin, this too is an erroneous defense. To begin with, keep in mind that genocide is constituted by the attempt to eliminate national, racial, and/or religious identities as such. Further, these identifying markers should not be interpreted too narrowly since, as I noted earlier, in a case like that of Cambodia, the outgroup was targeted by way of socio-economic and class-educational factors even down to something as seemingly arbitrary as *eyeglasses*.[249] Suffice it to say, the Canaanites are clearly presented as a distinct religious and national group with their own religious deity and cultic practices, practices which the Israelites believe to be uniquely wicked and thus worthy only of 'deicide,' as Merrill puts it. That desire to *kill* distinct Canaanite religious identity and practice is all that is required to classify the actions undertaken by the Israelites as genocidal. As for Taylor's additional assertion that this particular genocide was justified because of the wickedness of the Canaanites, once again, such claims do not change the fact that the act meets the legal definition of genocide.

What about the fact that the Israelites spared Rahab and her family as well as the Gibeonites? If some members of the group are spared by the genocidaires, does that exempt the overall act from being genocide? The simple answer is no, *of course not*. Just consider again our Rwanda example. Many Hutu husbands managed to have their Tutsi wives spared from the slaughter. Some even succeeded in getting the amnesty extended to the siblings and/or parents of those Tutsi wives. But would anyone seriously claim that such instances somehow warrant the judgment that Rwanda was thereby not a genocide after all? The suggestion is as absurd as it is offensive.

As for Rahab's family and the Gibeonites, it is worth noting that both of these groups were spared only due to their own resourcefulness in managing to extract an oath of protection

---

249 Power, *A Problem from Hell: America and the Age of Genocide,* chapter 6.

from the Israelites. In short, from the Israelite perspective, these were concessions required by circumstance not unlike that terrified Tutsi wife bargaining for her life. Furthermore, since genocide is focused on the eradication of the national, ethnic, and/or religious *identity,* one may spare individuals who bear an identity while continuing to seek to eradicate the identity itself, all the more so if the individuals who are spared aid the overall purpose of the genocide (as Rahab clearly did). After all, even the Nazis employed Jewish laborers.[250]

To sum up, these various attempts to exempt the Israelite actions against the Canaanites should be categorized collectively as a big basket of odiferous red herrings. One cannot exempt the actions of the Israelites from the category of genocide simply because they claimed they were carrying out divine commands or because they did not target Canaanite ethnicity *as such* or because they allegedly acted without hatred or fear in their commission of the acts. Such considerations play precisely no role in the legal definition of genocide. In short, the Just War theorists cannot preempt the "heavy rhetorical punch" of the 'genocide' label by way of a definitional technicality. The question remains, however, as to whether a close reading of the text will vindicate the central Just War Interpreter thesis of exaggerated rhetoric coupled with a justified forcible expulsion from the land. To that question we now turn.

From war crime to just war

At this point, we will turn to consider the more substantive defenses against the categorization of genocide. We will begin by providing a summary of the concept of just war. This concept

---

250 See, for example, Nikolaus Wachsmann, *KL: A History of the Nazi Concentration Camps* (Farrar, Strauss, and Giroux, 2015).

involves the notion that under particular, carefully circumscribed criteria, it can be right and just to go to war. As I noted above, there are two sets of criteria for just war: the right to undertake a war and the right way to carry out a war. Those who seek to categorize the Israelite action under the broad classification of just war are seeking to establish that, given the circumstances, Israel was justified in going to war and just in their conduct of war. As regards the criteria for going to war, these points include (but are not limited to) just cause, competent authority, last resort, and proportionality. So, for example, one might argue that the cause of the Israelites (including securing a homeland; stopping an egregiously sinful society; protecting their own community from that society; gaining rightful ownership of land from squatters) was just; the authority (God) was surely sufficient to warrant the battle; there were no other alternatives given their lack of homeland, the moral corruption of the Canaanites, and the lack of authority the Canaanites had to live on the land; and given the unique circumstances their actions were proportional to the needs and threat.

And so, even if the unique circumstances of direct divine command and divine intervention should distinguish this conquest from conventional warfare, from the perspective of the Just War Interpreters it should still be classified as just and thus conforming more broadly to the criteria of just war theorization. The real key to the Just War Interpreters comes in their careful reading of the text which leads to a nuanced understanding of the Israelites' actions. At this point, we will consider three key points made by Copan and Flannagan in their important book *Did God Really Command Genocide?* After summarizing those points we will take stock and see whether they are sufficient to move the conquest definitively away from the category of genocide and into that of just war.

To begin with, Copan and Flannagan point out that within Joshua the language of displacement, as in calls for the Canaanites to be *driven out* of the land, occurs more frequently than the language of eradication and that this actually provides us with the primary goal of Israelite actions.[251] As they put it, "Israel's chief responsibility was to dispossess or drive out the Canaanites rather than kill them."[252] And as Joshua Ryan Butler observes, "Being 'driven out' is the language of eviction, not murder."[253]

Second, Copan and Flannagan argue that it is misleading to refer to the settlements that provide the primary military targets of outright eradication (e.g. Jericho; Ai) as 'cities'. Rather, they follow Richard Hess in arguing that these settlements are best understood as military citadels or forts which included a commander (i.e. king) as well as "religious and political personnel."[254] Butler writes: "The cities Israel takes out are military strongholds, not civilian population centers.... So when Israel 'utterly destroys' a city like Jericho or Ai, we should picture a military fort being taken over—not a civilian massacre. God is pulling down the Great Wall of China, not demolishing Beijing. Israel is taking out the Pentagon, not New York City."[255] Butler adds, "Israel is taking on Napoleon and his militias, not Paris and her masses."[256]

Third, Copan and Flannagan argue that the passages which do refer to total slaughter (e.g. Deuteronomy 20:16-17a; Joshua 6:21), should be understood not literally but rather as hyperbolic war rhetoric. To that end, they provide multiple examples from ancient Near Eastern literature where formulaic language of total eradication is employed.[257] In addition, Copan and Flannagan

---

251 Copan and Flannagan, *Did God Really Command Genocide?* chapter 6. Cf. David Lamb, *God Behaving Badly: Is the God of the Old Testament Angry, Sexist, and Racist* (InterVarsity Press, 2011), 100.

252 Copan and Flannagan, *Did God Really Command Genocide?*, 81.

253 Joshua Ryan Butler. *The Skeletons in God's Closet*, 232.

254 Copan and Flannagan, *Did God Really Command Genocide?*, 101.

255 Butler, *The Skeletons in God's Closet*, 227.

256 Butler, *The Skeletons in God's Closet*, 227.

257 See Copan and Flannagan, *Did God Really Command Genocide?*, chapters 8,9.

argue that a careful reading of Joshua and Judges shows that the texts depict the Canaanites remaining in the land even after they are supposedly eradicated. In short, if we read the text as a unified work of a capable editor who would have been aware of glaring inconsistencies, we should conclude that the hyperbole thesis is confirmed by the texts themselves.[258]

Of course, even if the texts don't depict genocide, they do portray the Israelites as forcing the Canaanites off the land and killing at least some non-combatants in the process including the above-mentioned "religious and political personnel" living in strongholds like Jericho as well as any rural civilian population that remained behind. While this is still a problem, it at least appears more tractable than outright genocide. That said, a more tractable problem is still a problem. Is there more that can be said?

Indeed, there is. Copan and Flannagan argue vigorously that the Canaanites were squatters on land that was really the property of the Israelites.[259] At first blush, this might seem to be an extraordinary claim given that the Canaanites had lived on the land for *centuries*. However, Butler illustrates the point nicely by telling a story in which God plants a garden in California and then ejects the residents because they have abused it. They immigrate to Texas but then he calls one of them—Ol' Abe—back to California. The problem is that some of the rowdy residents of Texas have already settled in the garden given to Abe. So God benevolently allows these Texas squatters to enjoy a few hundred years on the land before he justly expulses them. Put within those terms, God and Abe's descendants look generous to a fault. And that, so Butler claims, is an apt description of the invasion of Canaan. The Israelites are merely delivering the

---

258 Cf. Nicholas Wolterstorff, "Reading Joshua," in *Divine Evil? The Moral Character of the God of Abraham*, eds. Michael Bergmann, Michael J. Murray, and Michael C. Rea (Oxford University Press, 2010), 236-256.

259 Copan and Flannagan, *Did God Really Command Genocide?*, 62 *ff*.

long overdue eviction notice to squatters who had no right to the land in the first place.[260]

Copan and Flannagan also emphasize the utter moral corruption of Canaanite society including institutionalized sinful acts like child sacrifice and temple prostitution.[261] Despite the unparalleled nature of their sinful corruption, God tolerated them on the land for *four centuries* before he finally sent his armies to drive them out. While some will call this an 'ethnic cleansing,' Copan and Flannagan insist that it "would be better termed 'moral cleansing'—or more specifically, long-awaited moral judgment on a wicked people whose time had finally come (Gen. 15:16)."[262]

Genocide and Ethnic Cleansing Revisited

At this point, we can take stock of the position of the Just War Interpreters and Copan and Flannagan's proposal in particular. To begin with, I'd like to dispense with some of the points that I consider secondary before turning to the main issue.

Let's start by agreeing that if God, the morally perfect creator and sustainer of all things, commands a human being to undertake an action, then that human being does have a moral obligation to carry it out. That said, the real issue we must consider is the *prima face* case for/against God's having commanded the actions in the first place.[263] And with that in mind, we can't help but note at the outset the degree to which this apologetic explanation conforms to standard justifications for genocide

---

[260] Butler, *The Skeletons in God's Closet*, 236-7.

[261] Copan and Flannagan, *Did God Really Command Genocide?*, Chapter 5.

[262] Copan and Flannagan, *Did God Really Command Genocide?*, 277.

[263] See the discussion in Rauser and Schieber, *An Atheist and a Christian Walk into a Bar*, chapter 4.

throughout history. As we saw in our survey of the Rwandan genocide, Hutus appealed to divine blessing and the sense of injustice sustained by the noxious Hamitic myth according to which Tutsis were otherized as illegitimate foreign squatters from Abyssinia. Needless to say, such defenses are of negligible value and a 'divine defense' would get precisely no traction in the International Criminal Court. To the objective observer not already committed to Copan and Flannagan's position, the defense of the Israelites looks every bit as implausible an instance of special pleading as a defense of the Hutus, the Khmer Rouge, or the Nazis. In short, the fact that the Israelites' claims conform closely to an established pattern of discredited defenses undermines the strength of their position. The more reasonable conclusion is that the Just War Interpreters are engaged in special pleading as they recycle already discredited tropes to rationalize the war crimes of their chosen ingroup.[264]

To sum up, unless Copan and Flannagan can make a case that the divine directives and Israelite actions are clearly *not* genocidal in nature, their proposal will suffer the same ignominious objections as those of the Genocide Apologists. Since the viability of this position ultimately depends on its ability to justify reclassifying these divine directives and consequent Israelite actions under the rubric of just war rather than genocide, we will now evaluate those points.

As we saw, Copan and Flannagan argue that the primary and controlling theme is not that of complete eradication (and thus genocide) but rather of displacement, driving the Canaanites out and thereby dispossessing them of the land. Further, they propose that the primary targets for military assault (and thus killing) are best thought of not as the populations of cities but rather of military forts or citadels, and thus primarily soldiers as well as political and religious personnel. And finally, the language of mass killing should be understood as hyperbolic in nature,

---

264 See Smith, *Less Than Human,* chapter 5.

exaggerated war rhetoric which was consistent with a proportion of the population continuing to exist, a fact tacitly recognized by the redactors of Joshua and Judges.

There is much to commend the approach of the Just War Interpreters. They provide important insights into the text as regards the oft-neglected theme of dispossession, the military nature of the 'cities', and the presence of hyperbolic rhetoric. In this relatively brief treatment I cannot do justice to the careful attention that Copan and Flannagan give to close readings of the biblical text and their nuanced engagement with related issues like international law and meta-ethics: their work truly is an interdisciplinary tour-de-force. But for all that, it seems to me that their herculean efforts are ultimately expended in defense of an indefensible thesis. And a closer look soon reveals just how indefensible that thesis is.

The first problem is that Copan and Flannagan are still clearly committed to the Israelite actions as ethnic cleansing, this despite their blushingly pained attempt to rebrand it as 'moral cleansing.' And while ethnic cleansing may not be as egregious a war crime as genocide, I hope we can agree that it is far from optimal when one's best defense consists of trading one war crime for another. But worst of all, it seems to me that a careful reflection on the implications of Copan and Flannagan's position supports the conclusion that, in fact, they still do support genocide in all but name.

To see why, let's begin by getting clear on the implications of this idea of dispossessing the Canaanites of the land. On the Copan and Flannagan reading, as the Israelites invade the region, Canaanites are driven out before them. This is precisely one of those points where we need to drop down from the clouds to ground level and contemplate what is actually being proposed. On this scenario, thousands of civilians are forced to flee for their very survival, leaving behind the only lives they've ever known, abandoning their beloved homes and communities and a land settled by their ancestors centuries before and setting off into the desert and the great unknown with whatever they can carry as smoke from the remnants of destroyed settlements like Jericho and Ai billows up on the horizon.

That scenario is terrifying enough, but it gets worse. In extreme conditions like these where people are scrambling to save their lives, what do you think would happen to the most vulnerable in the population including the severely mentally and physically handicapped, the small children, the sick, the indigent, the widows, and the elderly? How many of the weak and marginalized, those barely subsisting on the edge of society, would be left behind to face their terrible fate at the hands of the advancing Israelite armies?

It gets worse yet. If the Canaanites were really as uniquely cruel and wicked as the Genocide Apologists and Just War Interpreters claim, then we could expect the powerful among them to *offer up* the weakest and most vulnerable (and, by implication, the *least* culpable) from their communities as a diversion to save their own skin. In short, it would be *anticipated* that as the Israelites advanced on the abandoned settlements, they would find cowering, terrified children, struggling disabled adults, and confused elderly people left behind. And what would happen to those people, the least of these of Canaanite society, upon meeting the advancing Israelite soldiers? The answer is clear: anyone who remained behind would be slaughtered with sword and spear and whatever bludgeoning tools may lie about. Like the much lauded Phineas, the Israelite soldiers would turn themselves upon the victims in a pious religious frenzy, plunging their spears into the abdomens of squirming toddlers, hurling large rocks down on the skulls of crawling disabled adults, swinging their swords into the necks of shivering elderly women. And remember, all this horror is unfolding, all this blood is spattered, all this inhumanity is perpetuated on the ostensibly softer, *non-genocidal* scenario proposed by the Just War Interpreters.

Lest you think I am somehow reading too much between the lines, I will reply that some lines beg to be read between. As a prime example, consider the following revealing passage that Copan and Flannagan cite from Kenneth Kitchen: "as in the south, the Hebrew force defeated the opposition; captured their towns, killed rulers and less mobile inhabitants . . . ."[265] Let's pause and ask: who are these *less mobile inhabitants* that Kitchen refers to only in passing? They are the very people I just took the time to *humanize:* terrified children, disabled adults, and elderly men and women. In other words, *the weakest and most vulnerable members of Canaanite society would be the least mobile and thus the ones most likely to be butchered by the advancing Israelite armies.* Meanwhile the wealthiest and most powerful among the Canaanites, those who represent the corrupt institutions the Israelites were aiming to eradicate, would be the most likely to escape. We saw above that Copan and Flannagan attempt to rebrand the ethnic cleansing of the land as, in fact, a *moral* cleansing. But what sort of moral cleansing is it that effectively targets the most vulnerable and least culpable members of a community for cruel eradication while allowing all those profoundly evil ringleaders to escape with impunity so that they may live another day?

This brings us to perhaps the central question: does Copan and Flannagan's analysis at least allow them to sidestep the most serious of charges, namely that of genocide? They certainly believe so as they argue that "when we look more closely at international law's usage of 'genocide,' such accusations [of Israelite genocide] appear all the more misdirected. International law *does* assume that in order to count as genocide, the perpetrator's aim has to be killing off an entire people group."[266] Unfortunately, this statement appears to commit the fallacy of equivocation by conflating (i) *the intent to kill/destroy an identity* with *(ii) the intent to kill/destroy every person who bears that identity.* For an act to qualify as genocide it only needs to meet (i), not (ii). This is trivially the

---

265 Cited in Copan and Flannagan, *Did God Really Command Genocide?*, 89, emphasis added; Cf. 105-6

266 Copan and Flannagan, *Did God Really Command Genocide?*, 128.

case given that the crime of genocide lists killing members of the group as but one means of actualizing genocidal intent. For the Israelites' actions to qualify as genocide, they do not need to target every member of the group and thus as I said above, genocide is clearly consistent both with sparing Rahab and her family as well as the Gibeonites and also with forcibly driving mobile survivors from the land by way of ethnic cleansing. So long as all those actions were undertaken with the end of eradicating Canaanite society, culture and religion, then the actions qualify as genocide. For that reason, replying that the *primary* goal of the Israelites was to dispossess the Canaanites of the land such that some were spared from being killed is *simply not relevant to the judgment of genocide*. Indeed, one may properly deem that defense as yet another red herring, one which seeks to distract from the fact that the primary genocidal intent was to destroy Canaanite society, as such.[267]

In the very section where Copan and Flannagan seek to deflect the genocide charge by arguing for the primacy of the theme of expulsion from the land over-against mass killing, they cite William Lane Craig as support for their position: "The judgment upon these Canaanite kingdoms was to dispossess them of their land and thus destroy them as kingdoms."[268] This is a deeply revealing quote and an ironic choice for Copan and Flannagan given that it actually serves to rebut the very point they are trying to argue. When Craig says the intent of this 'dispossession' was ultimately to 'destroy' the Canaanites as *kingdoms* it is clear that he is referencing the destruction of Canaanite national, cultural, and religious identity.[269] Thus, yet again we see here evidence for a *textbook* instance of genocide.

---

267 Many other scholars likewise appear to believe errantly that genocide consists of the intent to kill individuals rather than an identity. For example, see Walton and Walton, *The Lost World of the Israelite Conquest*, 175, 179.

268 Cited in Copan and Flannagan, *Did God Really Command Genocide?*, 81.

269 Walton and Walton likewise offer an ironically damning attempt to distance

A closer look confirms the genocide interpretation. The Israelites are consistently seeking to eradicate Canaanite cultural identity. The actions by which they seek to do this include threats and public acts designed to terrorize the population, an aggressive military invasion, the destruction of all artifacts of Canaanite culture, a programmatic attempt to drive the Canaanites away from their homes, markets, temples, and communities and out of the land, and the killing of all Canaanite civilians that remain behind. If there is one thing that is clear in the Deuteronomic history (at least on the Copan-Flannagan reading), it is that God directs the Israelites to destroy Canaanite culture and identity and the Israelites attempt to carry out that desire to the full extent of their abilities.

It is also important to underscore the extent to which civilians are living within the 'citadels' and thus how these are, in fact, communities. To begin with, Rahab and presumably at least several members of her family are clearly civilians living in Jericho. Further, Copan and Flannagan recognize that there would be many other non-military individuals in the settlements at any given time. And when it comes to the destruction of Ai in Joshua 8, we read that after the soldiers defending the settlement are drawn off, the Israelites attack Ai proper. But who are they attacking if Ai is solely a military target and all the soldiers have left the 'fort' to fight the Israelites? The message is clear: the *community* still has many non-combatant civilians remaining inside its walls. At that point, we read the blunt description that "Twelve thousand men and women fell that day—all the people of Ai." (8:25) Even if Copan and Flannagan are correct that the numbers of casualties in battles like this are probably inflated,[270]

---

the action from genocide when they write "the purpose of the *herem* is to remove a community identity from use, not to kill individual people." *The Lost World of the Israelite Conquest,* 190. That "removal of community identity" is, in essence, the genocidal destruction of an identity.

270 Copan and Flannagan, *Did God Really Command Genocide?*, 100.

the fact remains that the text clearly specifies that non-military male and female *civilians* are the target at this point. As Eric Seibert observes, "Every indication we have from Joshua 6-11 is that entire populations were decimated. It requires special pleading to argue that women and children were absent."[271]

In their survey of biblical archaeology, Finkelstein and Silberman lend some credibility to Copan and Flannagan's reading, for they describe the settlements as follows: "They were mainly administrative strongholds for the elite, housing the king, his family, and his small entourage of bureaucrats, with the peasants living scattered through the surrounding countryside in small villages."[272] However, this support comes at a significant cost, namely that of calling into question the overall veracity of the Joshua account. Finkelstein and Silberman continue: "The typical city had only a palace, a temple compound, and a few other public edifices—probably residences for high officials, inns, and other administrative buildings. *But there were no city walls. The formidable Canaanite cities described in the conquest narrative were not protected by fortifications!*"[273] This is the tension that Copan and Flannagan face: if they want to avoid the charge of confirmation bias, they can't selectively choose which of the archaeological and documentary evidence they shall adopt and which they shall ignore. If we are to reject the narrative's description of Jericho and Ai as bustling cities with thousands of civilians, as Copan and Flannagan concede, then why not also concede the archaeologist's additional claim that these fledgling settlements altogether lacked the military prowess and fortifications also described in the narrative? And if we go that far, should we not consider questioning the historicity of the narratives altogether?

---

271 Seibert, *The Violence of Scripture*, 97.

272 Israel Finkelstein and Neil Asher Silberman, *The Bible Unearthed: Archaeology's New Vision of Ancient Israel and the Origin of Its Sacred Texts* (Touchstone, 2002), 77.

273 Finkelstein and Silberman, *The Bible Unearthed: Archaeology's New Vision of Ancient Israel and the Origin of Its Sacred Texts*, 77, emphasis added.

We will come back to the difficult but crucial question of history later. However, at this point I will simply state that in my view Copan and Flannagan's attempt to re-categorize the communities of Jericho and Ai as military settlements is misleading at best given the fact that *within the terms of the narratives these are undeniably described at least as regional community hubs with a heavy civilian presence which served the rural population* rather like the forts that once dotted North America. As a resident of Edmonton, Alberta, I am reminded of the founding of our city two centuries ago as Fort Edmonton, a regional trading and administrative center. Fort Edmonton was not simply an army barracks. It was a *community,* one that included many civilians (e.g. regional administrators, merchants and their families, voyageurs, and First Nations traders) at any given time.

Nor is this point merely applicable to the past: something similar is true of military bases today. They are not simply army barracks: they are self-contained *communities.* Consider, for example, Fort Hood, a major military base in Texas.[274] According to Wikipedia, Fort Hood is populated by 45,414 soldiers and 8900 civilian employees living together on base.[275] The census data for Fort Hood further identifies a diverse population including many children and some elderly and disabled persons.[276] Imagine if a Mexican army invaded Texas with the express goal of targeting all military bases like Fort Hood not only to the end of knocking out their military capacity but also to eradicate the entire populations living on base including civilian men and women, the elderly, disabled, and children. Such an action

---

[274] At the time of this writing, this military base is still named after Confederate General John Bell Hood. However, there is a growing movement to rename US military bases that are named after confederate soldiers, so that name may soon be changed.

[275] "Fort Hood," Wikipedia, https://en.wikipedia.org/wiki/Fort_Hood

[276] "Quick Facts: Fort Hood CDP, Texas," United States Census Bureau, https://www.census.gov/quickfacts/forthoodcdptexas

would be considered a war crime of the first order. And if it were undertaken as part of a plan to eradicate American identity *as such* then it would also properly be described as genocide. By the same token, there is no question but that the Israelite assault on Canaan qualifies as genocide and recasting settlements like Jericho and Ai as military citadels does nothing to change that.

The Aftermath

I briefly discussed above the two sets of criteria for initiating and conducting a just war: the criteria for justly going into battle and the criteria for justly carrying out a battle. In recent years, just war theorists have also begun to identify a third set of criteria, those that focus on justly concluding a war (*jus post bellum*). The just conclusion of a war includes attention to such diverse justice issues as environmental remediation, post-war resettlement and reconstruction, and treatment of physical injury and emotional trauma in the civilian and non-civilian population. The importance of considering the criteria of *jus post bellum* is evident in our WWII case study. While our reflection on the just conduct of the war focused on the ethics of the Allied targeted bombing of civilians in Operation Centerboard (Hiroshima) and Operation Gomorrah (Hamburg), the fullest ethical evaluation of the war should also encompass the conduct of Allied forces post-war. And here, too, there are significant moral lapses such as the abysmal failure of Allied powers to address the effects of radiation in Japan and the extensive Jewish refugee problem in Europe.[277]

The concept of *jus post bellum* highlights the importance of addressing the long-term multi-faceted lingering impacts of

---

[277] On the issue of Jewish refugees postwar see the Academy Award winning 1997 documentary *The Long Way Home*.

war on a society and the environment. While I have already determined that the Just War Interpreters have failed to recast Canaan within the broad confines of just war, it is worthwhile considering just how devastating a genocidal event of this degree would've been on the Canaanites who continued to exist in proximity to the genocidaires within the same region.

We can set the stage by returning to our case study and considering the horrific impact of the genocide of Rwanda on the population. According to a UNICEF study, five of six children had at least witnessed genocidal violence while many more within that group had participated in it. Long after the genocide was officially concluded, countless Tutsis lived in continued fear that the Hutu genocidaires would return at some later point to finish the job. Indeed, for at least two years after the genocide officially ended, Hutu militias continued killing Tutsis in sporadic eruptions of violence. This is hardly surprising: once you dehumanize a population to the point that you are willing to bring about their mass eradication through the most direct and intimate means possible, it is very difficult simply to turn off those impulses and to rehumanize them once again. As Gourevitch reflects, "Imagine what the totality of such devastation means for a society, and it becomes clear that the Hutu Power's crime was much greater than the murder of nearly a million people. Nobody in Rwanda escaped direct physical or psychic damage."[278]

On Copan and Flannagan's reading, the Israelites invaded the land, visiting debilitating psychological terror upon the Canaanites, decimating regional centers and slaughtering all the inhabitants therein including political and religious leaders and their families, butchering soldiers *in toto* on the battlefield, forcibly dispossessing civilians of land that their ancestors had possessed for centuries, setting their settlements and possessions on fire

---

[278] Gourevitch, *We Wish to Inform You that Tomorrow We Will be Killed with Our Families*, 224.

in an ancient Near Eastern version of *blitzkrieg*, and chasing down and slaughtering the "less mobile inhabitants" including the elderly, mentally and physically handicapped, small children, infants, and anyone else that failed to outrun the advancing Israelite army. Think about that and ask yourself: what would be the collective trauma, the devastating psychological pain, the hopelessness and anguish that would envelope the survivors of this extraordinary series of events? What kind of fear would survivors endure that the Israelites might yet return in the future to finish the job? How would that terror continue to haunt them in the years and decades after the genocide had ended? How would those traumas lodge themselves squarely into the collectively psyche of this ancient people?

The importance of the ongoing psychological terror that would have been experienced by the Canaanites post-genocide cannot be underestimated. Copan and Flannagan point out that the Canaanites continued to live in proximity to the Israelites. Needless to say, that does little to ameliorate the difficulty of the situation. Indeed, if anything the horror is compounded. On this view, a smattering of traumatized Canaanites are left behind, their possessions destroyed, their livelihoods lost, their families massacred. And now, like Tutsis reliving daily the horrors inflicted on them by the Hutu genocidaires, these Canaanites must live in proximity to *their* genocidaires, the very individuals who killed their families, destroyed their homes, and took their land.

The Rwandan genocide is commonly dated to April-July 1994. However, as I noted above, sporadic violence against Tutsis continued into 1996 as many Hutus remained intent on "finishing the job." In one particularly horrific event, multiple Tutsis seeking refuge in a monastery were slaughtered by Hutus.[279] The continued impact upon Tutsis of carrying the psychological and emotional scars of the genocide and living

---

279 Gourevitch, *We Wish to Inform You that Tomorrow We Will be Killed with Our Families*, 278.

under the terror that it might be completed in the future was devastating. As I noted, the long-term psychological and spiritual impact on genocidaires would also be profound, including nagging guilt and depression often countered with a continued dehumanization of the victims coupled with an internal impulse to finish the job.

This tendency is not only a natural outcome of the impact of dehumanizing others, but it is spurred on by the psychological process known as the *escalation of commitment* according to which individuals continue on a course of action despite increasingly negative results. The psychology of this action can be explicated in terms of the sunk cost fallacy in which one's prior investment that cannot be recovered (i.e. sunk costs) are taken as justification to continue a course of action. To note a trivial example, imagine that you are with a group of friends and you all decide to rent a movie. You recommend a particular film that you've heard good things about and you pay the fee. Your endorsement and paying of the rental cost constitute investments. As you start to watch the film, your friends are critical and show disinterest. And under normal circumstances, you would do so as well: it turns out that this isn't a great film. But because you recommended it and paid for it, you have sunk costs that you (fallaciously) want to recoup and so you counter their criticisms with an increasingly spirited (and pained) defense of a film that is, by any measure, a dud.

Now think much more radically about a genocidaire who has invested in the horrific program of attempting to eradicate the Tutsi population in Rwanda. After killing Tutsis and vocally defending his actions, the genocidaire is now committed and so, despite misgivings as to the rightness of his cause, he continues to defend his actions with increasing intensity coupled with violent outbursts at the target Tutsi population. These actions can be explained in terms of an attempt to rationalize and so justify the extraordinarily evil actions in which he has already invested so heavily.

To conclude, not only do Copan and Flannagan fail to defend the claim that Deuteronomy 7 and 20 and Joshua 1-12 do not qualify as genocide and ethnic cleansing, but they also seem to have no consideration at all for the terrible lot of the Canaanite survivors *post bellum*. There is a simple reason for this: in Copan and Flannagan's estimation, the Canaanites do not enter into the moral calculation: as hopelessly wicked people worthy only to be destroyed and driven out, they are *personae non gratae*. Those that survived should be happy that they escaped with their lives given that their less mobile family, friends, and neighbors were reduced to blackened, mutilated corpses in the smoking ruins.

Sadly, like so many other Genocide Apologists and Just War Interpreters, Copan and Flannagan are committed to a one-sided attempt to dehumanize and otherize the Canaanites as a people wholly irredeemable, a people who are only good to be sent to slaughter and driven into the hinterland. And so these apologists carefully cultivate a one-sided picture of Canaanite society as completely corrupt and without any redeeming merit, so terrible that it is worthy only of destruction as the surviving Canaanites are violently expulsed from their homeland and left to fend for themselves on the margins of existence.

This is the story of the Canaanites. But it is not their story alone: it is a story shared by countless victims of genocide throughout history, people like the Armenians, the Jews, and the Tutsis. If the Canaanites echo down through time to today, so do the cold, blood curdling defenses of their genocidaires. Indeed, one finds them on display in the meticulously reasoned and yet painfully errant rationalizations of Copan and Flannagan, as deftly argued a defense of the indefensible as one could hope to find.

Conclusion

When we surveyed the Genocide Apologists, we noted that not all of them recognized that they were defending actions which meet the legal definitions of genocide and ethnic cleansing. The Just War Interpreters initially present a more promising approach, one that appears to be more humane even as it is grounded in a close reading of the text. But the result still leaves us with an ethnic cleansing of the land. Furthermore, I argued that even this softer, modified view still meets the legal definition of genocide. And that means that the Just War Interpreters' approach in fact ends up collapsing back into little more than a repackaged Genocide Apologetic. The picture is even worse when considered under the criteria of jus post bellum. This genocide would have been profoundly corrupting of the genocidaires and obviously absolutely devastating for the surviving Canaanites. Copan and Flannagan devote their efforts to othering the Canaanites in order to justify the unmitigated slaughter and 'moral cleansing' of the land. As a result, these people are treated as *personae non gratae,* a tragic status which is shared by the victims of genocide throughout history.

Suffice it to say, when it comes to our criteria this position does not fare substantially better than the traditional Genocide Apologetic. With respect to the Perfect God criterion, it is utterly implausible to envision a morally perfect God commanding moral atrocities or an omnipotent God needing to employ as blunt and brutish a tool as genocide in order to secure a sufficient level of moral purity in his chosen people. Indeed, it makes no sense to speak of preserving moral purity by undertaking actions that have a devastating morally corrupting impact on the persons who undertake them including the dehumanization of the victims by way of behaviors like mockery, torture, mutilation, and rape. We are called to love our neighbors, not objectify and destroy them. And the Canaanite *is* our neighbor.

10

The Spiritualizers

For centuries, astronomers believed that the earth was the fixed center of the universe and that all celestial objects—sun, moon, and stars—orbited around it. This position was known as geocentrism (earth-centered) or the Ptolemaic theory (in honor of influential Greek astronomer Ptolemy). Geocentrism worked surprisingly well for more than a millennium, but eventually the evidence against it began to mount. For example, astronomers increasingly noticed perturbations in the movements of celestial objects which would fail to conform to the smooth orbits that the theory predicted. While this awkward fact presented a problem for the theory, Ptolemaic astronomers soon devised an ingenious solution to account for the back-and-forth movements: they added epicycles, smaller looped orbits moving occasionally around the circumference of the larger orbit.

For a while this tweak to the theory "saved the appearances" and allowed astronomers to continue to maintain that the earth was the fixed center of all things. However, yet more counter-evidence soon began to accrue against the modified theory. Even the addition of more epicycles could only offer a temporary solution and eventually the disconfirming evidence hit a critical mass that could no longer plausibly be addressed simply by adding yet more tweaks to the theory. At this point, astronomers found themselves contemplating another solution, a radical paradigm shift, one that replaced the now untenable geocentric theory with a heliocentric (that is, sun-centered) model of the universe.

So why begin this chapter by recounting the fate of Geocentrism? The simple reason is that the survey thus far suggests that epicycles are not sufficient and there is a need for a paradigm shift of equivalent proportion. The Genocide Apologists and Just War Interpreters have a shared theoretical commitment to the reliable historical reference of Deuteronomy and Joshua and the morally obligatory status of the actions commanded by God. When the Genocide Apologist's views are laid bare, and illumined by the horror of Rwanda, we recoil in incredulity at the prospect of defending genocide.

Enter the Just War Interpreters preparing to add epicycles to the theory by way of a recasting of the narrative in the terms of just war and displacement. While the proposal looks initially promising, upon closer examination it shows itself to be inadequate, like placing a Band-Aid on a gangrenous wound. As with geocentrism, the problems run to the core of the proposal and so they cannot be addressed merely by tweaking the system.

But if it is time for a paradigm shift, then we must ask: a shift to what? We will seek to outline an answer in the next two chapters, beginning here with a move away from viewing the Canaanite conquest as historical to viewing it as symbolic and spiritual. I refer to this approach as spiritualizing. Our survey and evaluation of the Spiritualizer approach will consider two well-known Patristic exemplars of the method in Gregory of Nyssa and Origen as well as some of the contemporary defenders like Jerome Creach and Douglas Earl. But we will first set the stage by considering an interesting model of spiritualization in the work of C.S. Lewis.

The Most Terrible Sentence in Fiction or History?

Before we turn to our primary focus on the Canaanites, we can unpack the basic idea of spiritualizing difficult biblical content with a modern defender of the approach. Doing so will help to provide a succinct introduction to the method as well as suggesting some of its potential weaknesses. Our test case will involve a brief consideration of the imprecatory (cursing) psalms and in particular what is perhaps the most disturbing psalm of all: 137. This notorious passage begins with the psalmist lamenting the fact that his society has been decimated and his people placed into exile by the Babylonians. As the lament continues to build, the psalmist gradually switches from grief to growing rage directed at the oppressors, finally culminating in the chilling cry of verse 9: "Happy is the one who seizes your infants and dashes them against the rocks." Atheist Dan Barker speaks for many when he asks, "Can there be a more terrible sentence ever spoken in fiction or history?"[280] No doubt, it is a pretty terrible statement. And every Christian reader must consider the question: what do you *do* with it?

Many readers, apparently driven by the assumption of the moral inerrancy of every utterance of the human authors of scripture, have assumed that the psalm requires us to justify the voice of the imprecatory psalmist, to vindicate his cries as morally upright calls to God to redress injustice and punish the wicked.[281] While one can readily envision instances where an oppressed person may rightly cry out for justice against their oppressors, it is quite another thing to apply that basic truism to this specific verse. It seems to me that the attempt to sanctify this cry to bludgeon the infants of one's oppressors is a nonstarter,

---

280 Barker, *God: The Most Unpleasant Character in All Fiction* (Sterling, 2016), 128.

281 See, for example, John Piper, Do I Not Hate Those Who Hate You, O Lord? The Verses We Skipped," Desiring God (October 3, 2000), https://www.desiringgod.org/articles/do-i-not-hate-those-who-hate-you-o-lord

regardless of who your oppressors may be or what they may have done. A curse like this simply cannot be considered morally praiseworthy or even permissible.

It is at this point that spiritualization offers a paradigm shift in thinking, one in which we move from a commitment to the moral authority of the psalmist and his literal sense, to the moral authority of the text with respect to the divine plenary sense. In short, this approach invokes the Two Authors Principle while identifying a morally errant meaning in the psalmist's voice and a morally appropriate meaning in the divine voice.

And what might that spiritually redemptive meaning look like? C.S. Lewis explores this approach in his book *Reflections on the Psalms*.[282] He first calls out the moral offense of the literal sense with refreshing candor. Rather than stick to the old paradigm that attempts some unconvincing defense of infant bludgeoning of one's enemies as just and right, he firmly aligns himself with the powerful moral intuitions that condemn such wishes as 'contemptible.' Since we can see that the psalmist's wish is flatly immoral, Lewis admonishes the reader not to attempt a defense of the old paradigm that would redeem the psalmist's voice as such: "we must not either try to explain them away or to yield for one moment to the idea that, because it comes in the Bible, all this vindictive hatred must somehow be good and pious."[283]

Since the human voice is in deep moral error, we must turn instead to the plenary sense of the divine voice for the final meaning of the psalm. Lewis begins by reiterating the idea that "all Holy Scripture is written for our learning",[284] a claim that I have reified into the Love Principle according to which we ought to read and interpret biblical passages in such a way that they

---

282 Origen defends a position very much like that of Lewis. See *Homilies on Joshua*, trans. Barbara J. Bruce, ed. Cynthia White (The Catholic University of America Press, 2002), 144.

283 Lewis, *Reflections on the Psalms* (HarperOne, 2017), 22-3.

284 Lewis, *Reflections on the Psalms*, 22.

increase love of God and neighbor. Given that commitment, how should we seek a plenary interpretation of Psalm 137:9, one which is consistent with right love of neighbor, a love that encompasses even our oppressors and their infants?

Lewis begins by emphasizing that we need to adopt a suitably nuanced understanding of the whole of Scripture. In an echo of my Canon Principle, he stresses that we should not think that each verse is itself a contained moral lesson that can be read in isolation apart from the whole. We need to recognize, instead, that Scripture is a complex text, one which occasionally includes errant and even wicked perspectives with respect to the literal sense of the human author. Lewis opines that the text's ultimate purpose with respect to our proper moral and spiritual formation is found as we engage with the plenary divine sense:

> The human qualities of the raw materials show through. Naivety, error, contradiction, even (as in the cursing Psalms) wickedness are not removed. The total result is not "the Word of God" in the sense that every passage, in itself, gives impeccable science or history [or, presumably, morality]. It carries the Word of God; and we ... receive that word from it not by using it as an encyclopedia or an encyclical but by steeping ourselves in its tone or temper and so learning its overall message.[285]

We can put it this way: you don't get a sense of the overall artistry of the painting by keeping your nose an inch away from the canvas and examining each individual brushstroke. Instead, you need to step back and take in the whole work. Only then will you see how each brushstroke contributes to the artistry of the entire picture.

If a reader analyzing the brushstrokes of Psalm 137 draws the lesson that hating one's enemies and longing for their infant children to be bludgeoned is consistent with Christian discipleship,

---

285 Lewis, *Reflections on the Psalms*, 130.

then that reader has failed to steep themselves in the tone and temper of Scripture and thus to learn its overall message. Instead, they need to step back and take in the whole of Scripture, recognizing that the individual brushstrokes of "naivety, error, contradiction and even wickedness" will only make sense in light of the entire picture. And how we will ultimately interpret those errant perspectives and thus see the total picture will depend on identifying the plenary voice as guided by the Jesus Principle and the Love Principle.

Insofar as the literal sense of the psalmist to exult in the bludgeoning of infants is irreconcilable with the life of Jesus and the love of God and neighbor, Lewis proposes that we have warrant to seek a plenary spiritual meaning in the text that *is* consistent with these principles. Much in the way that Jesus guides us to find a deeper spiritual meaning in his Parable of the Sower (Matthew 13:8), so we may find a deeper spiritual meaning in the voice of the imprecatory psalmist.

And what is that plenary meaning? At this point, Lewis proposes a spiritualization of the psalm such that we treat the infant as symbolizing sinful impulses which should be destroyed within us:

> From this point of view I can use even the horrible passage in 137 about dashing the Babylonian babies against the stones. I know things in the inner world which are like babies ; the infantile beginnings of small indulgences, small resentments, which may one day become dipsomania or settled hatred, but which woo us and wheedle us with special pleadings and seem so tiny, so helpless, that in resisting them we feel we are being cruel to animals. They begin whimpering to us "I don't ask much, but", or "I had at least hoped", or "you owe yourself *some* consideration". Against all such pretty infants (the dears have such winning ways) the advice of the Psalm is the best.

Knock the little bastards' brains out. And "blessed" he who can, for it's easier said than done.[286]

So the Christian is called to mortify the flesh and eradicate sinful impulses from one's life, and before these 'infant' impulses grow and mature into habituated patterns of behavior, they should be destroyed: as Lewis so memorably puts it, "Knock the little bastards' brains out." Lewis' reading of the babies as symbols for sinful, wicked impulses is certainly one way to appropriate this text consistent with the love of neighbor.

As you might expect, such a proposal will immediately invite an incredulous response from many readers who will see Lewis as engaging in nothing more than a strained and fanciful projection. I can readily understand that response from a non-Christian who rejects the five hermeneutical principles that under-gird my analysis of the biblical text. But the matter is very different for those who *do* believe that Scripture is a unified work including both divine and human voices, that the divine voice is that of a perfect God, that the nature of God is modeled in the life and teaching of Jesus, and that he purposes the whole text to cultivate within the reader a love of God and neighbor. Given those background assumptions, Lewis' proposal looks far more credible than it would otherwise.

Indeed, we might recall at this point the wise words of Sherlock Holmes: "when you have eliminated the impossible, whatever remains, however improbable, must be the truth." In other words, while a particular biblical interpretation may look implausible on its own, once we survey the alternatives set against our reading assumptions we may decide that each of those alternative interpretations is even more extraordinary. And in that case, rather than believe this requires us to surrender one or more of our background reading principles, we may conclude that the *prima facie* improbable reading ultimately wins the day.

---

[286] Lewis, *Reflections on the Psalms*, 159.

Thus, if we are committed to the view that Psalm 137:9 is part of God's inspired and authoritative Scripture and the alternative interpretation is that the psalmist expressed a praiseworthy wish to retribute violence on his enemies, as Christians we may find that Lewis' spiritualization reading suddenly looks far more plausible than it did at first blush. Here, at least, is a reading consistent with the life and teaching of Jesus and the love of God and neighbor.

At this point, the skeptics of Christian reading will have their own reply: "Perhaps the real lesson is that the Bible wasn't inspired by a perfect God who wants to make us followers of Jesus who love God and neighbor. Perhaps it is simply a flawed human collection of writings with some nasty stuff that should just be rejected. *Why not that?*" That, of course, *is* a possible response, just as it is possible that Stanley Kubrick is not as brilliant as once thought and that *The Shining* really is littered with glaring continuity errors and other 'goofs.' I will return to that question in the final chapter. For now I will simply note that my focus in this book is on seeking to define a specific problem, critique particular solutions, and to offer a range of other viable solutions consistent with my background theological and hermeneutical assumptions. Every reader will have to decide for themselves whether they have reached a critical threshold to consider rejection of those theological and/or hermeneutical assumptions. As for me, insofar as I believe I have enough independent reason to accept that Kubrick is a brilliant filmmaker, I will continue to work on understanding these puzzling scenes in *The Shining* as something other than goofs. I believe that I have more than enough independent reason to believe that God is perfect, that he has revealed himself uniquely in Jesus and that the Scripture is his inspired word to us.[287] And so, I will continue

---

[287] I am not claiming that I accept Scripture as plenary divine revelation by way of a discursive argument, however. For a critique of foundationalist/evidentialist defenses of Scripture, see Rauser, *Theology in Search of Foundations*,

to work on interpreting these troubling biblical passages in a manner consistent with those convictions.

The Canaanites and the Patristic Spiritualizers

Lewis' interpretation of Psalm 137:9 provides us with a capsule summary of the Spiritualizing approach, one in which the literal sense is found to be indefensible, thereby prompting a search for a spiritual meaning that is consistent with the life and teaching of Jesus and the love of God and neighbor. And just as we can find a spiritual meaning of a single verse which is compatible with those principles, so we can scale up the basic model to spiritualize entire sections and even books of problematic content in a way that is consistent with our reading principles.

The idea that the Christian reader is justified in seeking a spiritual, non-violent reading of biblical texts which is consistent with the revealed identity of God and Jesus and the ethical and spiritual formation of the reader is an ancient one.[288] We can find a seed for it in the second century "Epistle to Diognetes": "As a king sends his son, who is also a king, so sent He Him; as God He sent Him; as to men He sent Him; as a Saviour He sent Him, and as seeking to persuade, not to compel us; *for violence has no place in the character of God.*"[289] If it really is the case that violence has no place in God, then we need to seek another

---

chapter 2. For an alternative, non-evidentialist approach, see Alvin Plantinga, *Warranted Christian Belief* (Oxford University Press, 2000), chapter 12.

288 See John Franke "Introduction to Joshua Through 2 Samuel," *Ancient Christian Commentary on Scripture: Old Testament IV: Joshua, Judges, Ruth, 1-2 Samuel*, ed. John R. Franke (InterVarsity, 2005), xxii.

289 "Epistle to Diognetes," *Ante-Nicene Christian Library*, vol. 1, *The Apostolic Fathers*, ed. Alexander Roberts and James Donaldson (T&T Clark, 1883), 310, emphasis added.

meaning for the biblical texts that depict God as violent. And spiritualization has long been a possible solution dating back to the Patristic era.

A striking example of this kind of reasoning is found in the work of fourth century theologian Gregory of Nyssa who offers a bold approach in his work *Life of Moses*. When discussing the killing of the Egyptian firstborn in the Exodus, Gregory expresses horror at the idea that God would indiscriminately kill the firstborn child of every family of Egypt, from that of the house of Pharaoh to that of the poorest slave: "How would a concept worthy of God be preserved in the description of what happened if one looked only to the history? The Egyptian acts unjustly, and in his place is punished his newborn child, who in his infancy cannot discern what is good and what is not."[290] Gregory is disturbed that a child should be punished for the wickedness of the father: "If such a one now pays the penalty of his father's wickedness, where is justice? Where is piety? Where is holiness? Where is Ezekiel, who cries: *The man who has sinned is the man who must die* and *a son is not to suffer for the sins of his father?* How can history so contradict reason?"[291] In short, the literal sense of the text presents us with a divine action which appears cruel and unjust. And for that reason, Gregory concludes, it *cannot* be the final (plenary) word to us.

That leads Gregory to infer that there must be a deeper spiritual meaning in the text, one which is consistent with the love and mercy of God and the transformative ethical design of Scripture: "Therefore, as we look for the true spiritual meaning, seeking to determine whether the events took place typologically, we should be prepared to believe that the lawgiver has taught through the things said. The teaching is this: When through virtue one comes to grips with any evil, he must completely

---

290 Gregory of Nyssa, *Life of Moses*, trans. Abraham Malherbe and Everett Ferguson (Paulist Press, 1978), 75.

291 Gregory of Nyssa, *Life of Moses*, 75, emphasis in original.

destroy the first beginnings of evil."[292] And so, he reasons that the Lord is "explicitly calling on us to kill the firstborn of the Egyptian evils when he commands us to abolish lust and anger and to have no more fear of the stain of adultery or the guilt of murder."[293] In other words, Gregory proposes that we think of the killing of these firstborn children much as Lewis proposes thinking of Babylonian infants, that is, as symbols for the growth of sinful impulses which need to be opposed, combated, killed.

On Gregory's reading, we should think of Israelite and Egyptian in this narrative symbolically: "For now in the difference of the names, Israelite and Egyptian, we perceive the difference between virtue and evil."[294] In other words, Gregory is scaling up Lewis's proposal from a single verse in a psalm to an entire narrative: the 'Israelite' is in this narrative symbolic of the virtuous character whereas the 'Egyptian' is symbolic of a destructive character. And sanctification calls us to eradicate the sinful Egyptian impulses within. The spiritual authority of the text as part of canon resides in the fact that it can form us into faithful disciples of Christ when it is read for this spiritual meaning, rather than as a historical record of God's past actions with respect to Israel's literal escape from Egypt.

Spiritualization offered a way for many people troubled by aspects of the literal meaning to make sense of Scripture. Augustine was famously won over to the depth and profundity of the biblical text by way of Ambrose's allegorical preaching, for example. John Chrysostom likewise amassed a following with his rich and creative spiritualized readings of biblical narratives. But undoubtedly the most famous of the Patristic-era Spiritualizers was the third century theologian Origen. He was deeply influenced by reading principles similar to the Jesus Principle and the Love Principle. Origen embraced an incarnational

---

292 Gregory of Nyssa, *Life of Moses*, 75-76.

293 Gregory of Nyssa, *Life of Moses*, 76.

294 Gregory of Nyssa, *Life of Moses*, 76.

understanding of Scripture, one according to which the reading of Scripture is a sacramental act: "As the people listened to Scripture, letting the words penetrate their minds, they were partaking of the body of Christ."[295] In Origen's view, every word in the text has a purpose to bring us to Christ and thus to dispense Christ's transforming grace to us. Additionally, Origen was deeply influenced by the Philonic tradition.[296] And he held to a tripartite view of scripture in correspondence with the tripartite view of the human person as body, soul, and spirit. On his view, the body encompassed the literal sense, the soul the moral sense, and the spirit the deepest allegorical or spiritual sense and it is on this final spiritual reading that we shall focus. In his reading, Origen always seeks to understand everything he reads in Scripture in light of the life and teaching of Jesus and that extends to his reading of Joshua. And he notably produced the only collection of sermons on Joshua in the early church.[297]

In his *Homilies on Joshua*, Origen deals squarely with the genocidal violence of the *herem* destruction of the Canaanites. Given that a literal reading of slaughtering one's neighbors is unworkable, Origen seeks an alternative spiritual reading of the text in which he follows the same basic template as C.S. Lewis and Gregory of Nyssa by suggesting that we view 'Canaanite' as a symbolic representation of sinful inner impulses that the Christian needs to eradicate in pursuit of holiness. However, Origen's symbolic reading is surprisingly detailed as he turns the text into a complex allegory of the spiritual life. In his view, Jericho is a sign of the present age encompassing all that is opposed to God's kingdom. He tells us that Jesus has overthrown the walls

---

[295] Cynthia White, "Introduction," in Origen, *Homilies on Joshua*, 6.

[296] See a helpful overview of Origen's spiritual exegesis see Franke, "Introduction to Joshua Through 2 Samuel," xviii-xxiii. For the Greek origins of allegorical reading in Homeric interpretation, see Boyd, *The Crucifixion of the Warrior God*, Volume 1: *The Cruciform Hermeneutic*, 420-23.

[297] Franke, "Introduction to Joshua Through 2 Samuel," xxviii.

of Jericho and that the trumpet blasts that herald the collapse of the walls are the writings of the New Testament.[298] Just as Christ's defeat of sin and evil is announced by Scripture so God's defeat of the ramparts of Jericho is announced by the trumpets, thereby eradicating "the walls of Jericho and all the devices of idolatry and dogmas of philosophers all the way to the foundations."[299] Notably, the collective shout of the people at the collapse of the walls is not limited to some spiritual elite, but rather is extended without special favor to all who fear the Lord.[300] When we learn the Scripture, Origen says that we actually fashion our own trumpets to defeat wickedness in our lives.[301]

And so, when we come to a passage like Joshua 6:16-17 in which we read that the Israelites devoted the entire city—save Rahab and her family—to destruction, Origen advises,

> This is what is indicated by these words: Take heed that you have nothing worldly in you, that you bring down with you to the Church neither worldly customs nor faults nor equivocations of the age. But let all worldly ways be anathema to you. Do not mix mundane things with divine; do not introduce worldly matters into the mysteries of the Church.[302]

Remember that the word *anathema* is the Greek equivalent of *herem*. Consequently, while the *herem* still very much concerns the contemporary reader, for Origen it is a *spiritual* concept. We see the same commitment manifested in the words of Paul in Philippians 3:8: "I consider everything a loss because of the surpassing worth of knowing Christ Jesus my Lord, for whose sake I have lost all things. I consider them garbage, that I may

---

[298] Origen, *Homilies on Joshua*, 74.

[299] Origen, *Homilies on Joshua*, 75.

[300] Origen, *Homilies on Joshua*, 76.

[301] Origen, *Homilies on Joshua*, 77.

[302] Origen, *Homilies on Joshua*, 78.

gain Christ." Thus, the lesson is to love neither the world nor the things in the world (1 John 2:15-17). Rather, allow Scripture to form you into Christ and recognize the triumph he has wrought. Finally, Origen suggests that Achan's sin (Joshua 7) lay in attempting to draw out worldly philosophy from carnal Jericho, and that provides us with a sober warning against the errors of the Gnostics of the early church (e.g. Valentinus, Basilides) who corrupted Christianity by blending it with pagan philosophy.[303] Presumably, this lesson offers an equally sober call to avoid the syncretistic union of Gospel to pagan philosophies in our own day. Ultimately, the call we receive in this passage is to devote ourselves wholly to Christ and to follow him in declaring *anathema* (that is, *herem*) the philosophies and base desires of this world.

Origen's symbolic reading often takes on a surprising level of detail which will appear quite fanciful to the contemporary reader. For example, in another homily he discusses the Gibeonites who famously trick Joshua into making a pact with them in Joshua 9. According to Origen, the Gibeonites represent immature followers of Christ. And as for the five kings who make war against them, Origen opines: "Now these five kings indicate the five corporeal senses: sight, hearing, taste, touch, and smell: for it must be through one of these that each person falls away into sin. These five senses are compared to those five kings who fight the Gibeonites, that is, carnal persons."[304] Once the 'kings' are interpreted as symbolic of the five senses, we can see that their 'killing' is really just a call to submit the senses to Christ in sanctification. Thus, Origen admonishes that we should not dwell on the cruelty that would be suggested by killing actual men, but rather on the spiritual chastening of bringing our senses into conformity to Christ. As he explains,

---

303 Origen, *Homilies on Joshua*, 83. Ironically, many of Origen's critics would've seen him as equally subject to this criticism.

304 Origen, *Homilies on Joshua*, 118.

Jesus destroyed the enemies, not teaching cruelty through this, as the heretics think, but representing the future sacraments in these affairs, so that when Jesus destroys those kings who maintain a reign of sin in us, we can fulfill that which the Apostle said, "Just as we presented our members to serve iniquity for iniquity, so now let us present our members to serve righteousness for sanctification." [305]

Let's consider one more example of Origen's hermeneutic. In Homily 15 he begins, "Unless those physical wars bore the figure of spiritual wars, I do not think the books of Jewish history would ever have been handed down by the apostles to the disciples of Christ, who came to teach peace, so that they could be read in the churches."[306] In other words, the only possible significance for followers of the Prince of Peace must be in a spiritual application. Origen then plaintively asks, given that fact, why God would command that the horses of the Canaanites be hamstrung in Joshua 11:8-11. Origen is perplexed by this command because the enemy is already defeated and Israel could have used the horses. (Alas, Origen makes no mention of the fact that this act constitutes terrible cruelty toward the animals.) Origen insists the counter-intuitive nature of these actions constitutes a clear signal that Scripture means something else in this description.[307] He then carefully builds a case arguing that the horses represent demonic agencies which must be destroyed.[308] "If we wage war properly under the leadership of Jesus, we ought to cut off their vices in ourselves and, taking 'the spiritual sword,' hamstring that whole stable of pernicious vices."[309] At that point, Origen then provides one of the best

---

305 Origen, *Homilies on Joshua*, 119.
306 Origen, *Homilies on Joshua*, 138.
307 Origen, *Homilies on Joshua*, 140.
308 Origen, *Homilies on Joshua*, 142.
309 Origen, *Homilies on Joshua*, 143.

summaries of his hermeneutical stance on Joshua in his entire corpus, and it is with this quote that we will end:

> A kingdom of sin was in every one of us before we believed. But afterwards, Jesus came and struck down all the kings who possessed kingdoms of sin in us, and he ordered us to destroy all those kings and to leave none of them. For if someone should keep any of them alive within, that person will not be able to be in the army of Jesus. Thus if avarice still reigns in you, or ostentation, or pride, or lust, you will not be a soldier of Israel, and neither will you fulfill the precept that the Lord gave to Jesus.[310]

Critiquing the Patristic Spiritualizers

In my view, this kind of spiritualization has at least a surface plausibility when it is kept generalized: e.g. Israel is 'virtue' whereas Egypt or Canaan is 'vice.' But the more one attempts to allegorize specific details within the narrative, as Origen is wont to do, the less plausible the general solution becomes. In this extraordinarily inventive and at times blushingly speculative manner, Origen aims to deflect the barbs of morally indignant critics and to deflate Christian cognitive dissonance by shifting our focus away from the ancient Near East and onto the spiritual life of the individual Christian who seeks to battle sinful impulses and be conformed to Christ.

While the Spiritualization option was influential in the early church, it has been relegated to a fringe position in the modern era and this for several reasons. At this point, we will consider three key objections to the Patristic Spiritualizers: first, transferring problematic moral content into a symbolic form does not

---

310 Origen, *Homilies on Joshua*, 145.

sufficiently address the moral problems presented by the text; second, spiritualization faces a dilemma: either accept that the events, in fact, occurred, in which case the symbolic-spiritual interpretation is mere distraction, or deny that the historical events occurred in which case one has effectively torn a rift in *Heilsgeschichte* (God's history); third, and perhaps most importantly, spiritualization falls victim to subjectivism and eisegesis given the lack of clear controls in identifying symbolic spiritual meanings.

Immoral Literal and Spiritual Meanings

In order to see the severe limits with spiritualizing problematic moral content, we can begin with Lewis' attempt to spiritualize Psalm 137:9 as the eradication of sinful desires. The obvious problem here is that the text still includes content that is morally problematic with respect to the literal sense of the human author. So leaving the problematic literal content unaddressed effectively amounts to the *distraction* reading strategy. To illustrate, imagine that instead of describing the act of smashing infants into rocks, the psalmist had mused about raping the young daughters of the oppressive Babylonians: "Happy is the one who seizes your girls and rapes them against a rock." Now imagine that a C.S. Lewis-inspired interpreter comes along and proposes that we can remedy the moral problematic presented by *this* horrifying text by spiritualizing it. We simply need to interpret the 'girls' as sinful impulses and *voila!*, those impulses can be mastered by one's forcible 'rape' of one's own will: "Against all such pretty girls (the dears have such winning ways) the advice of the Psalm is the best. Rape the little wenches' brains out. And 'blessed' he who can, for it's easier said than done."

Problem solved? Hardly. If raping children is an immoral act then *invoking a metaphor of spiritual growth that appeals to the image of raping children is also wrong*. Just as raping a child is a wicked act, so appealing to child-rape as a metaphor for sanctification is an inept, indeed wicked metaphor. The same, of course, would apply to a description of infant bludgeoning. That, too, is an inept and wicked metaphor. An evil, violent action like that simply cannot be 'redeemed' by way of symbolic spiritualization. Rather, it would seem that it should be repudiated outright.[311]

Similar problems arise with Gregory of Nyssa's and Origen's attempts to defuse the problem of othering violence through spiritualization. An excellent capsule summary of the problem is found in Gregory's own words: "in the difference of the names, Israelite and Egyptian, we perceive the difference between virtue and evil." While Gregory's intentions to address the problem of God indiscriminately killing the first-born of the Egyptians are noble, his solution of spiritualizing 'Israelite' to represent goodness/virtue and 'Egyptian' to represent evil/vice is problematic precisely because *these are two real ethnic/national identities*.

To illustrate the problem, consider the classic 1969 anti-war song "One Tin Soldier" by Canadian band The Original Caste. The song describes the conflict between two groups, the pure Mountain People and the wicked Valley People. The Mountain People have a treasure which they want to share peaceably with the Valley People. However, the Valley People are not interested in sharing: instead, they want it all for their own. And so they attack the Mountain People, killing them and seizing the booty. The song poignantly ends with the Valley People opening the treasure and discovering a simple but profound message: "Peace on Earth."

In this song, the two peoples are generalized types and obviously do not refer to actual ethnic or national groups; thus, there is no problem with the fact that they represent nobility/goodness vs. ignobility/badness. In this way, the story functions

---

311 The matter is somewhat more complex when we encounter well-established metaphors. For example, while I am not a fan of the idiom "There is more than one way to skin a cat," given that it is already a commonly recognized expression, one could defend it by way of established usage. That said, even if a metaphor of sanctification as infant bludgeoning were well-established I would still advise against its usage given that the act here is unequivocally immoral.

effectively as a parable for each one of us, and all without slurring or impugning any actual group of people. But imagine if the song instead used the designations of white people to represent goodness and virtue and black people to represent evil and vice. In that case, explaining that the song doesn't describe *actual* events but is only intended as a parable in which whites vs. blacks represents a *symbolic* struggle between good and evil, virtue and vice, would do nothing to address the moral offense of those particular labels. The fact would remain that the song perpetuates prejudice, *rhetorical violence* and othering of one actual group of real people by equating that group with the symbolic identity of evil or vice.

This problem affects Gregory's spiritualization. By mapping actual ethnic and national identities onto virtues and vices (Israelite=virtue; Egyptian=vice) his reading promotes prejudice, rhetorical violence, and othering against real Egyptians. And the same basic problem affects Origen's attempt to spiritualize another historic people, the Canaanites, as a symbol of a wicked worldliness that needs to be extirpated, eradicated, razed and ruined. Incidentally, it is worth pointing out that there is new genetic evidence that identifies people living in Lebanon today as the modern descendants of the ancient Canaanites.[312] So always remember: this was a real people. Thus, while spiritualization does address the problem of actual historical violence, it appears to solve that problem only by creating another: the rhetorical marginalization of actual ethnic/national/religious groups.

Distraction or the Denial of Heilsgeschichte

The Spiritualization approach has an undeniable benefit in terms of removing the potential for these violent texts to be used to justify violence against others. To note one particularly striking

---

312 Lizzie Wade, "Ancient DNA reveals fate of the mysterious Canaanites," *Science* (July 27, 2017), https://www.sciencemag.org/news/2017/07/ancient-dna-reveals-fate-mysterious-canaanites

example, Douglas Earl points out that while it is commonly assumed that the medieval crusaders must have appealed to Joshua as a primary biblical text to justify their campaigns against the Muslims, such medieval appeals are, in fact, surprisingly rare. Rather, the medievals commonly looked to the Book of Maccabees for a biblical precedent to justify the campaigns. Earl argues that one important reason for this fact traces back to the deep influence of Origen's spiritualized reading of Joshua on the church of the first millennium.[313] By establishing a normative reading of the text as an internal spiritual struggle in the life of the Christian, Origen usurped the text's ability to provide a viable precedent to justify violence against other groups like Muslims. By contrast, given that Maccabees was read as a historical account of Israel overthrowing illegitimate occupants of the land, it provided a far more natural textual precedent for the campaigns.

Conversely, it is worth noting that not long after Origen's spiritualization fell into disfavor following the Reformation, Joshua was being co-opted to justify assaultive actions including Oliver Cromwell's genocidal invasion of Ireland and Cotton Mather's genocidal campaign against the American Indians.[314] This is not surprising for once one allows that God has commanded genocide due to special circumstances in the past it is an open question as to whether other special circumstances may arise once again. And when you're in the fog of war, it can become perilously easy to believe those conditions have been met and thus that new Canaanites have arisen in one's own day.

Sometimes the spiritualization of a text is presented *alongside* the problematic literal reading rather than as an alternative to it.[315] As I said with respect to Lewis on the imprecatory psalms, that solution is inadequate at best as it only serves to distract

---

313 Douglas S. Earl, "Joshua and the Crusades," in *Holy War in the Bible*, 42.
314 See Jenkins, *Laying Down the Sword*, 129-35.
315 For an attempt to combine allegorical and historical reading in the case

from the moral offense. When it comes to historical narratives like the Exodus or the Canaanite conquest, merely adding a spiritual meaning (e.g. Israelite good; Egyptian/Canaanite evil) without addressing the historical-ethical questions is arguably the worst option of all. Not only does the ethical problem of history still remain waiting to be addressed, but the reader has opted to distance him/herself from that violence by a strategy that maps the symbolic binary opposition of good and evil onto real groups, thereby perpetuating the problem of othering and dehumanization. Consequently, if the spiritualization response is to be effective, it will need to take the next step of rejecting the historical referent altogether.[316]

Given the argument I have presented based on Rwanda as a model of ethical intuitive reflection, the only viable way forward is to deny the history of the Canaanite genocide, for our moral intuitions will not allow another option. If genocide is intrinsically wrong when it targeted Tutsis, then it is intrinsically wrong when it targeted Canaanites. Simply adding a spiritual application for the contemporary reader onto a morally indefensible literal meaning is equivalent to addressing rust on a car with a new paint job. You may not be able to see the problem for a time but it is still there, festering underneath the surface. Philip Jenkins puts it well: "We can no longer resort just to allegorizing the defeated, seeing them as prowling demonic forces. They were real people, and we can make an imaginative effort to recapture their experience. Canaanites once had voices too."[317]

If we are to cut the proverbial Gordian knot we will need to consider the broader question of how this denial of mundane

---

of the Midianite killing see David L. Stubbs, *Numbers*, Brazos Theological Commentary on the Bible (Brazos, 2009), 233.

316 For a discussion of the debate over Origen's view of the historicity of Joshua, see Boyd, *The Crucifixion of the Warrior God*, Volume 1: *The Cruciform Hermeneutic*, 433-36.

317 Jenkins, *Laying Down the Sword*, 239.

history affects our understanding of God's salvation history. Questioning that history raises both a *theological question* (what does this do to Christian belief?) and a *historical question* (is this conclusion supported by the historical record?). Let's turn to answer each question, beginning with the theological concern.

The theological concern is often framed in terms of a slippery slope: once we question Joshua, do we also question Moses, Abraham, Adam? Or to go in the other direction, if the first Joshua is non-historical, then why believe the second one is historical? As G.W. Ramsey once wryly put it, "If Jericho was not Razed, is our faith in vain?"[318]

First, let's set the stage. The German word *Heilsgeschichte*, or 'salvation history,' captures the idea of a theological-historical narrative chronicling the great works of God from creation to redemption to new creation. That story constitutes the backbone of the biblical narrative,[319] extending from the creation of Adam and Eve to the calling of Abraham, the Exodus under Moses, the occupation of the Promised Land under Joshua, the period of Judges, the establishment of the monarchy with Saul and David, the defeat of the Northern Kingdom by Assyria in 722 BCE, the defeat of the Southern Kingdom to Babylon in 587/6 BCE, the Exile and Return. This history establishes a royal lineage that leads ultimately to Jesus Christ as memorably summarized in the genealogy of Matthew 1:1-16 (proceeding from Abraham to Jesus) and the genealogy of Luke 3:23-38 (proceeding from Jesus back to Adam). If we begin to question aspects of that history from Adam to Abraham to Joshua to Jesus, do we indeed find ourselves on a slippery slope? To put it bluntly, is the denial of historical correlates in the narrative the proverbial loose thread that threatens to unravel the entire theological sweater?

---

318 Cited in Douglas Earl, *The Joshua Delusion* (Cascade, 2011), 1.

319 For an example see Craig G. Bartholomew and Michael W. Goheen, *The Drama of Scripture: Finding Our Place in the Biblical Story* (Baker Academic, 2004).

A particularly effective way to see the problem brought to life is with the great Hall of Faith chapter of Hebrews 11 which seeks to inspire the contemporary reader with illustrations of devotion from past saints. The story begins with Abel who provided a faithful offering to God (v. 4). The narrative then recounts the faith of a long list of saintly figures including Enoch, Noah, Abraham, Isaac, Jacob, Moses, and Rahab and many, many others. The writer concludes, "These were all commended for their faith" (v. 39). Needless to say, the whole point of the writer to the Hebrews is that these are *real people* who did *real things* which are exemplary of faith and thus which provide inspiring guides to the disciple in our own day. Thus, if these stories are really just that, *stories*, mere historical fiction, then the entire chapter is evacuated of its motivational *gravitas*.

To illustrate, a baseball coach who wants to inspire his team may pump them up with the great achievements of Babe Ruth or Hank Aaron or Jackie Robinson. But he will not spend any time recounting the achievements of Roy Hobbs because Mr. Hobbs is a *fictional character* from the film *The Natural* (and the 1952 novel of the same name). You might invoke Hobbs to illustrate a point, but if you want to *inspire* an athlete you tell them the story of another *real* athlete: you don't tell them a fiction. By the same token, if you want to inspire a real *spiritual* athlete, you tell them stories of other real spiritual athletes who accomplished great things: you don't tell them a fiction. Why does the writer of Hebrews refer to the *actual* collapse of the walls of Jericho (v. 30) and the *actual* faith of Rahab (v. 31) if not to inspire an equivalent faith response in the reader?

That brings us to a pivotal question: while it could certainly be disconcerting to learn that particular segments of the narrative of God's action in history are not, in fact, historical, does that denial actually affect essential orthodox doctrinal confessions? The answer would seem to be: it depends. There certainly are places where historical confession is essential to Christian orthodoxy. This is definitely the case with the life, death, and resurrection of Jesus. As Paul famously observed, if Christ has not been raised, our faith is in vain (1 Corinthians 15:14). So it is clear enough that orthodox Christianity is predicated on the historical life, death, and resurrection of Jesus. But beyond that limited historical scope, how many of the other events that form the great narrative we call *Heilsgeschichte* are likewise absolutely non-negotiable for a Christian? That is, how much of this putative history is an essential part of Christian dogma? How much of it is necessary to secure orthodoxy? Must one believe that God literally created Adam in a garden, that he called Abram out of Ur, that he appointed Moses to lead his people out of Egypt, that he sent Joshua and his people into Canaan, and so on? Are all those beliefs *required* of the orthodox Christian?

It would seem that the most reasonable place to begin evaluating these claims is by considering the content of central Christian creeds, for these are the confessions that aim to articulate essential Christian doctrinal confession. The truth is, however, that beyond the life, death, and resurrection of Jesus, the central creeds such as the Apostles' Creed and the Nicene Creed simply do not include beliefs about these additional figures and events that comprise *Heilsgeschichte*. This is not to say that belief in other major figures and events of God's salvation history are *irrelevant* to Christian belief: far from it. But it does suggest that they are not *essential*. And that would allow for the possibility of an orthodox Christian denying specific historical claims concerning these individuals or events if one believes the historical and/or theological evidence warrants doing so.

Few of us are *mere* Christians, however, so at this point it may be worthwhile to consider how this stance might relate to a specific denominational tradition. Since I am a member of the evangelical North American Baptist denomination, I will consider the implications of the view I'm exploring here for my affinity with this tradition.[320] Our centering confessional statement is the

---

[320] For a very fine defense of the importance of creeds and confessions to the

North American Baptist Statement of Belief.[321] Notably, while this six-page document summarizes major Christian, evangelical, and baptistic doctrinal distinctives, it offers minimal details as regards *Heilsgeschichte*: it refers to the fall of Adam and the Law of Moses and of course the life, death, and resurrection of Jesus. But in that six pages it makes no mention of figures like Abraham or David, major events like the flood, Exodus, or conquest of Canaan, or even the name of Israel. Consequently, beyond the life, death, and resurrection of Jesus there is a very minimal set of explicit confessional requirements as regards specifically historical claims.

Given that I approach matters from a Baptistic perspective, it is also worthwhile to highlight my view of the important baptistic concept of *soul competency*. As R. Stanton Norman observes, within the Baptist tradition, soul competency refers to "our ability to think, render moral decisions, grapple with issues of immortality, and contemplate the mystery and majesty of the cosmic order."[322] In short, soul competency underscores the importance of each individual maintaining a God-given graced ability to reason about doctrinal matters. The idea is not one of *individualism* for we are all essentially tied to community. Indeed, I have argued elsewhere about the importance of recognizing that confession is a *shared* experience.[323] But it does mean that each of us is responsible to work, to the extent that we are able, toward *owning* our personal convictions. In the famous words of Thomas More (who was no Baptist, of course!), "I never intend, God being my good Lord, to pin my soul to another man's back . . . ." Thus, the importance of reasoning through

---

health of the church, see Carl Trueman, *The Creedal Imperative* (Crossway, 2012).

321 "Statement of Beliefs of the North American Baptists," https://nabconference.org/wp-content/uploads/2019/02/2.-NAB-Statement-of-Beliefs-and-Affirmation-of-Marriage-ADOPTED-by-Triennial-Delegates-July-5-2012_0-1.pdf

322 R. Stanton Norman, *The Baptist Way* (Broadman and Holman, 2005), 161.

323 *What's So Confusing About Grace?*, chapter 26.

difficult doctrinal issues and being informed by our moral reasoning in the process is all part of soul competency.

Norman does offer an important caveat, however, as he adds that one should not construe soul competency in a way that "usurps biblical authority." As he puts it, both General and Particular Baptists of the past recognized that "a person's conscience could be mistaken and that Scripture was the corrective to and guide for conscience. Freedom of conscience cannot be used as a license to supplant orthodox doctrine."[324] To that I would offer three replies. First, while the right reading of Scripture may indeed correct an errant reading of conscience, *a right reading of conscience may likewise correct an errant reading of Scripture.* After all, our reading of Scripture is no more secure from error than our reading of conscience. Second, I do not believe that I am in any way "supplanting orthodox doctrine": I affirm plenary biblical inspiration and even inerrancy (appropriately defined *qua* the divine plenary meaning) along with all the other major doctrinal confessions in the North American Baptist Statement of Belief as well as the Apostles' Creed and major ecumenical creeds like Nicaea. Finally, while other Christians will undoubtedly disagree with me at points, it is to be expected that Baptists who truly embrace soul competency will inevitably have some significant disagreement in the practical outworking of their understanding of doctrine. And thus, there should be room for principled disagreement of conscience. Indeed, how could it be otherwise?

At this point, it might be helpful to consider the parable of the two canoes that Brian McLaren shares in his book *A Generous Orthodoxy*.[325] The parable begins with two groups of travelers heading downstream in their respective canoes. Gradually they enter into white water, and as the rapids become larger and more dangerous, each group has a very different response. The first group chooses to remain in the river and ride out the rapids even

---

324 Norman, *The Baptist Way*, 161.

325 McLaren, *A Generous Orthodoxy* (Zondervan, 2004), 141-143.

though staying afloat in the rough water requires them to toss items overboard. By contrast, the second group is unwilling to throw anything overboard, and so their solution to keep from sinking is to pull out of the river altogether and begin a laborious overland portage while keeping all of their baggage in the boat.

Within the parable, the rapids represent the varied challenges that modernity presents to Christian faith while the canoers represent two very different responses we can make to the rapids of modernity. The canoers who withdraw from the river and begin to portage exemplify the 'conservative' response that rejects the 'rapids' of modernity and opts to leave the water altogether. By contrast, the canoers who throw some particular gear overboard in order to ford the rapids represent the 'liberal' response that revises traditional Christian beliefs in order to meet the challenges of modernity.

While McLaren's parable aims to describe various different responses as the church journeyed through modernity, it applies equally well to the practical decisions that must be faced by *every* Christian. As we encounter evidence that appears to challenge our current understanding of Christian belief, whatever those beliefs may be, we need to consider whether to retain our beliefs as is despite the challenge (i.e. to pull out of the river and portage) or to revise our beliefs accordingly (i.e. to stay on the river and abandon that specific doctrinal claim).

When McLaren presented his parable, he framed it in a rather stark binary fashion that appears to pit two groups—conservatives and liberals—against one another. And so, the liberals choose to toss the freight of particular doctrines while conservatives leave the river of modernity and retain the baggage. Although this is a decent starting point, the reality is far more complicated than that story would suggest. Rather than think of two discrete groups, one that portages and another that stays on the river, we should recognize that each one of us is going to leave the river at some points and remain on it at others. In that sense, we're all 'conservatives' about some matters and 'liberals' about others.[326]

Christians who come out of a conservative evangelical background often need to consider whether to revise their beliefs about issues like a young earth and a global flood. They need to consider particular theories of biblical inerrancy which seem to run afoul of various lines of scientific, historical, or ethical evidence. They need to consider whether they will retain a belief in Mosaic authorship of the Torah or Pauline authorship of the Pastoral Epistles. They need to consider whether the particular theory they currently hold of the divine nature or the incarnation is logically coherent, theologically orthodox, and/or pastorally defensible. In these and countless other areas, each Christian must decide whether they will take the step of throwing a doctrine they currently hold into the river in order to ford the rapids or whether faithfulness requires them to pull out of the river, doctrine intact, in order to begin a laborious portage.[327]

The evangelical Christianity in which I was raised approached this issue from a *maximalist* perspective in which one strived to retain as much as possible of their current beliefs, often driven by the assumption that the loss of *anything* would threaten the loss of *everything*. In this way, my first forays into apologetics as a keen teenager included spirited defenses of young earth creationism and the global flood.[328] The assumption was that all these historical claims mattered to orthodox confession and if they weren't quite as essential as the life, death, and resurrection of Jesus, they were certainly close. Reject the historicity of one

---

326 See Randal Rauser, *You're Not as Crazy as I Think: Dialogue in a world of loud voices and hardened opinions* (InterVarsity Press, 2011), chapter 7.

327 In *What's So Confusing About Grace?* I provide an extended discussion of my own process of doctrinal reflection and revision.

328 For example, I argued that the modest amount of dust on the surface of the moon supported a young earth and that there was good evidence that Noah's Ark had been discovered atop Mount Ararat.

of these events and you would indeed be sent down a slippery slope to denying the resurrection.

In retrospect, it seems to me that this all-or-nothing thinking is simply mistaken. For example, one can reject young earth creationism and a global flood and still retain all the central Christian confessions like the Trinity, the fall, the incarnation, the atonement, and the resurrection. Thus, rather than demonstrating a slippery slope, I would submit that this type of reasoning illustrates a slippery slope fallacy.

Another somewhat more nuanced two-tiered approach would still remain committed to the importance of retaining the overall historical narrative while recognizing that some biblical stories are literary cul-de-sacs relative to the main narrative and thus they might be dehistoricized without significant loss to the integrity of the main storyline. Thus, on this view, one would distinguish between *central* historical elements in the narrative which are essential to the narratival integrity of the whole and those *peripheral* cul-de-sacs which can be dehistoricized if the evidence warrants. The peripheral elements would be defined as stories which do not form an essential part of the narrative stretching from Adam to Israel to Jesus. They may be part of that narrative in a broader sense—as we might say, they occur in the same 'universe'—but they are nonetheless self-contained narratives such that the loss of them as historical would not create a rift in the whole. The books of Job, Jonah, and Esther would all be examples of peripheral narratives by this definition. By contrast, however, the narratives in Deuteronomy and Joshua would most certainly be central on this view. As Jerome Creach observes, "The story appears in Joshua 1-12, but Exodus (17:8-16), Numbers (13; 21:1-3, 21-35; 31; 32; 33:50-56), and Deuteronomy (1:1-4:43; 7; 20) anticipate the taking of the land, and the narrative books that follow Joshua present its completion (see especially Judg. 1-3; 1 Sam. 15). Therefore, this story cannot be dismissed as a minor part of the Old Testament."[329]

While I have some sympathy with that two-tiered approach, ultimately I think it places too much doctrinal emphasis upon the need to root every aspect of the main narrative in a historical referent. As I suggested above, I don't think that kind of conservatism is justified given the fact that the primary creeds simply do not require belief in those historical elements of God's actions. Belief in Noah's Ark, Abraham's call, Moses' Exodus, and Joshua's conquest of Canaan are among the major events of the Judeo-Christian narrative of salvation history, but as events that occurred in spacetime, *they are not of themselves articles of Christian faith*. And while I concede that the writer to the Hebrews appears to have viewed this full catalogue of events as historical inspiring models of faith, I cannot accept that this fact is itself sufficient to oblige the Christian to accept the historical occurrence of all these stories as written. And of course, I believe that the moral argument I have presented along with the guiding reading principles I have proposed collectively constitute an excellent reason to deny the historicity of the conquest of Jericho. Thus, we have at least one historical event in Hebrews 11 which should be read non-historically.

Let's try this one more time. I have argued that the life, death, and resurrection of Jesus clearly are essential to Christian confession. But can we extend that same necessity to a broader swath of history? We could try reasoning like this: As divine, Jesus could not make mistakes about history; nor could he lie about it. So it follows that if he believed some person existed in the past and/or some event occurred in the past then we ought to believe this as well. And as one Christian puts it, "Jesus believed every event of the Old Testament."[330] To note a few examples, Jesus refers to Adam and Eve (Matthew 19:4-5), Noah and the ark (Luke

---

329 Creach, *Violence in Scripture*, 97.

330 Mike Matthews, "Jesus Believed Every Event of the Old

17:26), Abraham, Isaac, and Jacob (Matthew 22:31-32), the calling of Moses in the burning bush (Mark 12:26), the miracles of Moses (e.g. John 3:14, 6:32), Elijah and Elisha's miracles (Luke 4:25-25), King David and King Solomon's rule (Matthew 12:3, 42), and so on. What is more, in the Transfiguration, in particular, Moses and Elijah actually appear with Jesus (Matthew 17:1-8; Mark 9:2-8; Luke 9:28-36). All of these events form the tapestry of *Heilsgeschichte*, and you cannot begin to tear holes in that tapestry without undermining the Gospels themselves since these narratives are simply extensions of the stories of God's great actions from the creation of Adam onward. Or to switch analogies, the events of *Heilsgeschichte* form the planks of a bridge that carries us across a deep canyon to the Gospel. As we remove each plank, we open up gaps in the bridge that eventually make it unable to carry us to that Good News.

This is a serious challenge and it deserves a careful response. That response builds on the essential concept of accommodation. Accommodation refers to the idea of *contextualized* communication in which the speaker/instructor presents the informational/educational material relative to the current state of understanding of the student so as to maximize understanding for that student. An example will serve to illustrate the point. My book *God or Godless* consists of twenty short debates with atheist John Loftus. In one of those debates, Loftus argues that the Bible demonstrates ignorance of modern science and that this supports the conclusion that God did not, in fact, author the Bible. Loftus assumes that if God were to reveal himself to an ancient people, he would have done so in the modern language of Big Bang cosmology, plate tectonics, and evolutionary biology.

But is that so obvious? I don't think so. The problem, as I point out in my rebuttal, is that "such an account of the world wouldn't have made any *sense* to the ancient Israelites. Can you

---

Testament," Answers in Genesis (April 1, 2011), https://answersingenesis.org/is-the-bible-true/jesus-believed-every-event-of-the-old-testament/

imagine people who considered a chariot cutting-edge technology trying to get their minds around $E=mc^2$? If God had revealed himself to the ancient Israelites in the science of the twenty-first century, he would have ensured their inability to understand the text."[331] It is essential to keep in mind that the primary focus of Genesis 1 and 2 is to establish a doctrine of God's absolute role as creator and sustainer of all things. But the text was written first and foremost for the ancient Israelites, and that end would hardly have been served by placing it in the language of incomprehensible twenty-first century scientific theories. Thus, I argue that God revealed a doctrine of creation in the ancient science of the Hebrew people, the very people that he desired to reach. Contrary to Loftus's argument, the fact that the revelation comes in the guise of ancient science is not evidence against its divine origin since a wise divine revelator would be *expected* to reveal himself in a way that is understandable and winsome for the target audience.

One could argue that we have a similar situation in the present case. Jesus came to reveal God to us (John 14:9), to reveal the purpose of the Law (Matthew 5:17), and to offer us a way back to the Father (John 14:6). By contrast, his primary purpose was *not* to provide an authoritative and final account of the historical veracity of every person and event of Jewish history to which he refers in his life and ministry. Thus, it is certainly possible that he could have accommodated particular errant assumptions about history which were widely shared by his audience given that sorting out those issues was simply not germane to *his* purpose. Conversely, if he had determined to correct every errant historical assumption whenever he spoke, that would have led to alienation, confusion and misunderstanding no less significant than if God had revealed Big Bang cosmology and plate tectonics to the ancient Israelites. To sum up, in the same

---

[331] John Loftus and Randal Rauser, *God or Godless: One Atheist. One Christian. Twenty Controversial Questions* (Baker, 2013), 120.

way that God could accommodate to the fallible and incomplete science of the ancient Israelites in order to reveal a doctrine of creation, so it is possible that Jesus could accommodate to the fallible and incomplete history of his audience in order to reveal the nature of God and the true meaning of salvation.[332]

Given the possibility that Christ accommodated to errant human opinions for his own pedagogical ends, I think it is simply misguided to believe that the question of history can be settled by way of a simplistic syllogism like this:

1. God cannot lie.
2. Jesus is God.
3. Therefore, Jesus cannot lie.
4. Therefore, any time Jesus refers to a person or event of Jewish history, we can know that this person existed or that this event occurred.[333]

Such a seemingly simple argument hides many dubious assumptions. Rather than assume that the history question can be settled *a priori*, we need to recognize that it can only truly be addressed *a posteriori* as with my extended moral argument. However, one may also assess the credibility of the story directly by considering the historical evidence for it. And so at this point we will evaluate the contemporaneous textual and archaeological evidence for the conquest of Canaan. Is belief in the events of Deuteronomy and Joshua well evidenced on historical grounds? Should these texts compel belief from every reasonable person who

---

[332] One could also argue that in his human mind, the incarnate Christ non-culpably believed many false claims about matters concerning topics like history and science. A claim of that sort would be consistent both with a Chalcedonian (two-minds) christology and a Kenotic christology.

[333] I am purposefully using ambiguous language in premises 1 and 2. This could be cleaned up by changing 'God' to 'a divine being'. But most people who invoke arguments of this type simply refer to 'God' simpliciter.

considers the full weight of historical evidence? More modestly, do these texts at least provide a very *plausible* interpretation of the available historical evidence? Or does the evidence support the conclusion that these texts are products of a much later time, a fact that would call the veracity of their historical claims into serious question?

The fact is that the Deuteronomic narrative faces some significant problems as history, and we can contextualize those problems by way of a comparison and contrast. In short, once we consider how impressive the historical evidence is for the life of the *second* Joshua (that is, Jesus) we will have a better sense of the relatively scant historical evidence for the life of the *first* Joshua and the events associated with that life.

Christian apologists love to talk about the historical evidence for the life, death, and resurrection of Jesus. For example, they point out that we have multiple independent sources testifying to Jesus and that these texts are all within a few decades of the purported events. The New Testament includes four distinct Gospel accounts, Matthew, Mark, Luke, and John, which draw upon additional independent witnesses.[334] These Gospels are generally dated from 40-65 years after the life of Jesus (i.e. from 70-95 CE). However, some scholars date the earliest Gospel, Mark, into the mid-50s. And many scholars believe that the Gospels themselves are based on eyewitness testimony.[335]

Equally important, the New Testament also includes several epistles, letters that circulated from as early as the late 40s, and those letters provide a surprising amount of very early information on Jesus. For example, 1 Corinthians 15 includes a truly impressive creedal confession that Paul cites in verses 3-7. This confession states belief in the atoning death and resurrection

---

334 For example, Matthew appears to include testimony from an 'M' source, a 'Q' source, and a Markan source.

335 Richard Bauckham, *Jesus and the Eyewitnesses: The Gospels as Eyewitness Testimony*, 2nd ed. (Eerdmans, 2017).

of Jesus and the fact that he was seen alive resurrected by several eyewitnesses including Peter, James, the Twelve, and five hundred others. All in all, this is a very impressive proto-creed which summarizes the core kerygmatic proclamation in the death and resurrection of Jesus.

So how early is this proto-creed? First Corinthians was written in 54/55 CE and when he cites the proto-creed Paul is recalling a teaching that he had shared earlier with the Corinthians on his previous visit in about 51 CE. It is a teaching which Paul had himself previously received (see the rabbinic language of receiving and passing on in verse 3). So when did *Paul* receive it? Using the rough timeline we can reconstruct from Galatians 1-2, it seems quite likely that Paul received it no later than the time he traveled up to Jerusalem to meet with Peter and James (Galatians 1:18), i.e. about 37 CE. Thus, it would follow that the creedal confession was already circulating in Jerusalem by the mid-thirties. In fact, renowned biblical scholar James Dunn, who was no conservative, argued that this formula may be traced to within *months* of the death of Jesus.[336] This proximity of event to witness is truly impressive for any claim of ancient history. In short, the New Testament documents provide a diverse library of independent first century writings testifying to the life, death, and resurrection of Jesus. Christian apologists have rightly noted that there simply isn't an equivalent to this in the ancient world.

To sum up, the essential Christian claims about Jesus are extraordinarily well-attested on historical grounds. But what happens when we switch our focus from the second Joshua to the first? How good is the historical evidence for figures like Moses and Joshua? At the outset, I think we need to recognize that, where historical evidence is concerned, we are in a radically different situation. To illustrate the nature of the shift, imagine that you are watching the weather forecast. The meteorologist

---

[336] James D.G. Dunn, *Jesus Remembered: Christianity in the Making*, vol. 1 (Eerdmans, 2003), 855.

tells you that it will be hot and sunny tomorrow with a risk of thunderstorms late in the afternoon. And from there, he continues to give you the fourteen day forecast, outlining in some detail what to expect for the next two weeks. It is important to note that the meteorologist does not qualify the anticipated accuracy of his forecast day by day. But be assured that with every day he extrapolates into the future, the accuracy of the forecast diminishes significantly. For example, he does not tell you that the forecast for tomorrow is 90% likely to be correct while the forecast for three days from now is only 60% likely to be correct and the forecast for two weeks from now is statistically no more likely to be accurate than just guessing. Thus, if you didn't know better you could fall into the trap of thinking that this weather report provides a reliable narrative summary of meteorological conditions for the next two weeks. In fact, it does no such thing: there's a world of difference between '90% accurate' and 'just guessing.'

We are in a similar situation when we begin to move back in *Heilsgeschichte* from the relatively strong confidence we have in the life, death, and resurrection of Jesus. So what happens when we move centuries into the past to consider other purported events in the history of God's people? What, in particular, can we say about the Canaanite conquest?

The obvious place to begin is by considering when Deuteronomy and Joshua were authored. The traditional view is that Deuteronomy was written by Moses and Joshua was written by Joshua himself.[337] Consequently, on this view, we should think of the narratives in these books as, in essence, reliable approximately contemporaneous accounts of the events they describe equivalent to the Gospel accounts of the life, death, and resurrection of Jesus. Defenders of the traditional view appeal to internal textual evidence including the fact that various

---

337 See "Who Wrote the Book of Joshua?" Thomas Nelson Bibles (August 28, 2018), https://www.thomasnelsonbibles.com/who-wrote-the-book-of-joshua/

biblical passages refer to Moses writing things down and they also refer to the law of Moses (e.g. Exodus 24:4, Joshua 1:7-8, Daniel 9:11, Malachi 4:4). In addition, they note that Jesus appears to describe Moses as the author of Torah in Mark 7:10 and Luke 20:37.[338]

However, even among conservative scholars it is increasingly common to find a more modest claim, not that Deuteronomy was written by Moses but rather that the text has a connection back to "essential Mosaic authorship." In other words, the source material traces back to Moses, but the text was likely compiled in its current form by some anonymous editor/narrator at a much later date. This would also explain the fact that the text includes features that appear to derive from a period long after the time of Moses.[339]

We seem to be in a similar situation with Joshua. As for the authorship of the book, Daniel Timmer (a professor at Puritan Reformed Theological Seminary) points out that it is anonymous. While there are some elements in the narrative that appear to date to the second half of the second millennium, Timmer adds that "the book also contains many 'until this day' statements that show the author's perspective to be one degree or another later than the events narrated . . . ."[340] Timmer concludes, "These and other data allow us to affirm that the book, although composed after Joshua, contains and faithfully preserves sources that go back to his time."[341] Here too we see a significant retreat from the traditional position of Joshua as author to the far more modest view that there appear to be sources within

---

338 See "Pentateuch, Mosaic Authorship of," in Geisler, *The Big Book of Christian Apologetics*; Archer, *Encyclopedia of Bible Difficulties*, 153-4.

339 John Scott Redd, "Deuteronomy," in *A Biblical-Theological Introduction to the Old Testament*, ed. Miles V. Van Pelt (Crossway, 2016), 134.

340 Timmer, "Joshua," in *A Biblical-Theological Introduction to the Old Testament*, 161.

341 Timmer, "Joshua," 161.

the text which can be dated back to the *time* of Joshua. Thus, we see that even relatively conservative commentators offer a significantly more modest position on authorship and dating than their conservative forebears.

To be sure, the traditional conservative stance on Deuteronomy/Joshua authorship and reliability is still defended in some circles. Some conservatives attempt to sidestep the historical challenges by appealing to *a priori* theological arguments based on assumptions about divine veracity and Jesus' testimony. For example, conservative evangelical Norman Geisler argues that while Jesus could accommodate to human limitations, he could not accommodate to human error. The reason, so Geisler claims, is that this would be *lying*,[342] and as God the Son, Jesus cannot lie (Titus 1:2; Hebrews 6:18).[343] Therefore, if Jesus testified to Mosaic authorship, we can trust that Moses was, in fact, the author of Deuteronomy. Geisler rounds out his argument by claiming that the scholars who disagree with him are guilty of an anti-supernatural bias: "Most modern critics deny Mosaic authorship and organize the writings around a much later, complex set of priestly scribes and editors. The objective has been to avoid the books' accounts of supernatural occurrences and divine authority."[344]

Those kinds of *a priori* theological arguments may have been influential among conservative Christians in the past, but how successful will they be against the rapids of historical biblical criticism and modern archaeology? Let's start with Geisler's claim that while God can accommodate to limited understanding, he cannot accommodate to error because that would be dishonest. This is a spurious distinction. Accommodation is always, to some degree, an accommodation to the limited and thus *errant* perspective of the audience. That is undeniably the

---

342 Geisler, "Pentateuch, Mosaic Authorship of," 7.
343 Geisler, "Pentateuch, Mosaic Authorship of," 8.
344 Geisler, "Pentateuch, Mosaic Authorship of," 431.

case with the biblical authors as the Bible exhibits abundant evidence of accommodation to errant scientific, historical, and ethical perspectives. Robin Parry provides an excellent survey as regards science and history in his book *The Biblical Cosmos: A Pilgrim's Guide to the Weird and Wonderful World of the Bible*. Parry begins by explaining how the Hebrew Bible assumes a flat earth surrounded by a sea inhabited by mythological chaos monsters like Rahab and Leviathan, fantastical creatures which would be at home in Tolkien's Middle Earth.[345] Even more extraordinarily, this worldview then posits another vast sea held above the earth by a hard dome or firmament so that the "floodgates of heaven" opened up in Noah's day to allow this sea in the sky to inundate the earth.[346] As bizarre as all this may seem to be to the contemporary reader, perhaps the strangest detail of all is the realm of the dead which they believed to exist underneath our feet, quite literally a shadowy netherworld that holds the souls of the dearly departed.[347] Parry points out the disturbing way that this background belief informs the description of an earthquake consuming people in Numbers 16:23-34:

> I used to read this story in the light of my modern worldview; I thought that this was simply an earthquake that split the ground under the rebels causing them to fall to their deaths in the crack. But it is clearly more than that. The earth split open and the rebels went down into [sic] alive *into sheol*, the dead zone. Clearly, sheol was thought to be *literally under the ground*.[348]

---

[345] Parry, *The Biblical Cosmos: A Pilgrim's Guide to the Weird and Wonderful World of the Bible* (Cascade, 2014), 32-37.

[346] Parry, *The Biblical Cosmos: A Pilgrim's Guide to the Weird and Wonderful World of the Bible,* 38-39

[347] For a discussion of a related topic pertaining to the ascension, see Randal Rauser, *Faith Lacking Understanding: Theology through a glass darkly* (Paternoster, 2008), 113-21.

[348] Parry, *The Biblical Cosmos,* 79, emphasis in original.

The Bible is revealed to the Hebrew people in terms of this strange three-storied universe with a flat earth, a sea held up in the sky above, and a vast cavernous underworld populated by the dead. These are the terms under which God chose to revel himself to the ancient Israelites. Yet, we can now say that all these details of this worldview are literally false: the earth is not flat, there is no ocean held up in the sky by a dome, and there is no subterranean cavern beneath us holding the spirits of the dead. These are all *errors* in the beliefs of ancient peoples. And yet, God clearly did not see fit to correct these errors at the time of revelation. Instead, he revealed himself to the Israelites in accord with this profoundly errant view of the world. Virtually nobody today continues to defend these obsolete elements of this worldview. And as Parry points out, even the most diligent Christian conservatives will tacitly concede at least some errors: "If fundamentalists really were to have the courage of their convictions then we would see membership of the Flat Earth Society boosted significantly. What happens instead is that this is a bridge too far, even for hard-line fundamentalists, and biblical texts are thus reinterpreted to fit with modern cosmology."[349]

I mentioned above that the Bible accommodates to errant scientific, historical, and ethical perspectives. The three-storied universe may provide a good reason to accept some degree of scientific and historical accommodation, but what about *ethical* accommodation? If the Bible is revealed to conform us to Christ and increase our love of God and neighbor, then how can God have allowed any *ethically* errant thinking to enter its pages?

While I understand the concern, once again, whether there are errant ethical perspectives represented by any biblical authors is first and foremost a question that can only be settled *a posteriori*. If it should turn out that there are such perspectives then the next question would be why the Perfect God included them and thus how they ultimately serve as part of a larger collection to

---

349 Parry, *The Biblical Cosmos*, 165-66.

bring about our positive spiritual formation into disciples of Christ quite in contrast to the problematic moral content of those passages.

If we want evidence of ethically problematic content in the Bible, we need look no further than the topic of this book: the Canaanite genocide and the associated dehumanizing rhetoric that accompanies it. However, there are many less extreme examples one could consider as well. For example, in the introduction, I outlined the punishment of stoning in the Torah, an act that we would condemn unequivocally as cruel and unusual if it occurred today.

Another oft-overlooked example, one which, if less extreme is nonetheless more comprehensively present, is the biblical teaching on corporal punishment. Consistently throughout the Bible, authors commend the corporal punishment of children, slaves, and others. To this day many North American Christians believe based on their reading of the Bible that corporal punishment is the 'biblical' way to discipline children. However, their practice is typically (and mercifully) quite far removed from the actual biblical teaching. As William Webb observes, many Christian parents adhere to a 'two-smacks max' principle which advises open hand hitting of small children on the buttocks and never spanking in anger. While these two-smacks max spankers believe they are following the biblical teaching, in his book *Corporal Punishment in the Bible,* Webb argues that a collation of Old Testament instructions on corporal punishment reveals teaching that is far more severe and disturbing. Webb summarizes that teaching in seven principles:

1. Do not be duped by age restrictions. Teenagers and elementary school children need the rod just as much, if not more, than those in early childhood, and beatings *are* effective (not 'ineffective' for older children as presently claimed).
2. Forget the idea of a two-smacks-max limit. Apply a gradual increase

in the number of strokes so that it fuses better with the forty strokes cap for adults.
3. Get the location right. Lashes are made for the 'backs of fools' not for their bottoms.
4. Remove the 'no bruising' restriction. Bruises, welts and wounds should be viewed as a virtue–the evidence of a sound beating.
5. Pick the right instrument. A good rod (hickory stick) will inflict far more intense pain and bruising than a hand on the bottom.
6. Stop thinking about corporal punishment as a last resort. Use the rod for nonvolitional misdemeanors as well as for major infractions.
7. Drop the notion of 'love but no anger.' Mix in a little righteous anger with your use of the rod.[350]

To put this summary into concrete terms, according to these guidelines a biblically faithful father could take his six year old who surreptitiously takes a cookie from the cookie jar, and he could beat the boy across his back with a hickory switch until he is black and blue. What is more, he could take his sixteen year old who fails to top up the gas tank after borrowing the car and do the same, albeit with more lashes given the boy's greater age. Does that look like wise teaching? On the contrary, is it not clearly abusive, deeply physically and emotionally harmful, and clearly morally wrong?

Webb recalls how, when he was still writing the book, he sent several chapters of the manuscript to a student from Ethiopia named Fanosie. Webb wanted to know if Fanosie thought it would be good for Webb to speak out against this kind of abusive behavior during a planned speaking engagement in Ethiopia. Webb recalls the young man's stirring response:

> He said nothing, nothing at all. Instead, Fanosie bent down his head and showed me a series of welts, scars and ugly

---

[350] William J. Webb, *Corporal Punishment in the Bible: A Redemptive-Movement Hermeneutic for Troubling Texts* (InterVarsity Press, 2011), 52-53.

disfigurations. He is a tall man and his dark curly hair hid these marks fairly well. He explained to me that he could take off his clothes and show me more marks from beatings he had as a child. He described being raised in a typical Christian home, and how not infrequently, his father beat him with a stick. In fact, Fanosie told me how it was still acceptable for many Christian husbands in Ethiopia to beat their wives as an act of corrective discipline.[351]

That is the real-world impact of attempting to apply faithfully the teaching of the biblical authors on corporal punishment: physical scars and deep emotional trauma. And it illustrates the essential role of moral intuitions and intimate acquaintance in informing and guiding our theological engagement with the text.

So if the right approach to this abusive teaching clearly cannot involve the perpetuation of what are clearly abusive disciplinary methods, how should we think about these troubling passages and their inclusion within Scripture? Webb proposes a redemptive-movement hermeneutic in which the reader can identify moral development in Scripture and we should interpret the earlier (e.g. violent and abusive) texts in light of the liberating revelation of God in Jesus Christ.[352] At the very least, we should be able to recognize that this teaching is itself in error and thus we have one particularly stark example where biblical authors promote unethical and unwise practices. Once we have recognized this one instance, we need to consider whether there are others. And as we have seen, there are indeed other cases, preeminent of which is teaching on the presence of divinely commanded genocide. Thus, from the perpetuation of genocide to corporal

---

[351] Webb, *Corporal Punishment in the Bible: A Redemptive-Movement Hermeneutic for Troubling Texts*, 18-19.

[352] Also see William Webb, *Slaves, Women & Homosexuals: Exploring the Hermeneutics of Cultural Analysis* (InterVarsity Press, 2001).

punishment, we should recognize that the Bible includes some material that represents morally errant authorial content.

The fact is that Christians already widely recognize that the entire cosmology in which *Heilsgeschichte* is set is an accommodation to ancient Near Eastern understandings of cosmology. And even Christians like those two-smacks max spankers recognize intuitively that the language of corporal beatings in the Bible is indefensible. Thus, it follows that Christian readers are grappling, tacitly if not explicitly, with the fact that some views endorsed by biblical authors are immoral and imprudent. If we are to retain our accommodation framework then we would need to concede the evidence supports the conclusion that God has accommodated to multiple levels of error in his progressive revelation in Scripture. For example, he accommodated to the scientific and historical errors that constitute the three-storied universe which forms the backdrop for Israelite understanding of the world. And he accommodated to the ethical errors of believing that corporal punishment by way of beating is a morally justifiable and prudential way to exercise discipline over one's children (to say nothing of slaves). One could readily multiply examples of accommodation in the Bible including God's accommodation to the errant theology of polytheism and henotheism in ancient Israel, the socio-economic institutions of slavery and polygyny, and the sheer brutality of many of the punitive punishments in the Torah.

Given this extensive evidence for error in the views expressed and assumed by biblical authors in terms of science, history, and ethics, error that I have proposed interpreting in terms of accommodation, to what degree might God have accommodated to errant understandings of the events that constitute *Heilsgeschichte*? Might God have accommodated to errant belief in a historical Adamic fall, Noahic flood, or Abrahamic calling by the inclusion of these stories into an inspired narrative even if those stories do not actually correspond to recognizable past events in spacetime? Given that we have multiple examples of errancy in the literal sense in all these other cases I don't think we can settle this question *a priori* by arguing that God would be 'lying' to include such material given that we already have multiple other cases where errors have been included.

Instead, we need to address this question *a posteriori* by considering the evidence for and against specific events. And with that, we can turn back to the Canaanite conquest. So let's begin by setting up a timeline. While the setting for the conquest of Canaan is commonly dated to around 1220 BCE,[353] the actual sources recounting the narrative appear to have originated centuries later. The key passages of Deuteronomy and the conquest narrative of Joshua are commonly dated to the period of the reforms that unfolded under King Josiah in the late 7th century BCE, although portions of the texts may be dated two centuries earlier. The context of their compilation is Josiah's attempt to bring about religious reforms including a new emphasis upon Yahweh worship as described in 2 Kings 23.[354]

By any reasonable measure, there is a very significant time gap between the alleged historical sequence and its recording in these 7th century BCE documents. Philip Jenkins puts the resulting time-gap into context: "The book's authors were as far removed from the conquest as we today are from the time of Martin Luther or Christopher Columbus."[355] Even if we grant the long-term stability of oral tradition, that is a significant span of time from the event to its literary recording. For the Christian used to debating the historicity of the New Testament where the timeline between events and their recording ranges from years-to-decades, it can be a shock to realize that the time-gap between the alleged events and the Deuteronomic history that purports to record them spans *centuries*. To return to our illustration, when we move from the history of Jesus to that of

---

353 Finkelstein and Silberman, *The Bible Unearthed*, 76.

354 See Creach, *Violence in Scripture*, 98.

355 Jenkins, *Laying Down the Sword*, 53-4.

Joshua, we are undertaking the equivalent of moving from a weather forecast for tomorrow to a long-term forecast for two weeks or more into the future. The historical evidence for the first Joshua is simply not comparable to the second.

If the details of the conquest narrative were independently corroborated by archaeological evidence and contemporaneous period documentation then that enormous time-gap could be overlooked. However, the evidence does not favor the events as described in Joshua 1-12. As Earl notes, the weight of archaeological evidence has been building against the historical reading of Joshua since Kathleen Kenyon established that the walls of Jericho did not fall in the era predicted by the conquest narrative.[356] In their influential survey *The Bible Unearthed*, Finkelstein and Silberman argue, "Despite the fact that the ancient cities of Jericho, Ai, Gibeon, Lachish, Hazor, and nearly all the others mentioned in the conquest story have been located and excavated, the evidence for a historical conquest of Canaan by the Israelites is . . . weak."[357] For example, Finkelstein and Silberman point to the rich trove of period documentary evidence which establishes that Canaan at the time was an economically depleted region controlled by Egypt with not more than 100,000 people. Suffice it to say,

> It is highly unlikely that the Egyptian garrisons throughout the country would have remained on the sidelines as a group of refugees (from Egypt) wreaked havoc throughout the province of Canaan. And it is inconceivable that the destruction of so many loyal vassal cities by the invaders would have left absolutely no trace in the extensive records of the Egyptian empire. The only independent mention of the name Israel in this period—the victor stele of Merneptah—announces

---

356 Earl, *The Joshua Delusion*, 3. Cf. Sharon R. Steadman, *Archaeology of Religion: Cultures and Their Beliefs in Worldwide Context* (Routledge, 2009), 287-289.

357 Finkelstein and Silberman, *The Bible Unearthed*, 73.

only that this otherwise obscure people, living in Canaan, had suffered a crushing defeat.[358]

When contemporaneous documentation and archaeological evidence from the region do not support the claims of documents composed *centuries* later, the wise course is to go with the weight of documentary and archaeological evidence. And that means that we should conclude based on the evidence that the conquest of Canaan likely never occurred in the manner described.

So if the Israelites did not invade and conquer Canaan in the thirteenth century BCE after just having departed Egypt, from where did this people originate? As Finkelstein and Silberman note, the only period reference to this people, that of the victor stele of Merneptah, already identifies them as an obscure people in Canaan. There are many theories and conjectures as regards the origin of the Israelites including the view that they gradually emerged from the Iron Age Canaanite population. Regardless, the consensus among scholars is that whatever their origins, it appears to be very different from the abrupt violent overthrow described in the Canaanite conquest.[359]

As we have seen, even conservative evangelical scholars like Copan and Flannagan who are keen to defend the history of the narrative concede that the numbers of armies and casualties are grossly inflated. Further, they also concede that the settlements were not actually cities, from which it would follow that thousands of male and female civilians were not, in fact, massacred at Ai. But if they are willing to concede that much, what grounds their conviction in the overall historicity of the narrative?

To sum up, while I believe that the concern about the slippery slope with dehistoricizing *Heilsgeschichte* is perfectly legitimate, the fact remains that beyond the core claims about the life, death, and

---

358 Finkelstein and Silberman, *The Bible Unearthed,* 79.

359 Ariel Lewin, *The Archaeology of Ancient Judea and Palestine,* trans. J. Paul Getty Trust (Getty Publications, 2005), 8.

resurrection of Jesus, most of the major events of biblical history are simply not of central doctrinal import for the Christian. Nor do I believe that passages like the genealogies in Matthew 1 and Luke 3 and the Hall of Faith in Hebrews 11 compel such a commitment. Consequently, while I think it is wise to retain a general conservatism that treats narratives as historical unless there is some good reason to believe otherwise, I am persuaded that in the case of the Canaanite conquest, I have provided such reasons. My reasoning began with a moral argument and guiding reading principles, but it has subsequently been corroborated by significant historical problems with Deuteronomy and Joshua including the fact that these texts were likely composed centuries after the purported events they describe and that they do not conform in significant details with the archaeological record and contemporaneous documentary records of the region.

Needless to say, one cannot settle these issues *a priori* as folks like Norman Geisler attempt to do with his claim that God cannot lie, still less with his uncharitable attempt to slur the motivations and presuppositions of those who disagree with him as being borne by an 'anti-supernatural bias'. To be sure, we can and indeed *must* still seek to inhabit the narrative, recognizing it as God's final revelation to us, but that engagement with the narrative world of the text need not be hamstrung by concerns over the historicity of narratival details which are incidental to mere Christian orthodoxy.[360] And we should always keep in mind that the reader's engagement with the text is to the end of our

---

360 This immersive and transformative engagement with the biblical narrative was famously described by Karl Barth in his address "The Strange New World Within the Bible," in *The Word of God and the Word of Man* (Harper, 1957). For a conversation between this existential and immersive engagement with the text and the evangelical concern with correspondence to historical events, see George Hunsinger, "What can Evangelicals and Postliberals Learn from Each Other? The Carl Henry/Hans Frei Exchange Reconsidered," *Disruptive Grace: Studies in the Theology of Karl Barth* (Eerdmans, 2000), 338-60.

proper formation in love of God and neighbor. When we find a nexus of moral, textual, and archaeological factors all testifying against the historicity of a narrative as such, we should be ready to surrender, severely qualify, or reinterpret the history. Indeed, one would think this fact would provide a welcome relief from the moral horror presented in Joshua 1-12. Christian faith most emphatically does not depend upon Jericho being razed.

Subjectivism and Eisegesis

This brings us to our third problem, and for many critics this may be the most serious objection of all: the lack of *control* and subjectivism that attends to the proposed spiritual interpretations of the text. The issue is well stated by Eugene Merrill in his critique of C.S. Cowles' spiritualized reading: "In effect, ordinary historical-grammatical exegesis of the Old Testament must be suspended where offensive texts are concerned. If they fall short of our perception as to God's love, they must be radically reinterpreted. *Such subjectivism of method is most disquieting and dangerous.*"[361]

Nor are these concerns new. While the fourth century theologian Basil of Caesarea was a fan of much of Origen's work, he remained skeptical of Origen's spiritualization of the text. In the following passage he offers a rather dry critique of Origen's treatment of the doctrine of creation, in particular: "I know the laws of allegory, though less by myself than from the works of others. There are those truly, who do not admit the common sense of the Scriptures, for whom water is not water, but some other nature, who see in a plant, in a fish, what their fancy wishes . . . . For me grass is grass or plant, fish, wild beast, domestic animal, I take all in the literal sense."[362] Read between the lines

---

[361] Merrill, "A Response to C.S. Cowles," *Show Them No Mercy: 4 Views on God and Canaanite Genocide*, 50, emphasis added.

[362] Cited in Franke, "Introduction to Joshua Through 2 Samuel," xxiv.

and one may see a penetrating critique of spiritualization: the plain meaning threatens to be obscured by unmoored speculation.

There is a significant problem here and I'll say more about it in a moment. However, it is also important to keep matters in perspective. And in my estimation, the spiritualization of genocide is not half as disquieting and dangerous as the Genocide Apologists' spirited defense of the literal sense. In my view, we should always counterbalance concerns about spiritualizing with the significant concern of *failing* to address the violence of the text. Allow me to give an illustration. Some years ago in a debate with an atheist, conservative American talk show host Dennis Prager posed the following question: "If you were in a dark alley in South Central Los Angeles and saw 10 young men walking toward you, would you be more at ease if you knew the men had just come from a Bible study?"[363] Setting aside the racist overtones of Prager's scenario (about 90% of South Central Los Angeles is black or Latino), the next question I'd want to ask is this: *what kind of Bible study?* If those ten young men were studying the Good Samaritan then yeah, I'd be relieved. But what if they were studying Joshua as a potential model to prepare for future 'biblical' warfare against an ill-defind group of latter day 'Canaanites'? In that case, I don't think I'd be at ease at all: quite the opposite, in fact. (And lest you are inclined to dismiss the whole scenario as fantastical, I would admonish you to consider how often Christians in history have managed to justify atrocities by labeling people in their own day as new 'Canaanites' or 'Amalekites.')

So I am quite serious when I say that I really do find the Genocide Apologists' style of argument more disquieting than the sometimes wooly hermeneutics of the Spiritualizers. As we have seen, when Joshua *was* widely spiritualized the book was not invoked to justify violent war against others. But when it was historicized again, it quickly provided a pretext to justify

---

363 Cited in Paul A. Elwell, *The Search for Truth* (iUniverse, 2010), 23.

the eradication of outgroups like the Irish and the American Indian. These are *real dangers*. And we would be foolhardy to think that we have now somehow past a point in history where we are no longer prone to those same tendencies to otherize and dehumanize that corrupted the witness of many Christians before us. Consequently, we should recognize those readings as potentially incendiary and we should seek to bar the door to them at all cost. So the risk of doing nothing is itself significant.

But while I believe that the Genocide Apologist has a *more disturbing position,* that in itself cannot be taken as grounds to nullify the subjectivism concern with the Spiritualizers' hermeneutics. This approach does appear to lack controls to identify meanings, resulting in something that looks to critics a lot like eisegetical subjective free association. And so, the spiritualization position will be significantly stronger if this concern can be addressed.

We can illustrate how problematic this kind of apparent free association unmoored to historical-grammatical exegesis can be by considering how it looks when the spiritual associations are invoked in favor of non-Christian theological assumptions. As an example, consider how LDS theologians appear to adopt a similar method of free symbolic association to make the claim that Ezekiel 37 miraculously predicts the future revelation of the Book of Mormon. This is how LDS interpreters Eric Shuster and Charles Sale explain it:

> Ezekiel foretells of the stick of Judah (the Bible) and the stick of Ephraim (the Book of Mormon) coming together to become "one stick" or "one in thine hand" (Ezekiel 37:15-20). The joining of these two records to validate each other accomplishes the Lord's law of two witnesses (Matthew 18:16; 2 Corinthians 13:1)—the Bible witnessing for the Book of Mormon and the Book of Mormon witnessing for the Bible.[364]

---

364 Eric Shuster and Charles Sale, *The Biblical Roots of Mormonism* (CFI, 2010), 83.

LDS theologians may think that Ezekiel 37 constitutes a powerful prophecy confirming the Book of Mormon, but you can bet that few if any Christian (or Jewish) theologians will find their exegesis compelling. On the contrary, they will likely dismiss this reading as a bald projection on the text. To be sure, the Mormon is free to appeal to Ezekiel 37 as a prophecy of the Book of Mormon if she likes, but she should not expect those who do not already accept her hermeneutic to find this to be a plausible reading.

Needless to say, the same hurdle is faced by attempts to spiritualize the divine directives of Deuteronomy 7 and 20 and the narrative of Joshua. The Canaanites represent sinful impulses that must be eradicated? The five kings slaughtered represents the five senses that must be sanctified? Who decides such things? Isn't this all simply driven by the subjective whim of the Christian interpreter?

While there certainly is a problem here, we should at least keep in mind that spiritualizers like Origen and Gregory of Nyssa did not simply propose their interpretations out of whole cloth. Rather, they reasoned stepwise to their particular readings by way of several methodological considerations including the morally problematic nature of the literal sense and its incompatibility with the life and teaching of Jesus and the love of God and neighbor. From their perspective, at least, they believe the consideration of all the relevant information led them to this plenary interpretation.

That said, it does seem to me that the Patristic Spiritualizers generally lack a method which is sufficiently linked to the text to justify their spiritual renderings. However, that does not mean the spiritualization project is lost. There are other ways to finding a symbolic, spiritually sanctifying meaning in the text, and these readings are less susceptible to the free association charge. At this point, we will turn to consider some key themes that emerge from interpreters that I view as New Spiritualizers including Jerome Creach and Douglas Earl.

The New Spiritualizers

While the spiritualization approach has been widely criticized for centuries, there are a few voices in our day advocating what I would call a neo-spiritualization of the text. In this section we will survey some of the approaches of the New Spiritualizers. These individuals are aware of the fact that allegorization appears to lack sufficient hermeneutical controls. And so, they seek deeper spiritual meanings by reasoning their views carefully from internal clues within the text.

In his book *Violence in Scripture* Jerome Creach explores a spiritual reading of the Canaanite conquest which is driven by recognition of the moral problematic presented by the literal meaning of the text. Creach's approach explores the familiar theme that the texts are calling the reader to total devotion to Yahweh while eschewing commitment to the things of this world. Within that context, the language of *herem* represents the need to consecrate a people wholly for the Lord. Think, by comparison, of a critical admonition in a passage like 1 John 2:15-16 where we are called to love not the world or to allow ourselves to be taken by the diversions of this life. In like manner, Israel was called to radical love of God and faithfulness to his call and so are we.

The problem, of course, is that this total devotion is presented in narrative terms that describe the actual destruction of people and their culture. So what more can be said to illumine that problem? To begin with, Creach points out that the texts are not contemporaneous accounts of destruction but rather were written centuries after the events they describe, at a time when the Canaanites were no longer a distinct people in the land. In his view, the texts were initially written around the time King Josiah led his religious reforms (c. 620s BCE), with the texts reaching final form only after the Babylonian destruction (587/6 BCE). In other words, the narrative was first composed and read at a time when Israel was "incapable of any such military or violent activity."³⁶⁵

This context is important because it means that the original audience hearing of this call to total fidelity was not a community reveling in recent military success but rather an oppressed and beleaguered people struggling with a way to maintain their own integrity and distinctiveness in the midst of exile: "the story of Israel's sweeping conquest of Canaan was told by people who themselves had no land and who were powerless before the great empires of their day."³⁶⁶ That fact should shape the way that we read the story by allowing us to see it not in terms of military conquest but rather as a spiritual call for faithfulness in exile.³⁶⁷ In this way, we can begin to read the text not as a triumphal narrative of destruction but rather as "a metaphor for complete devotion to God."³⁶⁸

From this perspective, the directives of Deuteronomy 7:2-5 and 20:10-18 take on a very different significance. Creach points out that the command of Deuteronomy 7:2-5 follows the Shema's call to love God completely (6:5) and is followed by a call not to intermarry. This instruction underscores the theme of faithful living as a minority community in (Babylonian) exile.³⁶⁹ Walter Brueggemann makes a similar point when he observes that the fact that the seven peoples targeted for destruction in 7:2 had long since disappeared by the time this passage was composed suggests that "the list of seven nations is an archaic slogan that represents, in context, any alien culture with its religious temptations for Israel."³⁷⁰ Likewise, the language of Deuteronomy 20:10-18 should be read primarily as a call for

---

365 Creach, *Violence in Scripture*, 98.

366 Creach, *Violence in Scripture*, 113.

367 Creach, *Violence in Scripture*, 115.

368 Creach, *Violence in Scripture*, 99, cf. 105.

369 Creach, *Violence in Scripture*, 108.

370 Brueggemann, *Deuteronomy*, 94.

spiritual distinction written to a people who are a threatened minority.[371]

As we read the narrative of the conquest itself, we should note that Joshua seems to be based on the portrait of King Josiah in passages like 2 Kings 23. These parallels provide a clue that the message is a non-literal description of complete devotion to Yahweh: "the language must be read as figurative, as an emblem of something higher and nobler, however reprehensible the background of the figure might be."[372] In addition, a close reading suggests internal clues in the narrative which offer a critique of the violence in the text.[373] For example, Joshua 8:35 suggestively refers to foreigners living among the Israelites.

The sharp ingroup/outgroup boundaries are further undermined by the fact that a Canaanite, Rahab, plays a key role and is presented as resourceful and wise. Creach points out both that Rahab was considered to have become the wife of Joshua in Rabbinic tradition and she is named as an ancestor of Jesus in Matthew 1:5.[374] Douglas Earl argues that the narrative intentionally juxtaposes Achan to Rahab in a way that subtly marginalizes ingroup/outgroup boundaries. While Rahab is the outsider who is vindicated and is included in the ingroup, Achan is an insider who is expelled to the outgroup. According to Earl, the extreme nature of the *herem* is required by the rhetorical form of the narrative in order to highlight the extent to which the standard ingroup/outgroup boundaries are actually being subverted:

> if it was not extreme then the stories of Rahab (Josh. 2) and of Achan (Josh. 7), whose story the tale of Jericho introduces, would not work. If the destruction of Jericho was not total, then Rahab might have got lucky and been one of the survivors.

---

371 Creach, *Violence in Scripture*, 109.
372 Creach, *Violence in Scripture*, 107.
373 See Seibert, *The Violence of Scripture*, chapter 7.
374 Creach, *Violence in Scripture*, 121.

> She might have lived through good fortune rather than as a result of the oath made. Moreover, if plunder could be taken then Achan would not be guilty of taking some of the plunder in disobedience to the command given (Josh. 6:18)—he, and many others would have been fortunate in being able to obtain great riches from the spoils of war.[375]

Thus, on Earl's view, the stark absolutes of the *herem* ironically serve to highlight the themes of grace and inclusion and to break down simplistic ingroup/outgroup distinctions.[376]

Of course, Rahab is not the only outsider who is brought into the group. The Gibeonites, one of the groups fated to destruction, also find their way into Israel's covenant. While some critics of this reading may retort that the trickery and deception they use is hardly laudatory, one could actually read it positively as an echo of Jacob the trickster from whom Israel receives their name. Creach goes further, arguing that the Gibeonites' resourcefulness exhibits a "covenant desire" that contrasts favorably with the Israelites who have taken their covenant status for granted. In this way, the singular contrast of Rahab/Achan now assumes a corporate contrast in the Israelites/Gibeonites and in both cases the ingroup/outgroup contrast is being subverted.[377] To sum up, both Rahab and the Gibeonites are viewed positively in the narrative as resourceful people who recognize the authority and power of Yahweh and desire to be part of the covenant. From that perspective, one might read this entire narrative as an elaborate exploration of themes reminiscent of Jesus' haunting parable of the Sheep and Goats in Matthew 25:31-46: many who believe they are sheep will find they are goats while many who are thought to be goats will find themselves to be sheep. So be

---

375 Earl, *The Joshua Delusion*, 73.

376 Many traditional conservative scholars have likewise noted these themes. See for example, Timmer, "Joshua," 167-8.

377 Creach, *Violence in Scripture*, 121.

on guard to ensure your faithfulness in exile while recognizing that you are not as unique and righteous as you might think.

The New Spiritualizers offer some suggestive ways of reading and processing the problematic violence in the text. As I conclude this section I will summarize what seem to me to be their most important points.

- First, the text should be read as the historical product of a marginalized, exiled minority group who are struggling to maintain their distinctiveness and faithfulness to the God of Israel in the presence of a hostile superior power. In that context, the meaning of *herem* to that beleaguered minority shifts from a focus on violent military conflict to that of maintaining covenant fidelity in a hostile land.
- Second, the conquest itself is presented as definitively God's doing. Thus, it doesn't provide a pretext for military engagement but rather a call to recognize Yahweh's supremacy in all things. Somewhat ironically, this fact should orient the attentive reader toward *non-violence* for the battle is the Lord's to fight (cf. Psalm 46:10) while the community's responsibility is to remain faithful to the call of purity.[378]
- Third, the absoluteness of the *herem* also functions to highlight the way that outsiders can be brought in by grace (Rahab; the Gibeonites) and the extent to which insiders can be turned out (Achan). This lesson, in turn, should prompt us all toward vigilance as we seek to introspect our own lives: "certainty of one's own righteousness is really the opposite of righteousness. Only those who approach God in humility as these Canaanites did, will find God's favor."[379]

When we read the text from this perspective, we have not a pretext for violence, a justification for triumphalism, or a precedent

---

378 Creach, *Violence in Scripture*, 123.

379 Creach, *Violence in Scripture*, 123.

to demonize outsiders. Rather, we have a sober warning about our own lack of spiritual awareness and holiness and a call to recognize holiness in the outsider to our community even as we seek to address spiritual waywardness from within our ranks.

Critiquing the New Spiritualizers

The New Spiritualizers offer a far more modest approach to the text than the heavily allegorical flights of fancy to be found in the Patristic Spiritualizers. As a result, this modesty also looks far more plausible.[380] While Origen often seems merely to be projecting meaning onto the text in an uncontrolled free association, the New Spiritualizers pay detailed attention to the text, its historical origin, and the conditions and perspectives of the original audience. And from that perspective, they undoubtedly highlight some very important themes. There is no doubt that the prominent status of Rahab (and to a lesser extent, the Gibeonites) both in the narrative and the subsequent Jewish and Christian tradition can be viewed as a tantalizing subversion of othering. By the same token, the exclusion of Achan is a sober reminder of the tenuous nature of ingroup membership which should prompt humility and introspection. And reading the entire text from a perspective of an oppressed minority rather than a triumphal military power definitely changes the overall context and implicature.

While this is all much to be admired, arguably the main problem with the New Spiritualizers is that their proposal is simply too modest and does not go far enough to address and neutralize the violence of the text. Creach says that the message must be

---

[380] If I may indulge in a baseball analogy, Origen swings for the fences and strikes out while the New Spiritualizers are content to bunt, but at least they get on base.

interpreted as "higher and nobler, however reprehensible the background of the figure might be." But we still need a more direct treatment of the fact that so much of that background is indeed *reprehensible*. We can put it this way: one could readily envision all manner of non-violent stories and images which could drive home the important lessons of covenant fidelity, personal introspection, and the call for faithfulness in a foreign and hostile land without invoking a brutally violent narrative of conquest which is prone to misinterpretation. So why communicate these very important truths in this extremely violent and deeply ironic way?

Perhaps most disturbing is the fact that the text is, on this reading, utilizing extreme violence in such an extraordinarily subtle manner. It would be one thing if the text was read in a morally problematic way only by casual lay readers unfamiliar with the nuances of the text. Think, for example of the benighted reader of *Animal Farm* who reads the story as a fantastical tale of animals rebelling against their human overlords because nobody ever explained the text as an allegory of the Russian Revolution. But once the deeper reading is explained everyone can see that this is *obviously* the deeper meaning: there just is no dispute about the real point of *Animal Farm*.

The fact is, however, that no such consensus has emerged on the deeper spiritual meaning of the Canaanite conquest and even expert interpreters are notoriously divided in how to interpret these chapters. As Creach observes, "That some very fine biblical scholars read Deuteronomy 7:2 as a clear command to slaughter people is evidence enough that even more lay readers will take it the same way."[381] Indeed. So why would God communicate such an important message in a way so prone to misunderstanding?[382]

---

381 Creach, *Violence in Scripture,* 111-12.

382 We shall return to this question squarely in chapter 12 as the problem of miscommunication.

From my perspective, the somewhat strained nature of this reading actually highlights the extent to which moral intuitions play a tacit role in our Bible reading and application. I am not threatened or disturbed by the extent to which these readings appear strained. In fact, I think it is a noble and beautiful thing that careful Christian readers expend effort to interpret these difficult texts in a way consistent with their moral intuitions and theological convictions This leads us back to the Sherlock Holmes principle: "when you have eliminated the impossible, whatever remains, however improbable, must be the truth." While we might wish that these spiritual readings were clearer, it could be that when all the evidence is amassed they nonetheless remain the best option given one's total data set and background interpretive assumptions.

However, it still seems very implausible to claim that God could not have communicated these enlightened spiritual truths about covenant faithfulness and the tenuous nature of ingroup boundaries in a way that wasn't prone to misunderstanding and written against the backdrop of extraordinary violence. As James Barr trenchantly observes: "The problem is not whether the narratives are fact or fiction, the problem is that, whether fact or fiction, the ritual destruction is *commended*."[383] In short, the morality of the reader seems to demand something more from us than reading the text for the plenary sense that is consistent with the life of Jesus and the love of God and neighbor. It further requires us to read in such a way that the literal sense itself with all its moral ugliness, becomes part of the divine witness to us. And that brings us to our final position.

---

383 Cited in Seibert, *The Violence of Scripture*, 98.

11

The Providential Errantists

We began our exploration of the Spiritualizers in chapter 10 with a test case based on one of the darkest verses in the entire Bible: "Happy is the one who seizes your infants and dashes them against the rocks." (Psalm 137:9) The psalm presents us with a rather bald problem: how could anyone wish something so vicious, vile, and cruel? This verse provided a capsule test case to explore one response from a famous Oxbridge don. As we saw, C.S. Lewis's proposed solution was a spiritual reading in which we may think of the 'infant' in the terms of sinful impulses: and of course, it is perfectly okay to bash *sinful impulses* against the proverbial rocks.

While Lewis offers us one way to think about the psalm, his proposed plenary meaning reveals significant weaknesses in the spiritualization option. To begin with, at the spiritual level the metaphor of infant bludgeoning to convey sanctification is clearly morally problematic no less than the spiritualization of another heinous act like rape. Further, in terms of the literal sense, it does appear that the human author is expressing a morally abhorrent wish which requires a more direct critique and censure from the reader.

When we scaled up this approach to the Canaanite conquest, the same problems appeared. We were encouraged to read the stark binary contrast between the divinely chosen Israelites and the corrupt, irredeemable resident nations from the perspective of a beleaguered minority exploring the meaning of fidelity in exile. While that certainly illumined the text from a more sympathetic perspective, it provided little by way of direct critical engagement with the decision to explore this call to fidelity in the terms of a narrative of genocidal annihilation. As with the imprecatory psalm, the Canaanite conquest forces us to consider the moral status of the text and the writers that composed it. If the psalmist's description evinces a morally problematic, incendiary hatred of Babylonian oppressors, the texts of the Canaanite conquest do likewise, albeit under the guise of the Canaanites of yesteryear. Once again, the text seems to demand more by way of a moral response from the reader. Unfortunately, the spiritualizing of the text does not offer a direct critical output for that type of engagement.

The resources for that moral critique are found in our final position, that of the Providential Errantist. The Providential Errantist is not necessarily opposed to the spiritualization of the text: indeed, the analysis of New Spiritualizers in terms of illumining the context and significance of the text provides many insights worthy of consideration. Instead, the Providential Errantist seeks to build on and supplement the insights of spiritualization by insisting on the importance of supplementing those insights with a clear and decisive critique of morally problematic aspects of the text. John Mansford Prior states the impulse that gives rise to the position: "In *Joshua* the genocide is ordered by God. The only reading that makes sense to me is that divinely sanctioned violence is a misguided manipulation of religion irreconcilable with faith in the Abba of Joshua the Nazarene."[384] Note the difference here with spiritualization. Prior

---

384 Prior, "'Power' and 'the Other' in *Joshua:* The Brutal Birthing of a Group

is not simply proposing that we can find a laudatory spiritual meaning to make sense of the violence. He is insisting that we also need to identify the literal sense of portions of the text as *misguided*, as *morally errant*, as *wrong*; we need to recognize that they are inconsistent with the life and teachings of Jesus, and that they need to be read from that critical stance.

Some people might erroneously assume that the Providential Errantist is thereby proposing a redrawing of the boundaries of canon or a qualification of levels of inspiration. But that is quite emphatically not the claim. We must keep in mind that we begin with a commitment to the Perfect God Principle and the Canon Principle. Just as we can reasonably conclude that *The Shining* has no genuine continuity errors that weren't intended by the director, so we can most definitely conclude that the Bible has no moral errors present in the voice of the human author which were not purposed as part of the canonical text by the divine author. The question before us, and that which involves the Providential Errantist, concerns the matter of *why* God providentially included these specific errors in the text. Yes, we can understand how the meaning of a Canaanite conquest changes when we interpret it as the story of a people grappling with covenant fidelity in exile. But the overall narrative itself is still profoundly problematic. Why not instead explore covenant fidelity with the image of a disciple praying daily in his window despite the social power and threats of those around him (e.g. Daniel 6)? Why express these various themes instead through a narrative of *genocide*? What is God doing with these passages?

In this chapter, we will explore the possibilities with the Providential Errantist's analysis of moral error within the text. We will begin with a return to Psalm 137 to outline a fuller approach which scales up from two elements: identification and transformation. It begins with a sympathetic identification with the wicked or immoral beliefs, actions, and/or impulses of the author/characters precisely because one important challenge may be to find *ourselves* in these troubling passages. Next, it considers the call to transformation in Christ when these passages are read in canonical perspective. After that, we shall explore ways to apply that template to the Canaanite conquest beginning with Greg Boyd's claim in *The Crucifixion of the Warrior God* that God accommodated to the Israelites' false view of their Lord as a violent warrior. We will then conclude the chapter with Eric Seibert's invitation to explore a sympathetic reading *with* the Canaanites.

However, before we get to all that, the very first thing we must do is to devote some time to framing the Providential Errantist's engagement with the text firmly within Israel's prophetic tradition of wrestling with God.

A Text of Prophetic Engagement

The film *Last Flag Flying* tells the story of a Vietnam vet named Larry (Steve Carrell) who is going to retrieve the body of his son who died fighting in Iraq. Along the way, he picks up two friends, fellow vets, including the Reverend Richard (Laurence Fishburne) and hard-bitten Sal (Bryan Cranston). At one point, the Reverend and Sal get into an argument over God's responsibility for the evil in the world. As you can imagine, the Reverend takes the pious high road of defending God. Sal, meanwhile, boldly insists that he would call the creator to account if given the chance:

> I reckon that I would take the opportunity to stand at attention and say to God, "Hey, where were you when they were raping children and the genocide and all that? Where were you when they flew planes into the buildings and killed thousands of people who were just going to work? Where were you when

Doc's kid was just buying Cokes for his buddies and a raghead come up and shoot his face off? Huh? Where were you?" And you see, I'm not going to stand there and try to explain myself to him. I'm going to make God explain *himself*, ah *yeah*. And I think that by the end of it he'll say "Hey come on, get in here. You! You're my kind of dude. Gimme one of these!"[385]

There are many Christians who would be shocked and appalled at Sal's monologue. They would censure it as inexcusably flippant if not outright sacrilegious. But Sal clearly thinks otherwise: indeed, he actually suggests that God might *approve* of his fearless inquisition. So who is right?

Many Christians will be surprised to learn just how much there is to be said for Sal's perspective. The fact is that his willingness to question and challenge God comports with a surprisingly common theme in Scripture, one which is regularly found among those who are most intimately related to God. This striking stance is evident in Abraham's determination to argue with God over whether Sodom should be destroyed (Genesis 18:23-24). It is present in Moses boldly holding God to the covenant he made with his people (Exodus 32:9-14). One finds it in Job who demands an explanation for his suffering; despite the directness of his complaint and his demand that God be called to give an account, Job is ultimately found to be the only person in the whole conversation who spoke truth about God. What is especially ironic here is that God spends chapters 38-41 giving Job a truly cosmic tongue-lashing, and yet at the end of it all he turns to address Eliphaz the Temanite and he says, "I am angry with you and your two friends, because *you have not spoken the truth about me, as my servant Job has*" (Job 42:7). If I may borrow a line from Sal, it's almost as if God is saying,

---

[385] *Last Flag Flying*, directed by Richard Linklater, Amazon Studies, 2017. By the way, Sal's use of the racist and xenophobic term 'raghead' is indefensible, but that doesn't diminish the important truth in his overall stance.

"Hey Job, come on, get in here. You! You're my kind of dude. Gimme one of these!" And let us not forget the psalmist who is never afraid to share the full gamut of emotions. Doubts, questions, frustration, disappointment, nothing is off the table, it's all there: "Why, O LORD, do you stand far away? Why do you hide yourself in times of trouble?" (10:1) "Why have you forgotten me?" (42:9) "Why do you forget our affliction and oppression?" (44:24) Notably, there is no evidence that God is offended by these pained and gritty questions. Rather, they are an integral part of the full human experience of the psalmist. And they have been an integral part of the spiritual journey of untold numbers of readers ever since.

When you add it all up, you could well conclude that Sal just might be right after all. God seems to welcome those who are not afraid to question and challenge. You might even say the one who honestly questions the text and boldly seeks answers is indeed God's kind of dude. But this is not simply a matter where the reader is an observer to the whole story. Abraham, Moses, Job, the Psalmist, and the rest are all exemplars along with Jacob of what it means to be *true Israel* as those who boldly struggle with God (Genesis 32:22-32). And insofar as the reader desires to join that discussion, he or she is welcomed in to that same pious struggle with the divine voice in the text.

Is it any wonder then if it should turn out that the Bible itself is actually *designed* to provide ample opportunity for the reader to engage critically with the text by identifying and critiquing providentially morally errant perspectives which are illumined as such in light of the model of Christ? Indeed, it seems to me that this is *precisely* the kind of feature that we should expect from a book designed to engage and thereby form readers into true disciples of Christ, people of Israel who are *defined* as those who wrestle with God. That is, we should expect that a text written to form a people who are defined as those who wrestle with God will provide occasion for precisely that kind of wrestling in the reader.

As with the alleged continuity errors in *The Shining* or the alleged grammatical errors in *Ulysses*, these are not in fact errors at all from the divine perspective. And so, the Providential Errantists invite us to read the text attentive to the distinctions illumined by the Spirititualizers but also ready to go further as need be in illumining, critiquing, and learning from the errors providentially included within Scripture. Bible reading is not like a church service you merely observe but rather one in which you are expected to participate.

From this perspective, the refusal to engage with a moral critique of the text is not a sign of a deep piety and submission, but rather a failure to seek a more holistic, honest, and potentially transformative engagement. It could reflect a failure to read in the tradition of Israel, as one who honestly *wrestles* with God. What if the spiritual formation of the reader into being a disciple of Christ is brought about precisely as they engage critically with troubling moral content? What if the reader is formed into Christ as they critically engage with cruel and brutal Torah punishments? What if the reader is expected to recognize the immorality of the modes of corporal punishment so enthusiastically embraced by many biblical authors, to question the adequacy of accommodating to an institution of slavery, to explore the ubiquity of patriarchal language, and to speak with a fierce prophetic indictment on behalf of the forgotten and demonized Canaanite? What if, in those moments, the reader is not abandoning piety? What if they are instead daring to assume the mantle of Abraham, Moses, Job, and the Psalmist? What if the reader is expected to wrestle with the text as Jacob wrestled with the angel? What might that wrestling look like as the reader seeks to wrest the meaning from texts that are *meant* to invite precisely an engaged moral critique from the reader? What if engaging providential errors in the text which can form us is precisely the kind of reading that makes us God's kind of dude?

Progressive Revelation and Accommodation

Two very well established concepts provide an important framework for Providential Errancy: progressive revelation and accommodation. According to progressive revelation, God gradually reveals theological truths over time. For example, the ancient Israelites originally thought of God in a monolatristic and henotheistic context, and then gradually moved to monotheism. After the New Testament, the church eventually moved toward a fully articulated *Trinitarian* monotheism. Progressive revelation is also clearly evident in ethical understanding for there can be no question but that by fulfilling the meaning of the Law, Jesus also offered correctives as to how the Law was to be understood.

As for the notion of accommodation, a concept to which we've already devoted significant attention, it may be viewed as the handmaiden of progressive revelation, the means by which God gradually reveals a fuller understanding of his nature (theology) and will (ethics). As we noted above, God accommodates to limited human understanding in several areas including history, science, ethics, and theology. Thus, divine accommodation involves the fact that God meets limited human creatures in our present understanding in order to bring us to a fuller understanding. It involves a divine condescension to the horizons of the reader to the end of achieving greater understanding, and that may involve God accommodating to various degrees of misunderstanding or false belief in the audience.

Needless to say, these are essential concepts when we are seeking to understand the ethical problems of the Canaanite conquest. In his article on 'Conquest' in the *Dictionary of Scripture and Ethics*, L. Daniel Hawk observes that with the rise of historical biblical criticism "the conquest traditions could then be understood as an early and primitive expression of Israel's religious thought in contrast to the more mature sentiments of peace and mercy reflected in later texts."[386] In other words, God allowed people to understand and relate to him in comparatively 'primitive' terms but he did so to the end of bringing people ultimately to a more fulsome, appropriate understanding. As Hawk explains,

> the idea [is] that God entered ancient Israel's experience at the level of its own understanding and then gradually led the nation to a higher spiritual and moral vision. Here again, the conquest materials could be understood as reflecting an early, more "worldly" vision that, although a necessary first step, faded in relevance as God revealed a more excellent way during the history of Israel's life as a people.[387]

Hawk concludes, "God had to enter and identify with a violent world in order to establish the basic understanding of human dignity that would form the foundation for more refined ethical sensibilities."[388] Hawk provides a clear outline of the basic proposal according to which God providentially accommodated to an errant understanding in order to move people gradually beyond that understanding.

Christopher Wright picks up this theme when he suggests that God may have accommodated to the ancient Near Eastern standards of warfare including the practice of slaughtering civilians indiscriminately:

> Is it possible (and as I say, I am not convinced I can answer this one way or the other to my own satisfaction), that in a fallen world where struggle for land involves war, and if the only kind of war at the time was the kind described in the Old

---

[386] L. Daniel Hawk, "Conquest," *Dictionary of Scripture and Ethics,* ed. Joel B. Green (Baker, 2011), 166.

[387] Hawk, "Conquest," 166.

[388] Hawk, "Conquest," 166.

Testament texts, this was the way it had to be if the land-gift promise was to be fulfilled in due course? If anything along these lines can be entertained—that is to say, if *herem*-style warfare can be even contemplated in the same moral framework as slavery and divorce (and many might reject the thought outright)—then we might be dealing with something God chose to accommodate within the context of a wicked world, not something that represented this best will or preference.[389]

There are at least two ways to interpret Wright's proposal and since I lack imagination, I'll just refer to them as the weak and strong interpretations. On the weak interpretation, Wright would be proposing that while God did indeed command the genocidal eradication of a people, he did so not because it reflected his perfect will but only because it was the very imperfect practice of warfare current in that day and, for whatever reason, it would not have been practical relative to God's ends to challenge that approach to war at that time.

It seems to me that there are at least two very significant objections to the weak interpretation. The first objection brings us back to divine omnipotence. What are we to make of the claim that an omnipotent God was simply *unable* to reveal his will for the Israelites apart from allowing them to think in the categories of standard ancient Near Eastern war practices, practices that included actions we today recognize as grossly immoral and baldly genocidal? This seems utterly implausible to me. After all, Jesus fundamentally challenged assumptions in his day. When the Jews interpreted the Messiah in deeply errant terms of secular political power, Jesus didn't allow them to believe such false notions. Instead, he challenged them, insisting that his kingdom is not of this world (John 18:36). (Needless to say, Jesus challenged many other assumptions as well such

---

[389] Wright, *The God I Don't Understand: Reflections on Tough Questions of Faith* (Zondervan, 2008), 89, emphasis in original.

as beliefs about righteousness, purity, and the boundaries of the Kingdom of God.) If an omnipotent God was perfectly able to challenge errant assumptions about messiahship and much else, why should we believe he was unable to challenge entrenched errant assumptions about war and national purity of an earlier time?

Second, this position faces a slippery slope objection: if God could command an evil like genocide simply because it was a common practice of war at a particular time in history, then what other common moral horrors of war could he accommodate on similar grounds? For example, rape and cannibalism have often been practices of warfare at various points in history.[390] Does that mean that it is possible that God could accommodate to those practices by *commanding* soldiers to rape and cannibalize defeated foes if he decided to reveal himself at a time when *those* practices were commonplace? Surely not! But if we say no, why should we think that God could accommodate *genocide* in this way? After all, as horrific as rape and cannibalism are, I see no reason to think they are somehow categorically *worse* than genocide.[391] Indeed, it turns out that this may not be a slippery slope after all: if rape and cannibalism are *not* worse than genocide then this interpretation *starts out* at the bottom of the slope. In other words, if this proposal is not vulnerable to a *reductio ad absurdum* that is only because it has already been reductio'd!

This brings me to the strong interpretation. On this reading, Wright is flatly denying that God ever commanded these actions at all. Rather, on this interpretation God allowed the Israelites to form the *false belief* that he had commanded this, and this accommodation to errant belief constituted part of his overall trajectory of incremental revelation much in the way suggested

---

[390] For example, in *Hidden Horrors: Japanese War Crimes in World War II* (Routledge, 2018), chapters 3, 4, Yuki Tanaka documents evidence of systematic rape and cannibalism carried out by Japanese soldiers in WWII.

[391] Indeed, as I noted earlier, rape is a standard *component* of genocide.

by Hawk. This seems to me to be a significant improvement and it moves us into the sphere of Providential Errancy. However, no proposal is without cost, and this one does invite the question: why would God allow the Israelites to believe wrongly about a matter so important?[392]

Identification and Transformation in a Cursing Psalm

The best way to appreciate the strength of Providential Errancy is by considering a specific case where error may serve our overall moral formation in critical engagement with the text. With that in mind, let's return to the infamous Psalm 137 with the starting point that the psalmist's desire to destroy the infants of his enemy is morally irredeemable and thus that spiritualizing the infants as wicked impulses is insufficient to resolve the problem. Given that fact, what more can be said of the psalm?

Before we engage in a critical stance *against* the voice of the author we need to consider a stance *with* the author by way of identification. Why? Because a good reader must begin in empathy. We need to invest the time to understand as well as we can what the author says and *why* he says it. To understand the emotional space of the original hearers, we should try to enter into the same anguish as the embittered author (and original audience) of Psalm 137 who is facing unimaginable misery and hopelessness in Babylonian exile. Yehezkel Sama effectively

---

[392] Wright is thinking of God accommodating the Israelites as they invaded the land in Joshua. But, of course, the proposal is quite different and more tractable if one envisions God accommodating *accounts* of the Israelites invading the land which were compiled centuries after the purported events and which are largely, if not solely, non-historical.

captures the sense of anguish and loss that would have been experienced by these people:

> They all wept over the Babylonian exile. What is the reason? Because, as it is written, they had enjoyed the pleasures of kings: "the precious sons of Zion," etc. [Lamentations 4:2]. Now they were descending into exile with collars around their necks and their hands tied behind their backs. When they were in the Babylonian exile, they thought that they had no chance to exist in the world, for the Holy One [had] left them and would never watch over them.[393]

That sense of hopelessness and abandonment provides an invitation to understand the perspective of the psalmist in the pain experienced by his community. And that can, in turn, help us to cultivate sympathy and understanding for those who suffer in our midst and who may act out in inappropriate ways as a result.

In order to pursue that deeper engagement with the psalm, I will suggest that we begin with a true contemporary story of loss.[394] On September 27, 2015 a Ferrari driven by a man named Marco Muzzo crashed into a van driven by Gary Neville who was at the time out with his three grandchildren: Daniel (age 9), Harrison (age 5) and Milly (age 2). Neville and his three grandchildren perished in the crash but Muzzo was uninjured. Muzzo was subsequently convicted of drunk driving and sentenced to ten years in prison.

At Muzzo's sentencing, the grieving mother, Jennifer Neville-Lake, delivered a searing impact statement to the Court. As you can imagine, she did not hold back against the man who

---

393 Yehezkel Sama, "Toward Penitent Return and Restoration," *Wrestling with God: Jewish Theological Responses During and After the Holocaust*, ed. Steven T. Katz, Shlomo Biderman, Gershon Greenberg (Oxford University Press, 2007), 136.

394 This example is based on a discussion in *What's So Confusing About Grace?* chapter 21.

had killed her three precious children. These are her words to Muzzo: "I would not wish this horror I am living on anyone *but you. You deserve to know exactly what it feels like to have every single child you create meet someone like you.*"395 Think about that. With those blistering words, Neville-Lake says she wishes that this young man, Mr. Muzzo, could know what it is like to experience the loss of *his* children. In essence, she says that she hopes any children he may have in the future *would be killed* for the sole reason that Muzzo may suffer the anguish and unimaginable grief of their loss.396

From an ethical view, it must be said that Neville-Lake's victim impact statement, while not quite as graphic as the psalmist, nonetheless has the same horrific desired end: *dead children*. From that perspective, we can say that the wish is, in itself, inexcusably cruel and morally wrong, a wish that belongs in the same dark moral sphere as that of Psalm 137:9. How could you wish for *any* child to be killed as retribution against a parent no matter what their parent may have done?

At the same time, the determination to understand Neville-Lake's context, to perceive truly why she says what she says, that really does alter our evaluation of the situation. To be sure, heeding that context does not suddenly vindicate her words. But it does allow us to see that this ugly curse is the understandable heart cry of a grieving mother. And there is nothing wrong with a mother being honest in sharing her indescribable grief and anger, even when stated in this, the darkest of wishes.

---

395 "'I would not wish this horror on anyone but you,' Neville-Lake says to Muzzo at sentencing hearing," *CP24* (February 23, 2016) https://www.cp24.com/news/i-would-not-wish-this-horror-on-anyone-but-you-neville-lake-says-to-muzzo-at-sentencing-hearing-1.2788882?cache=ahlalmzxbysj, emphasis added.

396 Muzzo was granted full parole on February 9, 2021. See "Marco Muzzo, drunk driver who killed children and their grandfather in 2015 crash, granted full parole," CBC News (February 9, 2021), https://www.cbc.ca/news/canada/toronto/marco-muzzo-parole-board-hearing-february-2021-1.5906691

As important as a sympathetic reading is, it is incomplete unless we take the next step of moving toward a truly incarnate reflection. As the venerable old saying goes, *before you judge an Israelite, walk a mile in his sandals.* It is at this point that we move from sympathy, a shared understanding at a distance, to true *empathy* as we attempt to understand what it would be like from the perspective of the speaker or author. Have you ever had reason to hate someone the way that the psalmist hates his Babylonian oppressors or the way that Jennifer Neville-Lake hated Marco Muzzo? If so, you may find yourself in Psalm 137 as you empathetically reflect on those moments where you similarly experienced intense hatred. If you are fortunate enough to have *not* been exposed to the kinds of conditions that would give rise to such volcanic hatred, you at least owe it to the psalmist to attempt some imaginative reflection by considering how you *would* react in that situation. Had I been expelled from my home like the Israelites, or had I lost three children like Neville-Lake, I cannot begin to imagine how I might respond. Suffice it to say, I find I'm not in a place to judge their anguished responses.

As we reflect on the curse of the psalmist through the moral call to find sympathy of perspective with all parties in the narrative, we might find two things happening. First, we find a growing empathy as we identify with the conditions under which the psalmist uttered his enraged cry. And second, we find a disturbing realization that the rage of the psalmist resides in us as well. We too have the potential to lash out at others when offended against in the most terrible of ways. Had we experienced the unimaginable suffering of Jennifer Neville-Lake, what would we say at the sentencing of the man who killed our children? If our societies had been destroyed and we'd been sent into exile, how would we protest against our oppressors?

This is the beginning of the prophetic engagement with the text as we start to explore the ways that the psalm can critically engage the reader. But it is only the beginning. As we turn to read the psalm canonically we must do so through the life of

Jesus. Jesus did not call for us to hate our enemies but rather to love them and to pray for those who persecute us (Matthew 5:43-44). When Peter, in a bold attempt to be magnanimous, suggested that we forgive our enemies seven times (Matthew 18:21) Jesus responded by upping the bar considerably to *seventy-seven times* (18:22). In a case of allegorical speculation that would make Origen proud, Augustine argues that 77 represents the total number of possible sins. Why? He reasons that since 10 represents the Ten Commandments, it follows that 11 goes beyond God's commandments as a sinful violation of the divine law; and since 7 is the number of completion, we may conclude that $11 \times 7 = 77$ represents the total number of sins of all history. And so, Augustine concludes that Jesus asks us always to be ready to forgive any and every sin, no matter what it may be.[397] In other words, we should never stop forgiving.

While contemporary commentators may not agree on Augustine's allegorical journey, most are in full agreement with the destination: Jesus' call to forgiveness is radical and unlimited. For example, Grant Osborne argues that Jesus may be referring back to Lamech's "'seventy-seven'-fold vengeful spirit" (Genesis 4:24): "Lamech celebrated his vengeance; Jesus here abrogates it altogether."[398] According to McNeile, with these words, "The unlimited revenge of primitive man has given place to the unlimited forgiveness of Christians."[399] The lesson is indeed that Christian forgiveness should truly be without limit.

If ever a person had a basis in history to pray a curse on their enemies, it was surely Jesus on the cross. And yet, instead, in that decisive moment looking from his place of torment on

---

[397] Augustine also points out that 77 is the number of generations from Christ back to Adam in the Gospel of Luke. *The Works of St. Augustine:* Sermons. Volume III: Sermons 51-94. Trans. Edmund Hill, O.P. (New City Press, 1991), 384-5.

[398] Grant R. Osborne, *Matthew*, Exegetical Commentary on the New Testament, ed. Clinton E. Arnold (Zondervan, 2010), 693.

[399] Cited in Osborne, *Matthew*, 693.

the very religious leaders who had just called for his death, Jesus asked for them to be forgiven (Luke 23:34). And in this act, he models the radical call for forgiveness that we all face when encountering those who've wronged us, a forgiveness that we are then called to as we preach in his name to all nations (Luke 24:47).

It is one thing to speak in general terms about radical forgiveness, but it is quite another to imagine oneself being called to forgive in the most extreme of circumstances. I am reminded of a powerful story shared by Corrie ten Boom. She recalls how after the war she was speaking in 1947 about the importance of forgiveness when she recognized in the audience one of the soldiers who had tormented her at Ravensbruck concentration camp. To her dismay, that man came up to her after her speech, unaware that she was one of the thousands of prisoners from the camp in which he'd worked. With a warm smile, he shared that he had become a Christian since the war and had repented of his great sins and changed his life. And then came the request: this former Nazi, a man with untold crimes against humanity to his name, was now extending his hand and asking Ten Boom to grant him forgiveness for what he had done.

In his famous book *The Sunflower*, Simon Wiesenthal describes being in a similar situation, one in which he, a Jew who had suffered enormously from Nazi evil, was asked to hear the confession of a dying SS soldier. As he stood at the man's bedside, the Nazi felt the need to confess. He told a horrific story of throwing grenades into a Jewish house which set the structure ablaze. The soldier then recalled that he and his colleagues trained their rifles at the building, ready to shoot anyone who would attempt to escape. Choking in anguish, the Nazi then recalled: "Behind the windows of the second floor, I saw a man with a small child in his arms. His clothes were alight. By his side stood a woman, doubtless the mother of the child. With his free hand the man covered the child's eyes . . . then he jumped into the street. Seconds later the mother followed. Then from the windows fell burning bodies . . . We shot . . . Oh God!"[400] After recalling this horrifying vignette, no doubt selected from a much longer catalogue of additional moral horrors, this dying man then asked Wiesenthal to forgive him for his crimes. But Wiesenthal offered no reply: instead, he turned and left the room without saying a word. Still, he could never shake that image of the dying man and his pained request. Years later, Wiesenthal reflects, "Was my silence at the bedside of the dying Nazi right or wrong? This is a profound moral question that challenges the conscience of the reader of this episode, just as much as it once challenged my heart and my mind."[401]

Ten Boom was facing a similar situation. A man who had committed untold moral atrocities was now standing before her, requesting her forgiveness, a remission for even the most heinous of sins. Although Ten Boom had just been expostulating as a Christian in front of an audience on the crucial importance of forgiveness, now, in this moment, she was being asked to live out her own message and she didn't know how to respond:

> And still I stood there with the coldness clutching my heart. But forgiveness is not an emotion. . . . Forgiveness is an act of the will, and the will can function regardless of the temperature of the heart. ". . . Help!" I prayed silently. "I can lift my hand. I can do that much. You supply the feeling."
>
> And so woodenly, mechanically, I thrust my hand into the one stretched out to me. And as I did, an incredible thing took place. The current started in my shoulder, raced down my arm, sprang into our joined hands. And then this healing warmth seemed to flood my whole being, bringing tears to my eyes.
>
> "I forgive you, brother!" I cried. "With all my heart!"
>
> For a long moment we grasped each other's hands, the

---

[400] Simon Wiesenthal, *The Sunflower: On the Possibilities and Limits of Forgiveness* (Schocken Books, 1998), 42-3.

[401] Wiesenthal, *The Sunflower: On the Possibilities and Limits of Forgiveness*, 97.

former guard and the former prisoner. I had never known God's love so intensely as I did then.[402]

Ten Boom offers an important insight: forgiveness, like love, is not about a warm emotional feeling but rather about an *act of will*. Moreover, it was an exercise of will borne of *obligation*, a sense that she was called to forgive as she had been forgiven.

At this point, we now have a moral critique to bring back to the imprecatory psalmist. Though we have identified with his pain and anger, we also recognize that we cannot remain there. As Christians, we have an obligation to exercise our own wills and initiate a process of forgiveness. In some cases, that act may, in fact, be the journey of a lifetime, but we are nonetheless called to take the first step. And this is precisely the moment when the text invites the performative engagement of the prophetic reader who is willing to read from the perspective of Jesus and consider what that kind of radical forgiveness would look like when brought into the world of the imprecatory psalmist.

With that question in mind, we can consider another contemporary example of a terrible vehicular accident in which parents who suffered egregious loss responded in a very different way to Jennifer Neville-Lake. In this case, a young man named Chandler Gerber was driving down a country road in Pennsylvania texting his wife early in the morning. Suddenly, while he was looking down at his phone he heard a sickening crash. As his van came to a stop, two small bodies rolled off the roof of the vehicle and onto the highway. Gerber had slammed into the back of an Amish buggy killing three children and injuring four others.

A few weeks later, Gerber received a letter from the grieving Amish parents, Martin and Mary Schwartz. As you can imagine, Gerber expected to receive a letter of vitriol and rage, and rightly so: as with Jennifer Neville-Lake, who could possibly fault a

---

402 Cited in Amy-Jill Levine and Ben Witherington III, *The Gospel of Luke*, New Cambridge Bible Commentary (Cambridge University Press, 2018), 191.

parent for responding in anger and bitterness? But instead, the letter read as follows:

> Dear ones,
>
> Trusting in God's ways, how does this find you? Hope all in good health and in good cheer. Around here we're all on the go and try to make the best we can. I always wonder if we take enough time with our children. Wishing you the best with your little one and the unknown future. I think of you often. God is always there.
> Sincerely,
> Martin and Mary Schwartz.[403]

The lesson here is not simply that Neville-Lake offered the 'wrong' response while Martin and Mary Schwartz offered the 'right' response. On the contrary, the imprecatory psalmist shows that there is a place for the voice of Neville-Lake as part of the honest, raw grieving process. Those feelings are real, genuine, and should not be denied.

Nonetheless, the fact remains that when read within the canonical context of the life and teaching of Jesus, we cannot allow words of hate to be the *last* word. This extension of extraordinary forgiveness embodies the concept of grace—God's unmerited favor—that is at the heart of Jesus' teaching: our call to love and forgive others as we have been loved and forgiven: to refuse to forgive in perpetuity only serves to hurt ourselves and to mar our relationship with God and others.

Gerber recalls that after receiving the extraordinary gift of forgiveness from the Schwartzes, he adopted "Beauty from ashes" as his motto and since that day he has sought to speak out to various groups about the dangers of texting and driving.[404] We

---

[403] Cited in Ross Pomeroy, "The Power of Forgiveness," Big Think (August 27, 2013), https://bigthink.com/experts-corner/the-power-of-forgiveness

[404] Alec Grey, "Hoosier who caused fatal crash works to prevent others from

are called ultimately, as Ten Boom and the Schwartzes demonstrate, to move toward forgiveness of others as we, ourselves, have been forgiven. And a critical engagement with the Psalmist can be part of our process of coming to terms with that call. So, it turns out that Psalm 137 need not simply be spiritualized. Indeed, to read it in that manner threatens to lose some of the most profound insights the text offers us as we seek to identify with the suffering and rage of the psalmist and then, in Christ, be challenged to move beyond it.

Scaling Up Providential Errancy to the Conquest

In chapter 10, we saw that the method of spiritualizing the psalmist's curses can be scaled up to entire chapters and books of the Bible that include problematic moral content including the Canaanite conquest. How might we scale up an analysis of providential error vis-à-vis the textual depiction of Israel and the Canaanites?

The starting point should be obvious for it begins by humanizing the voices that cause us trouble and offense, attempting to understand matters from their perspective just as we engaged empathetically with the psalmist. Thus, we can begin to humanize the narrative by understanding the circumstances under which the psalm was written, appreciating that these are texts composed in the midst of pain, uncertainty, and anguish. Just as we commit to understanding Neville-Lake's curse and the psalmist's curse in context, so we should work to understand the entire conquest in the light of an anguished people considering faithfulness as they enter into exile. Then we can begin to understand their hatred

---

texting and driving," Indy Star (August 20, 2013), https://www.indystar.com/story/news/2013/08/20/hoosier-who-caused-fatal-crash-works-to-prevent-others-from-texting-and-driving/2679117/

of their oppressors much as Neville-Lake hated the drunk driver who killed her children or as Ten Boom hated the Nazi guard who so tormented her.

But if we must be honest about these feelings of hatred and rage, we should not stay there. Our journey toward redemptive reading should move us beyond this anger and hatred to reading these words in light of the forgiveness of Christ. We too are called to forgive as we have been forgiven. In order to take the hand of the Savior, you must first unclench your fist: forgiveness of others is essential to the forgiveness of oneself (Matthew 18:21-35).

The idea that the literal sense of the text sometimes includes errors not only of science and history but of morality and that any such moral errors which may exist are providentially included for the formation of the reader brings us to the position of the Providential Errantist: do not simply spiritualize morally errant views that emerge in the text; rather, critically engage with them, confident that they are included to form the faithful reader into a lover of God and neighbor.

The Crucifixion of the Warrior God

In my view, Greg Boyd has made the most significant contribution to the debate over biblical violence in recent decades. He commenced work on a book on the topic in the mid-2000s, initially from what appears to be the Just War Interpreter paradigm.[405] But gradually, Boyd came to recognize that this approach was unworkable and so he began again with a clean slate working from an Anabaptist perspective. The result is the 2017 publication of his monumental two-volume treatise *The Crucifixion of the Warrior God*. This is a work of size and scope to rival that of the best seventeenth century Protestant Scholastics (that's a compliment, by the way). Needless to say, our engagement with

---

[405] Boyd, *The Crucifixion of the Warrior God*, Volume 1: *The Cruciform Hermeneutic*, xxix-xxxii.

this landmark 1492 page tome will be very cursory and will focus on the specific topic of the Canaanite conquest.

Boyd endorses the Augustinian rule (what I have parsed out as the Jesus Principle and Love Principle). However, he astutely argues that the rule requires more precision since different readers may find different things to highlight in Jesus' life. If, for example, one is drawn to Jesus' use of sharp rhetorical language against his opponents and his table-turning protest in the Temple, one might be able to justify violence against opposing groups, as Augustine himself did against the Donatists.[406] Boyd thus proposes that the principle should be founded on the Crucifixion as the ultimate revelation of God.[407] "The thread that weaves together everything Jesus was about is the nonviolent, self-sacrificial, enemy embracing love of God revealed on the cross."[408] With a nod to Anselm, Boyd states that "the cross is that revelation beyond which none greater can be conceived."[409] This event provides the culmination and interpretive framework for the life of Jesus and the whole of Scripture.[410]

On Boyd's view, when God reveals himself, he accommodates to human misunderstanding and error. However, error does not

---

406 Boyd, *The Crucifixion of the Warrior God*, Volume 1, 150-151.

407 Boyd, *The Crucifixion of the Warrior God*, Volume 1, chapters 4-6.

408 Boyd, *The Crucifixion of the Warrior God*, Volume 1, 142.

409 Boyd, *The Crucifixion of the Warrior God*, Volume 1, 155.

410 Should Boyd's point warrant a revision of the principle as I defined it in chapter 7? I'm not convinced for two reasons. First, I believe that an appropriate engagement with the life and teaching of Jesus alone could be sufficient to ground the appropriate attitude toward the outsider. That is why I began the book by appealing to the pivotal Parable of the Good Samaritan. Second, there are many problematic views of the crucifixion as well, so a focus on that event does not secure a non-violent result. That said, I do believe Boyd makes an important point worth considering, and there is no doubt that the *fullest and most adequate* interpretation of the life of Jesus will be that which frames it in terms of his atoning death.

enter the text willy-nilly without purpose. Rather, when we find errors in the text, we should look for a deeper divine purpose in allowing them: "While OT authors often reflect their fallen and culturally conditioned understandings of God by attributing violence directly to him, the Cruciform Thesis discloses that 'something else is going on.'"[411] The template is the crucifixion, the ultimate event where God allows human beings to behave in a wicked, misguided manner while disclosing a deeper redemptive and non-violent meaning behind human violence. Indeed, that deeper meaning is God bringing about reconciliation with an alienated creation, and despite the ugliness of the crucifixion, that deeper story is beautiful beyond description. In like manner, God allows wickedness and error to enter the text elsewhere and when he does we should interpret it as a literary crucifix which invites a search for a deeper meaning pointing to that story of non-violent redemption. Boyd provides a helpful overview in the following passage:

> if we resolve to "know nothing except Jesus Christ, and him crucified" (1 Cor 2:2) as we interpret these genocidal portraits of God, we are empowered to see through their sin-mirroring surface to discern the cruciform God stooping to become the sin and curse of his people within the written witness to God's covenantal faithfulness (2 Cor 5:21; Gal 3:13). We can see that God is bearing the sin of his people—including the sin of believing him to be a genocidal ANE warrior deity—and thereby taking on a literary apperance that reflects that sin. As such, these ghoulish portraits of God become for us literary crucifixes that bear witness to just how low the heavenly missionary was willing to stoop to remain in covenant with, and to continue to further his historical purposes through, his ancient people.[412]

---

411 Boyd, *The Crucifixion of the Warrior God*, Volume 2: *The Cruciform Thesis*, 635.
412 Boyd, *The Crucifixion of the Warrior God*, Volume 2, 927.

On the cross, God allowed people to think about him wrongly even to the extent of crucifying the Son of Man. As for Canaan, he likewise allowed his people to come to believe that he was a divine warrior when, in fact, God was repudiating those very images.

It is important to note that Boyd does not deny the history of the Canaanite conquest as I have proposed. Rather, he adheres to what he calls a Conservative Hermeneutical Principle which commits him to maintaining as much of the (historical) narrative as is possible. What that means for the Canaanite conquest is that Boyd affirms that it always was God's plan to punish and displace the Canaanites as a people and to give their land to elect Israel. Thus, Boyd refers to "God's original dream of a nonviolent replacement of inhabitants in the promised land . . ."[413] a plan that included the intent to punish and expel the Canaanites 'non-violently' by way of a plague of hornets.[414] In addition, God had a plan to make the land temporarily uninhabitable for the people so that it would effectively 'vomit' the Canaanites out.[415]

Unfortunately, the Israelites did not heed that plan. Instead, they found recourse to violence by seeking to kill and expel the Canaanites themselves through military conflict. To illustrate the dynamic, I think of the pericope in which Jesus asks Peter to get out of the boat and walk on the water toward him. Initially, Peter obeyed but then he looked at the waves and began to doubt at which point he started to sink. Likewise, Boyd proposes that originally, the Israelites were promised that God would take the land without recourse to human violence; when they failed to trust God to do that the Israelites sank into their own delusion of the tribal warrior deity and the resulting divinely sanctioned violence.

---

413 Boyd, *The Crucifixion of the Warrior God*, Volume 2, 974.

414 Boyd, *The Crucifixion of the Warrior God*, Volume 2, 965-68.

415 Boyd, *The Crucifixion of the Warrior God*, Volume 2, 968-69.

And so, eventually, God's non-violent promises and plans are distorted and obscured in favor of the lure of God as violent warrior. This lapse into deep theological error involves "God allowing the fallen and culturally conditioned mindset of his people to act on him, thereby conditioning the results of his 'breathing,' just as he does on the cross."[416] The overall message is that the Israelites distorted God's plan to remove the Canaanites peacefully by projecting God as a violent deity. That distorted perspective turns these narratives into "sin-bearing, literary crucifixes."[417] Thus, God gave the Israelites over to their own errant delusions. But he did so with real purpose to bring justice on the Canaanites: "God would now use the evil of the Israelites' disobedient reliance on the sword to punish the evil of the Canaanites [*sic*] wickedness and idolatry."[418]

There are clues in the text for this original plan of a non-violent taking of the land including the above mentioned role of hornets as an original planned means of expulsion. Another clue as to God's original intention is found in the mysterious angelic commander of Joshua 5:13-15 who stands apart from the battle and does not take sides. This figure reflects "the Spirit of God breaking through the fallen and cultural conditioning of the author/redactors of this narrative to provide a direct revelation of God's heart."[419] Thus, we have a glimpse of the true nature of God as love that should guide our reading of these literary crucifixes of violence.

The Crucifixion of the Warrior God is a tour-de-force and Boyd provides a first-rate and very sophisticated example of the Providential Errancy position. However, as I said, our engagement is focused primarily on the (relatively brief) section where Boyd addresses the Canaanite conquest. While I find great merit in his

---

416 Boyd, *The Crucifixion of the Warrior God*, Volume 2, 973.
417 Boyd, *The Crucifixion of the Warrior God*, Volume 2, 980.
418 Boyd, *The Crucifixion of the Warrior God*, Volume 2, 982.
419 Boyd, *The Crucifixion of the Warrior God*, Volume 2, 976.

proposal generally, I do have some points of critique regarding his treatment of the conquest, and I will outline two concerns here. Both of these criticisms ultimately center on Boyd's Conservative Hermeneutical Principle.[420] While I am sympathetic with the principle, I believe that Boyd is *too* conservative in attempting to adhere to the 'original meaning' of a passage.[421] I will now argue the point with respect to history and violence.

The first point concerns history: I think Boyd goes too far in trying to theologize the narrative in a way that maximizes the historical backdrop. I made the point earlier with respect to my longterm weather forecast illustration: the forecast for tomorrow warrants much higher deference than the forecast for two weeks from now; by the same token, events in the life of Jesus warrant much higher deference (both on theological and evidential grounds) than the events of the Canaanite conquest. As Boyd himself has been a forceful defender of the evidence for the historical Jesus,[422] it puzzles me that he does not allow the comparatively poor historical evidence for the Canaanite conquest to have a greater impact on his theological reading of the text. One of the difficulties is that Boyd attempts, as he says, to restrict his discussion to "the world within the biblical narrative" rather than "actual history."[423] While I agree that we should continue to inhabit the strange new world in the Bible as a literary unity, I don't think that one can remove the question of actual history from the discussion of the conquest of Canaan any more than one can remove it from the conquest of sin on Golgotha. If there is strong evidence that the Canaanite conquest

---

420 Boyd, *The Crucifixion of the Warrior God*, Volume 1, 524.

421 Boyd rightly recognizes that this point places him at odds with those like myself who advocate what he (I believe wrongly) calls the 'Dismissal Solution.'

422 See Gregory A. Boyd and Paul R. Eddy, *Lord or Legend? Wrestling with the Jesus Dilemma* (Wipf and Stock, 2010).

423 Boyd, *The Crucifixion of the Warrior God*, Volume 2, 981.

never happened, as such, then we ought to allow that fact to inform our reading of and theological engagement with the text.

This brings me to the issue of violence. As we have seen, Boyd's Conservative Hemeneutical Principle commits him to the view that God did intend to expel the Canaanites and give the land to the Israelites, albeit non-violently. This raises an initial question: given the undeniable trauma of an entire community being uprooted from its land, why couldn't God allow the Israelites to live alongside the Canaanites? If Israel is called to be a blessing to the world (a world that includes Canaanites) then why not start by living among them as a transforming presence (e.g. Romans 12:2)? The answer, says Boyd, is that the Israelites would be negatively influenced by (i.e. conformed to) Canaanite culture.[424] Thus, God planned to remove the Canaanites himself to protect Israelite purity. Ironically, Boyd's scenario of an entire people being forcibly displaced from a land ends up looking surprisingly like ethnic cleansing, albeit with a divine rather than human agent working to bring it about.

There can be no doubt that Boyd's position is far less problematic than God *directly* commanding his human subjects to expel (let alone kill) the Canaanites. Nonetheless, it seems to me that it still faces significant difficulties not least of which is that lingering taint of ethnic cleansing. And then there is the question of the means by which God intended to cleanse the land. As we have seen, Boyd accepts as expressive of God's original intention the related metaphorical description of a people being *vomited out* of the land. Boyd's assurances of the divine desire for a non-violent displacement notwithstanding, the image of vomiting is indisputably a *violent* one. To see why, we only need remember back to the terribly unpleasant occasions when we have vomited: the agonizing build-up of nausea, the commencement of dry heaves, the spasmodic clenching of stomach muscles, and finally the evacuation of a toxic, acidic stew of foul nastiness.

---

[424] Boyd, *The Crucifixion of the Warrior God*, Volume 2, 978.

Indeed, vomiting is one of the most exceedingly violent bodily functions there is. So to choose that experience as the metaphor to describe the means by which God will remove people from a land surely invites the description of an exceedingly violent expulsion. It also suggests that an entire people should be viewed as being as toxic as vomit such that they needed to be expelled from the land. This kind of rhetorical description of a people group is disturbingly similar to the othering language we already noted in the Genocide Apologists.

Let's now turn our attention to the means by which God planned to 'vomit out' the Canaanites. Boyd gives us one primary mechanism: plagues of hornets. While that thankfully does not involve human-on-human violence, as a mode of expulsion it is nonetheless far from being *non*-violent. On the contrary, it seems to me that finding recourse to an incessant plague of stinging insects would seem to be an especially cruel and vicious way to displace a people. Boyd attempts to minimize the trauma by describing these teeming swarms in a relatively benign manner as 'unpleasant' and 'pesky.'[425]

We need to be clear: people don't abandon the only home they've ever known, a land their ancestors settled centuries before, because some insects have become merely unpleasant or pesky.[426] They abandon it because, as Boyd more accurately says elsewhere, life has become truly *intolerable:* "If only the Israelites could have trusted him," Boyd says, "Yahweh would have driven out the indigenous population, whether by performing signs and wonders, making the land uninhabitable, or by making it *intolerably insect-ridden.*"[427]

But what does that mean with respect to hornets, exactly? Again, we need to be very clear: an existence with stinging

---

425 Boyd, *The Crucifixion of the Warrior God*, Volume 2, 966, 968.

426 As a person who lives on the Canadian prairies where I annually endure an onslaught of mosquitoes in the summer, I speak from experience.

427 Boyd, *The Crucifixion of the Warrior God*, Volume 2, 970, emphasis added.

insects that becomes so unbearable that it is truly intolerable is one that would be quite literally, torturous. And to render a person's existence torturous as a punitive action against that person is, by definition, to torture them. Thus, Boyd's hornet claim entails that God's original 'non-violent' plan was to torture an entire civilian population in order to get them to clear the land for the Israelites in order to ensure the purity of the Israelites from that toxic vomitus race. On this scenario, Canaanite lives would have become unbearable, their crops dying, they would be covered in welts, their children would die an agonizing death from anaphylactic shock after being stung dozens of times while playing in the field, leaving a traumatized family mourning their loss. That's not merely *pesky*.

Again, we can be aided at this point in our moral reflection by our own personal acquaintance experiences. I remember vividly the day when my daughter, then a toddler, was swarmed by a nest of hornets. She was stung about five times before I managed to get her into the house: thirty times could have killed her. I can still envision her red, screaming face and wild eyes, consumed by the pain, desperate to take a breath, terrified. How many Canaanites would have been subject to this and much worse on Boyd's putatively *non-violent* scenario?

According to Justin Schmidt, the stings of yellowjackets and baldface hornets are "definitely more serious and attention grabbing than those of fire ants. They are bad. On the pain scale, both yellowjacket and baldfaced hornet stings muster the respectable pain level of 2 . . . ."[428] Schmidt concludes, "the stings of either produce instantaneous, hot, burning, complex pain that gets one's attention no matter what other thoughts were preoccupying the mind. The pain lasts unabated for about 2 minutes, after which it decreases gradually over the next couple

---

428 This is on 4 point scale. Justin O. Schmidt, *The Sting of the Wild* (Johns Hopkins University Press, 2016), 100.

of minutes, leaving us with a hot, red, enduring flare to remind us of the event...."[429]

Those would be the kind of torturous experiences that would plague an entire population subject to a divinely orchestrated aggressive hornet infestation. Note as well that hornets would often target the most vulnerable who are unable to protect themselves including infants, small children, and the mentally and physically handicapped.[430] And the torment would need to be extraordinary and perpetual in order to force people to abandon the land their ancestors settled centuries before. As I said, this act would meet any reasonable threshold for the definition of *torture*, both physical and psychological.

One more thing: in my book *Conversations with My Inner Atheist* I outline several critiera that need to be present for punishment to be just including limiting the punishment to the guilty parties in a subject population, exercising a punishment commensurate to the guilty action, and the subject(s) being made aware that the suffering endured is punishment for the guilty action.[431] These criteria are clearly violated when an entire people (including infants, small children, the mentally handicapped, and others) are indiscriminately attacked and stung by waves of hornets bereft of any interpretive context which would identify these plagues unambiguously to *all* victims as a specific punishment from the Israelite God *for specific sins and to clear the land for the Israelites*.

So while it is definitely laudable that Boyd denies God commanded a genocide, it is still worrisome that on his view God planned to expel the Canaanites violently, *vomiting them* out of the land with means that included swarms of potentially lethal

---

[429] Schmidt, *The Sting of the Wild*, 100.

[430] Note the ironic parallel with Copan and Flannagan: in both cases (Copan and Flannagan's soldiers or Boyd's hornets) a forcible expulsion would end up ironically targeting many of the most vulnerable and least culpable persons in the community.

[431] Rauser, *Conversations with My Inner Atheist*, chapter 10.

insects that would torture many of the most vulnerable until the entire community was forced to move in a last ditch, desperate attempt to survive.

    I do have one more concern about divine violence and punishment before we conclude. Boyd argues that in lieu of the hornets and other natural forces vomiting the Canaanites out of the land, God opted to expel them by allowing the Israelites to act on their own false beliefs about the warrior deity. Thus, Boyd believes that Israelites' violent actions against the Canaanites constituted a violent *punishment*, albeit one that involves God's passive allowance of misunderstanding rather than God's active command. Boyd appears to be making a moral distinction between active and passive punishment: God does not actively inflict punishment on the Canaanite society *in toto* but he passively punishes them by standing by and allowing them to experience the violence of the Israelites which is borne by their false beliefs about Yahweh. And it is punishment precisely because it is motivated by a punitive response to Canaanite sin.

    I would want to challenge the viability of that distinction. And to do so, I will appeal to James Rachels' famous thought experiment which challenges the moral contrast between active and passive euthanasia:

> Smith will inherit a large fortune on the death of his six-year-old cousin. Smith drowns his cousin in the bath and makes it look like an accident. In the case of Jones, he also stands to inherit a fortune on the death of his six-year-old cousin. He enters the bathroom and plans to drown his cousin in the bath. Jones sees the child slip, hit his head and fall face down in the water. Jones watches and does nothing while his cousin drown [*sic*] ... Smith acted to kill his cousin while Jones "merely" let the child die ... [but] Jones is no better than Smith even though he did not directly act to kill his cousin.[432]

---

    432 Cited in Frank William Lewins, *Bioethics for Health Professionals* (Macmillan,

I believe that Rachels is correct: Jones is no better than Smith. Why? Because they both desire the same immoral end: the murder of the six-year-old cousin. The point is that acts of omission can be as morally culpable as acts of comission, depending on the intention that underlies each and the means by which that intention is realized.

Boyd agrees with the Genocide Apologists and Just War Interpreters that God actively desired to punish Canaanite society *in toto* and to expulse them from—or vomit them out of—the land. On the view of the Genocide Apologists and Just War Interpreters, God did so by commanding the Israelites to invade the land, violently slaughtering and driving out the civilian population as they advanced through the territory. On Boyd's view, he did so by *allowing the Israelites to believe* he had commanded them to invade the land, violently slaughtering and driving out the civilian population as they advanced through the territory. To be blunt, I simply don't see a sufficient difference here. Thus, while Boyd goes quite far in addressing the problem of divine violence, in my view, he does not go far enough.

Learning to Read with the Canaanites

In recent years, pacifist biblical scholar Eric Seibert has been an important voice in calling for a critical reevaluation of the biblical text to align our understanding with our deepest moral sensibilities. Seibert argues that this requires us to distinguish between the 'textual God' and the 'actual God' by recognizing that many descriptions of God's being and action within the Bible may not be correct descriptions of who God, in fact, is.[433] While this might sound like a worrisome concession to some, the relative modesty of the claim should become clearer once we recognize the degree to which progressive revelation and accommodation qualify various descriptions of God within

---

1996), 29.

[433] Seibert, *Disturbing Divine Behavior*, 178.

Scripture. For example, when discussing omniscience we noted both texts that describe God as perfectly omniscient and texts that describe God as learning. Every Christian must decide how to resolve these contrasting depictions and which set of descriptions will provide the control. The same lesson applies to the various depictions of how God relates to violence. As Seibert observes, "There are many Old Testament views and perspectives on violence, and some of these are diametrically opposed to each other."[434] In those cases, I have argued that we need to read in a way that is consistent with the love of God and neighbor.

As Christian readers, we are raised from a very young age to read with the Israelites. After all, they are God's people. But as we know, sometimes that type of reading raises profound moral difficulties. While the Canaanite conquest has been our primary focus, similar problems can arise with other texts which generally are not viewed as problematic. Consider, for example, the familiar narrative of the Exodus, a story that shows God aligning with his people and lovingly and powerfully delivering them from slavery to a cruel, oppressive power.[435] For those long familiar with only thinking of the story in those terms, it can be a surprise to come to terms with how the story appears to those who do not accept the assumptions of that reading tradition. Consider, for example, how famous film critic Roger Ebert reacts to the film *Prince of Egypt* which is an animated retelling of the Exodus:

> The story of Exodus has its parallels in many religions, always with the same result: God chooses one of his peoples over the others. We like these stories because in the one we subscribe to, we are the chosen people. I have always rather thought God could have spared man a lot of trouble by casting his net

---

434 Seibert, *The Violence of Scripture*, 7.

435 This reading has had powerful resonance within liberation theology.

more widely, emphasizing universality rather than tribalism, but there you have it.[436]

In Ebert's view, the Exodus is not a story of liberation, but rather a story of *tribalism*, of God choosing one side rather than another.

One might protest that Ebert has misread the story, that he missed the point, that he failed to read from the perspective of the Israelites. Perhaps, but isn't it also possible that, to some degree, *we have failed to read from the perspective of the Egyptians?* Remember the point made powerfully by Gregory of Nyssa. He asks, why would God kill the beloved firstborn son of a deathly poor Egyptian peasant who is eking out a marginal life on the edge of the community, a man who himself had no part in the oppression of the Israelites? If we do not appreciate that Ebert and Gregory of Nyssa both have a point, are we not in danger of losing our neighbor in the reading?

With that challenge in mind, Seibert suggests that we enter the story of the Canaanite conquest from a very different angle by seeking to read the narrative not only from the view of the Israelites who are escaping oppression but also from the view of the people they are thereby seeking to kill and expulse. In short, Seibert is suggesting that we *read with the Canaanites*:

> When we read from this perspective, and choose to sympathize with the Canaanites rather than rejoice with the Israelites, the story looks very different and our perception of it changes dramatically. Reading with the Canaanites problematizes the

---

436 Roger Ebert, Review of *The Prince of Egypt,"* RogerEbert.com https://www.rogerebert.com/reviews/the-prince-of-egypt-1998#:~:text=%22The%20Prince%20of%20Egypt%22%20is,looking%20animated%20films%20ever%20made.&text=This%20is%20a%20film%20that,the%20category%20of%20children's%20entertainment.

violence of this narrative and raises doubts about the legitimacy of Israelite aggression.[437]

Seibert writes, "We must learn to see Canaanites as real people—moms and dads, aunts and uncles, brothers and sisters, nephews and nieces, grandmas and grandpas—who had hopes and dreams, strengths and weaknesses, virtues and vices, just like we do. They too were created in God's image."[438] The more that we seek to tell the story from the perspective of the Canaanites, granting them names and a place in history, and even a potential place in God's kingdom, and the more we use that exercise to develop a general commitment to reading from the margins,[439] the more we undermine the ability to co-opt these stories for violent acts that are irreconcilable with the way of Jesus.

One finds an example of this when Jesus travels to Tyre and Sidon in Matthew 15:21-28, a region that Frederick Dale Bruner wryly describes as representing 'paganland' for Jesus' pious Jewish audience.[440] The setting is shocking enough. But then, as if to compound the scandal, the story identifies a *Canaanite* woman coming to Jesus for help. Bruner writes: "To readers of the Hebrew Scriptures, the adjective 'Canaanite' means everything dangerous to the faith of Israel."[441] So when this woman has the temerity to ask for healing for her demon-possessed daughter, Jesus predictably shuts her down by saying it is not right to give the bread for children to *dogs*. If you are shocked by the term *dog*, then ask yourself: what else would you call Canaanites, a

---

437 Seibert, *The Violence of Scripture*, 101. See also Boyd, *The Crucifixion of the Warrior God*, vol. 1, 297-99.

438 Seibert, *The Violence of Scripture*, 101.

439 Seibert, *The Violence of Scripture*, 102-103.

440 Frederick Dale Bruner, *Matthew: A Commentary*, 13-28, rev. ed. (Eerdmans, 2003), 97.

441 Bruner, *Matthew: A Commentary*, 97.

people so irredeemably wicked that biblical history tells us they deserved only complete and total eradication?

But then something truly extraordinary happens. The woman is undeterred by this rebuff. In fact, she offers the perfect response to Jesus: *even dogs receive crumbs from the master's table*, she shoots back. And lest one think that by offering that quick witted reply, she has showed up the master, Jesus' mirthful reply reveals the truth. She has risen to the challenge as he knew she would and Jesus is delighted with the result.[442] R.T. France writes, "In refusing to accept the traditional Jewish exclusion of Gentiles from the grace of God, she has shown a truly prophetic grasp of the new perspective of the kingdom of heaven, which is now to be open to 'people from east and west' (8:11-12) on the basis of their faith rather than of their racial identity."[443] And keep in mind that this prophetic revelation comes courtesy of a Canaanite, a people believed to be so exceedingly wicked that they were once considered only good for slaughter.

So here is the question. Is Jesus signaling a change in policy where Canaanites are concerned? *They needed to be slaughtered in the past, but they've since improved sufficiently that at long last at least some of them may be fitting subjects for healing.* Or, more radically, is Jesus signaling that particular attitudes about Canaanites and their collective irredeemability were wrong all along? To put it another way, is Jesus ennobling this particular Canaanite woman? Or is he ennobling an *entire people*, a people that, like the Samaritans, had long been despised and mistrusted?

There is another side to this as well. Remember that Joshua tells the story that includes Rahab and the Gibeonites within God's story so it includes the sobering depiction of Achan cast off. As Donald Senior observes, this provocative pericope should

---

442 For my treatment of this story see *Conversations with My Inner Atheist: A Christian Apologist Explores Questions that Keep People Up at Night*, chapter 12.

443 R.T. France, *The Gospel of Matthew*, The New International Commentary on the New Testament (Eerdmans, 2007), 590.

be read in contrast to the motif within Matthew of Jesus being rejected by Jewish leaders. While the Jewish leaders condemn Jesus as "in league with Satan" the Canaanite woman stands up and is vindicated.[444] And so, there is a sober warning to the Jewish leaders and other insiders that they could miss God while the outsider like the Canaanite woman is embraced within God's kingdom. The lesson is not simply that the Canaanites can, at long last, be included as part of God's plan. Rather, I would submit the real revelation is that the Canaanites have *always* been a people who were part of God's benevolent care. The lesson is that Jesus truly loves *all* people: Jews, Gentiles, Samaritans, and yes, Canaanites too. So perhaps the next question is this: who are the Canaanites in our time and place? And how can we begin to read from the margins with them?

---

[444] Donald Senior, *The Gospel of Matthew* (Abingdon Press, 1997), 132.

12

The Ethics of Authorial Ambiguation:

Why isn't God clearer?

In this book I have sought to argue that we need to recognize the central role of moral intuition in hermeneutics and theology as we seek to understand the deeply troubling Canaanite conquest. I argued that the divine directives of Deuteronomy 7 and 20 and the Israelite actions of Joshua 1-12 meet the legal definitions of genocide and ethnic cleansing. Next, I articulated five guiding reading principles when engaging the biblical text which center on the perfection of God as author and the end of the text as being to form us into disciples of Jesus who love God and neighbor. From that point, I then critiqued the Genocide Apologists and the Just War Interpreters both of whom interpret the texts as narrating historical events which they believe were morally justified. Not only is that interpretation negated by moral intuition, but it violates the end of becoming like Jesus and loving one's neighbor. We then considered the approach of the Spiritualizers: while their careful attempts to discern spiritual meanings in the text consistent with the love of God and neighbor are to be admired, their proposal still lacks a deeper critique of the violent narratives through which those spiritual truths are communicated. In order to address that lack, we turned finally to the Providential Errancy view that cultivates formative critical engagement through a moral critique of the literal meaning which is consistent with the love of God and neighbor. By engaging strategies like reading from the margins, we can identify with the voice of the marginalized and oppressed in the narrative as we learn to be like Christ.

In this final chapter, we will turn to consider one remaining but very significant problem: if the purpose of the Bible is to shape readers and hearers into faithful disciples who love God and neighbor, then why does it often seem ill-suited to that task? For example, why does the text allow for very serious instances of miscommunication with readers, even very careful and diligent readers? Atheist John Loftus puts the issue like this:

> Dispensing higher critical studies and just taking the Bible at face value, what are we to make of the way God communicated, given the final canonical Bible? My claim is that God did a woefully inadequate job, especially since he's supposedly omniscient and knows how "sinful" people such as us could misunderstand his words.[445]

Loftus calls this the "problem of miscommunication" and it is indeed a problem as this book has made very clear: Christians have disagreed for centuries over how to interpret the Canaanite conquest and some of those interpretations have been used to justify terrible, unchristlike actions, even moral atrocities like genocide. It hardly needs to be said that this is precisely the opposite of the intended effect, i.e. to conform people to Jesus so that they love God and neighbor. And so, we must return to the question: why think God inspired these texts at all?

---

[445] John Loftus, "What We've Got Here is a Failure to Communicate," in *The Christian Delusion*, ed. John Loftus (Prometheus, 2010), 181-2.

In this final chapter, I will outline the problem of miscommunication as I see it and I will offer a response. I will then conclude with a call to church leaders to seek actively to *disambiguate* significant misunderstandings of the biblical text, particularly those that threaten to undermine or weaken the cultivation of love of God and neighbor. If, as I believe, particular readings of these texts offer a fundamental violation of our moral knowledge, then we cannot remain silent: it behooves us as morally serious readers who seek to be like Christ to rebut seriously errant readings and to defend interpretations consistent with our moral intuitions and the theological and ethical ends for which we believe the text was revealed.

The Ethics of Ambiguation

One way to think about the problem of miscommunication is that it constitutes an abdication of one's authorial obligation to achieve a minimal threshold of clear communication with the reader on an important topic. When there is a serious issue at stake, one can argue that the artist has a moral obligation to *disambiguate* their message and ensure that a clear moral stance is communicated relative to the problematic moral content. Since I have availed myself of cinematic examples before (most notably, *The Shining*) I shall do so once more here by considering the ethics of ambiguation in dialogue with the 2003 film *Elephant*.

Elephant, directed by Gus Van Zant, depicts a day at a typical American high school which culminates in a tragic school shooting. The film was released four years after the infamous Columbine High School shooting in Colorado. Upon its release it attracted a significant amount of attention not least because Van Zant offered no analysis of the violence depicted in the film, no consideration of the causes, no suggestion of how one should respond. As Roger Ebert observes, "It offers no explanation for the tragedy, no insights into the psyches of the killers, no theories about teenagers or society or guns or psychopathic behavior. It simply looks at the day as it unfolds . . . ."[446] This hands-off approach to the subject matter offended some critics. Todd McCarthy of *Variety* begins his review like this: "To make a film about something like the Columbine student shootings incident and provide no insight or enlightenment would seem to be pointless at best and irresponsible at worst, and that is what Gus Van Sant has done in 'Elephant'."[447]

However, other critics saw things differently. Far from viewing this as a violation of the ethics of ambiguity, they deemed Van Sant's ambiguous stance to be a bold, laudatory treatment of the subject matter. Ebert, for example, believed that Van Zant's refusal to engage in moral analysis of the events of the film was "a brave and radical act; it refuses to supply reasons and assign cures, so that we can close the case and move on." Ebert adds, "I think its responsibility comes precisely in its refusal to provide a point."[448] In short, Ebert believes Van Zant was wise to cede some control to the viewer, to insist that *they* figure out how they will respond to the story that has been told.

The debate over Van Zant's ethical stance as a storyteller perfectly illustrates the debate over the ethics of ambiguity. Is it permissible for an author to assume a posture of neutrality or ambiguity, to fail to guide the reader or viewer as to processing the moral content of the artistic work? McCarthy seems to think the creator is required to take a clear and unequivocal stance for the viewer. But Ebert, rightly in my view, insists that neutrality or ambiguity can be justified insofar as it serves the greater vision of the creator who aims to use the film to prompt

---

[446] Roger Ebert, Review of *Elephant* (November 7, 2003), https://www.rogerebert.com/reviews/elephant-2003

[447] Todd McCarthy, Review of *Elephant, Variety* (May 18, 2003), https://variety.com/2003/film/awards/elephant-2-1200541588/

[448] Ebert, Review of *Elephant*.

audiences to seek for *themselves* a deeper wrestling with the moral content of the artistic work. The ambiguity does not *detract* from the formative ethical force of the narrative. Quite the contrary, in fact: this more open-ended approach to the subject matter may be *more* effective in bringing about deep-seated change than having the film itself spoon-feed some particular mode of analysis to the viewer.

We may think of the Canaanite conquest in similar terms. If we accept that God does not approve of genocide, then God seems to have assumed a disturbingly detached perspective from the deeply troubling narrative.[449] Absent are the overt cues from the narrator that would signal the proper moral appraisal of the acts. Perhaps in this case as well, the logic is that "the responsibility comes precisely in its refusal to provide a point," at least in the confines of the immediate narrative itself. The reader is forced to confront deeply troubling moral content, the othering, expulsion, and mass killing of an entire population, by reading within the wider canon and reflecting in light of one's own spiritual formation in Christ.

Origen recognized that the spiritual meanings he was proposing were not readily accessible to the lay reader. But far from seeing this as a problem, he argued that the apparent obscurity and difficulty of the biblical text in conveying the right response to troubling moral content constituted a providential *feature* of the text, one that was intended by God to draw the reader into serious critical engagement and reflection.[450] Just as Van Zant declined to disambiguate the analysis of the shooting in *Elephant* for the sake of the viewer so God declined to disambiguate the Canaanite conquest for the sake of the reader.

Perhaps you could concede that in principle there is an ethical defense of ambiguation insofar as it serves some greater end.

---

[449] This would remain the case even if we grant the alleged cues of internal critique such as the juxtaposition of Rahab and Achan.

[450] Franke, "Introduction to Joshua Through 2 Samuel," xxii.

However, you might still insist that there are limits and that in the case of the Bible the degree of misunderstanding is sufficiently egregious that it is simply not plausible to defend it in those terms. Just as God might plausibly have morally sufficient reasons to allow *some degree of evil* in the world, you can concede that God might have morally sufficient reasons to allow *some degree of ambiguity* within the text. But just as a skeptic could retort that it is not plausible to believe that he had sufficient reason to allow *this much evil* in the world so you could retort that it is not plausible to believe that he had sufficient reason to allow *this much ambiguity* in the text.

At this point, we can reformulate the problem of miscommunication by way of another illustration, this one drawing upon the controversial performance legacy of the horrorcore rap group Insane Clown Posse (ICP). For years, ICP has been known for their exceedingly violent, vulgar, and sexualized lyrics (Samuel Buntz refers to "Lyrical misogyny of a sub-Eminem level"[451]), intense shows, and a rabid and violent fan base known as "Juggalos". To sum up, ICP is one of the most notorious acts in modern popular music.

Then in 2009, after almost twenty years building a notorious reputation and ravenous fan base, the duo that makes up ICP, Violent J and Shaggy 2 Dope, revealed that they are, in fact, Christians.[452] Allegedly, they based the entire mythology of

---

[451] Samuel Buntz, "The Insane Clown Posse's Juggalos Are Hungering Not Just for Food But For Faith," *The Federalist*, https://thefederalist.com/2017/09/27/insane-clown-posses-juggalos-hungering-not-just-food-faith/

[452] Tom Murphy, "Where's God? Insane Clown Posse's Violent J speaks frankly about God and religion," *Westword* (April 9, 2013), https://www.westword.com/music/wheres-god-insane-clown-posses-violent-j-speaks-frankly-about-god-and-religion-5715974 Whether they should be considered Christians is, in fact, far from clear. Violent J says, "I don't know the specifics of any certain religion or anything like that, but I've always believed you can hear your guardian angel on your shoulder telling you if what you're doing is evil or not. And I've always

"The Carnival," a theme which runs through all their albums, on God and the need to live in proper relationship with him.[453] Violent J explains,

> We've dropped little hints, and we've revealed that we're religious people from the beginning of our music. We've never hidden the fact that we believe in god. Behind the face paint, behind the brutality of our music, there's a fine message there that says this is entertainment, but in real life, live by that guardian angel on your shoulder and it'll tell you when you're doing something you shouldn't be doing. It'll tell you when you're being helpful, and you should listen to that voice.[454]

Not surprisingly, most of the Juggalos were utterly unaware of the allegedly redemptive, religious meaning of the band's oeuvre and many understandably felt betrayed. And it isn't hard to see why. Indeed, this unveiling raises some important ethical questions as Jon Ronson observes: "one might argue that 20 years was, under the circumstances, an incredibly long time for them to have pretended to be unholy, and that, from a Christian perspective, *the harm they did while feigning unholiness may even have outweighed the greater good.*"[455] Ronson's final observation summarizes the central problem: the harm of ICP allowing their message to remain ambiguous for so long *plausibly outweighs*

---

believed that good souls go to heaven and bad souls go to hell." Fortunately, we need not settle the theological orthodoxy of ICP for this illustration to serve my purposes.

453 Jon Ronson, "Insane Clown Posse: And God Created Controversy," *The Guardian* (October 9, 2010), http://www.theguardian.com/music/2010/oct/09/insane-clown-posse-christians-god

454 Cited in Murphy, "Where's God? Insane Clown Posse's Violent J speaks frankly about God and religion."

455 Ronson, "Insane Clown Posse: And God Created Controversy," emphasis added.

whatever greater good they may have hoped to achieve.[456] How many Juggalos took meth before an ICP concert or committed acts of violence afterward, all buoyed on by the lyrical content of the music and utterly oblivious to the terribly subtle ironic redemptive message buried within? Judging by the notorious reputation of these fans,[457] the answer is *more than a few*. So, assuming that the infamous duo is serious in their posture and messaging, one could reasonably object that they violated the ethics of ambiguation by promoting a message which was sufficiently ambiguous that it led to gross misunderstanding, pain and suffering that outweighed any greater good which could come about through that misunderstanding.

When we turn from ICP to the Bible we are not dealing simply with misunderstanding for two decades but for *two millennia or more*. Moreover, critics will insist that the damage that this has done to the credibility of the Bible and the witness of the church has been enormous. People reject Christianity because of crimes committed in the name of Christ and justified by way of biblical precedent. They reject Christianity because of very reasonable violent readings of the Good Book. They reject Christianity because even now many Christians continue to defend the ethics of divinely commanded genocide while dehumanizing Canaanites as cancer. This misreading of biblical violence is

---

456 Another case comes from the band Beastie Boys. On their 1986 album *Licensed to Ill*, Beastie Boys became famous with the title track "Fight for Your Right (to Party)". The song appeared to be a classic party anthem and was a big hit with kids. Unfortunately, Beastie Boys were intending the song *ironically* as a sardonic absurdist deconstruction of the party song. See Michael Diamond and Adam Horovitz, *The Beastie Boys Book* (Spiegel and Grau, 2018), 228. That subtle message was completely lost on the young audience.

457 In 2011, the FBI classified Juggalos as a "loosely affiliated hybrid gang." Buntz, "The Insane Clown Posse's Juggalos Are Hungering Not Just for Food But For Faith."

not limited to the past: it continues down to the present in the Genocide Apologists.

Of course, we could spend hundreds more pages enumerating examples of the alleged negative consequences of ambiguity, but let us just note here that some of the most painful and heartbreaking instances of this apparent miscommunication involve professing Christians who are led to undertake actions contrary to their own moral intuitions and which are inimical to their own love of neighbor because they honestly believe the biblical text compels this of them. For example, in the following passage, John Henry Hopkins recalls that he ultimately endorsed slavery, despite significant misgivings, because of his desire to adhere to what he believed to be biblical teaching:

> If it were a matter to be determined by personal sympathies, tastes, or feelings, I should be as ready as any man to condemn the institution of slavery, for all my prejudices of education, habit, and social position stand entirely opposed to it. But as a Christian . . . I am compelled to submit my weak and erring intellect to the authority of the Almighty. For then only can I be *safe* in my conclusions.[458]

Tragic examples like this could easily be multiplied. Just imagine, for example, how many of Cromwell's soldiers suppressed that moral voice within as they were killing Irish civilians in the misbegotten belief that they had the divine imprimatur? As atheist Dan Barker writes: "Paul wrote that 'God is not the author of confusion,' but can you think of a book that has caused more confusion than the bible?"[459] If Ronson may rightly question whether that two decade charade of ICP outweighed any

---

458 Cited in Webb, *Corporal Punishment in the Bible*, 124, emphasis in original.

459 Dan Barker, *Godless: How an Evangelical Preacher Became One of America's Leading Atheists* (Ulysses Press, 2008), 36.

conceivable good, how much more may one wonder the same about centuries of biblical misinterpretation?

In Search of the Greater Good

We can present the critic's objection in the form of a simple argument which goes like this:

1. If God is the primary author of Scripture then Scripture should be maximally effective in forming Christians into disciples of Jesus who love God and their neighbors.
2. The degree of ambiguity in Scripture is inconsistent with a text that is maximally effective in forming Christians into disciples of Jesus who love God and their neighbors.
3. Therefore, Scripture is not maximally effective in forming Christians into disciples of Jesus who love God and their neighbors.
4. Therefore God is not the primary author of Scripture.

I must admit that I have some questions and concerns about the first premise. To begin with, we might question our ability to discern what maximal effectiveness looks like. For example, the first premise fails to distinguish between maximal effectiveness for every individual reader/hearer vs. maximal effectiveness for the *greatest number* of readers/hearers. One could argue that John Henry Hopkins might *personally* have benefited from a clearer denunciation of slavery within the text even while insisting that the majority of readers over time would benefit from greater *ambiguity* around that specific question. And if the latter criterion (the greatest good for the greatest number) is the relevant one in this case, then the fact that particular individuals would have benefited in their spiritual formation from greater clarity on some specific issue would not of itself constitute a defeater to the claim.[460] Furthermore, it is also possible that a clearer denunciation of slavery in the text would not have been heeded by Hopkins despite his asseverations to the contrary. (We are not always the most reliable judges of how we might have acted under different circumstances.)

I can hear the voice of the critics: Surely it is *absurd* to say that *Hopkins* wouldn't have benefited overall in his spiritual formation had there been a clearer denunciation of slavery in the biblical text! I understand that incredulity and I am sympathetic to it, to be sure. But the skeptic must also appreciate here how much depends on our initial commitment to the perfection of the author. I may be unable to come up with any solution as to why a master filmmaker like Kubrick would include a continuity error like a missing door panel and yet if I am sufficiently persuaded that he is indeed an expert filmmaker and that he directed *The Shining*, I will continue to believe that it is not a genuine continuity error and thus that there must be some reason for the anomaly. And if I am persuaded overall that God is indeed the perfect primary author of Scripture then I will remain committed to recognizing its efficacious function for forming Christ followers, even when I am inclined to think that *I* would have done things differently.

Ultimately, everything hinges on premise 2: is the degree of ambiguity present really irredeemable relative to the ends of the spiritual formation God seeks to bring about in the reader/hearer? Much depends on what we expect the Bible to be, for I fear that many critics here are hampered in their analysis by a reductionistic understanding of the meaning and purpose of the Scriptures. I grew up in a tradition that tended to view the Bible as something akin to a glorified evangelistic tract which would summarize the doctrine of salvation in four easy laws

---

460 Keep in mind that acting to maximize the greatest good for the greatest number in one specific instance does not automatically commit one to a general utilitarian model of normative ethics.

that could readily be taught to others. God, of course, could have given us a tract if he had so desired, but he clearly chose not to do that. Instead, he gave us a complex library of diverse literary genres rich in textual ambiguity, vagueness, and irony.[461] If we expect a transfer of information-for-salvation, the text will frustrate our expectations of 'direct communication.' But in that case, the fault lies not with the Bible but with our errant assumptions about it.

In my book *An Atheist and a Christian Walk into a Bar*, my atheist coauthor Justin Schieber raises a similar objection to the problem of miscommunication though he dubs it the problem of 'Massive Theological Disagreement': if God has revealed himself, why didn't he make his revelation clearer? Why is there any room for debate and disagreement? Schieber presents the dilemma not in terms of the ethics of authorship but rather the ethics of parenting. He presents a scenario in which two children begin to fight because they disagree over the nature of the request that has been made by their parent. Once the fight erupts, the parent would surely intervene and clarify his/her wishes (if not before). And if they didn't, they would be a bad parent. So unless we think that God is a bad parent, we should surely expect God to intervene as well: "Hey, kids, I never meant to say that I *actually* commanded genocide!"

In response to Schieber, I give at least one reason why a parent would have morally sufficient reasons to allow conflict to arise between siblings. It could be, for example, that this conflict will provide the catalyst for the siblings to come to terms with some deep, ongoing problem in their relationship and as a result, the conflict will ultimately bring about a growth in that relationship. In addition, I point out that this basic scenario isn't implausible at all because "parents *often* do things like this. Based on their knowledge of their children and their desire to ensure that their

---

[461] See for example, Carolyn Sharp, *Irony and Meaning in the Hebrew Bible* (Indiana University Press, 2009).

children grow and develop in their character, parents may allow states of affairs to exist that might appear to the casual observer to be inept or improper."[462]

The conflict is similar to that which arises in misunderstanding or misreading Scripture, albeit scaled up to a level that spans millennia and encompasses millions of readers and hearers. But just as the problem is that much greater, so is the potential for unanticipated positive formative impacts on untold millions of people. For that reason, and given a commitment to the perfection of the author, it seems to me that we should chasten our opinions as to what degree of ambiguity would be considered to be ultimately inconsistent with the divine purposes.

Let's imagine that a writer wants to write a book against war. What would be the most effective type of book to generate the largest impact in terms of cultivating anti-war attitudes? I propose that we consider that question with respect to three different actual literary works.

The first volume is an anti-war essay: *War is a Racket* is a 1935 book published by Smedley D. Butler, a retired general from the US Marines. The book is based on a speech in which Butler lays out a critique of war by focusing on the degree to which business interests shape the battlefield. *War is a Racket* offers a straightforward, discursive argument based on a clearly articulated thesis with supporting data. In short, it is the kind of clear book that many critics think God should have written.

While there is much to be said for *War is a Racket* in terms of achieving the end of deterring people from military conflict, for many people, *story* will be a more effective mode of communication than a formal argument in essay form. And that brings us to our second alternative response. This approach surrenders the discursive, didacticism in favor of a riveting and moving narrative. When it comes to the history of anti-war novels, Dalton Trumbo's *Johnny Got His Gun* is one of the best. The novel tells

---

[462] Rauser and Schieber, *An Atheist and a Christian Walk into a Bar*, 75.

the story of a young man named Joe Bonham who loses his legs, arms, and face to a German bomb in WWI, but his mind is intact, unable to contact the outside world. This leaves him in a horrifying purgatory of sentient immobility, a prisoner in his own mangled body. The novel has been described by *The New York Times* as "perhaps the most bitter and graphic antiwar novel ever written."[463] There is no misunderstanding the strong anti-war sentiment of Trumbo's powerful story. While it lacks the clearly articulated argument, statistics, and other supporting evidence of *War is a Racket*, one could argue that Trumbo's novel more than makes up for it in terms of sheer emotive force. And in that regard, it could perhaps be even more effective in building antiwar sentiment in the long-term.

Our last book is also a narrative, but this one is notably more ambiguous than *Johnny Got His Gun*. Stephen Crane's *The Red Badge of Courage* made its young author a star upon its publication and it is today considered a classic American novel. *The Red Badge of Courage* tells the story of Henry Fleming, a young soldier with the Union Army in the Civil War who flees the conflict in fear only to return later, determined to acquire a wound on the battlefield (i.e. his badge of courage) and with it, to regain his honor.

There is no doubting the bracing anti-war sentiment of *Johnny Got His Gun*, but when it comes to conveying a view about the battlefield, *Red Badge* is a good deal subtler. One can read the novel as an ironic deconstruction of war and the values of machismo and courage that often underlie it. But one can also read it, as some do, as a straightforward depiction of a soldier who eventually finds his courage and becomes a man through the crucible of war. The critic might insist that if Crane really wanted to issue a powerful antiwar statement, he would have

---

463 Guy Flatley,"Thirty Years Later, Johnny Gets His Gun Again," *New York Times* (June 28, 1970), https://www.nytimes.com/1970/06/28/archives/thirty-years-later-johnny-gets-his-gun-again-johnny-gets-his-gun.html.

written a novel without ambiguity. Or perhaps he would have ditched the narrative form altogether and authored a polemical essay.

So which writing would be most effective at fomenting anti-war attitudes over the long-term: Butler's essay, Trumbo's novel, or Crane's novel? These are interesting questions, but I really don't see any way to arrive at a definitive answer. There are just far too many variables that one might consider. By the same token, I don't believe there is a compelling defense of premise 2 by way of this type of armchair theorizing.

I have the same sentiments when it comes to the Bible. I have assumed, rather simply, that the Bible has one goal: to cultivate disciples into being followers of Jesus (2 Timothy 3:14-17). However, it is possible that even if this is the primary goal of the Bible that it has other goals as well, and the text as it exists is ideally suited to the fulfillment of that ensemble of goals, not just the primary one that I have discussed here. Needless to say, a greater understanding of what additional goals God may be seeking to achieve with the Bible would be essential information before we could draw a final conclusion that it had failed in that end.

One more thing: as regards that specific primary goal on which we have focused, that of cultivating disciples who are like Jesus, I am just not persuaded that the skeptic has a good defense of premise 2 not least because I approach the text through the total experience and reasons I have for Christian faith. And so, I continue to defer to the wisdom of the master artist in achieving the ends he seeks to achieve within his work. That said, I understand how other people who assess the evidence may reasonably disagree.

Disambiguation and the Ethics of the Pastorate and the Pew

Bart Ehrman begins his book *Jesus, Interrupted* by describing how recent advances in archaeological, linguistic, and textual studies illumine our understanding of the Bible. While this rich repository of information is frequently communicated to graduate students and seminarians, it largely remains unknown in the pew. Why? The sad reality is that many pastors choose not to introduce this material to their congregants. Ehrman writes: "For all those who aspire to being well educated, knowledgeable, and informed about our civilization's most important book, that has to change."[464]

While I don't always agree with Ehrman, I heartily endorse this point. Pastors should not avoid these topics even if they are awkward or difficult or cannot be addressed satisfactorily within a Sunday morning sermon. Pastors and other church leaders should be committed to seeking to bring about a long term educational formation within their congregations and that should extend to a deepened understanding of the meaning and purpose of Scripture as well as various other complex topics like manuscript evidence, pseudopigraphy, and archaeology.

To the extent that a seemingly unacceptable degree of ambiguity exists as to the meaning and significance of violent texts in the Bible, I would argue that pastors and other church leaders must shoulder some of the blame. I am reminded of a cartoon that depicts two men discussing the problem of evil. The first man asks why God allows evil and the second replies, "Maybe God allows evil so that we can learn how to fight against it . . . ." But before he can finish his thought, the first man cuts him off: "Hey quiet Charlie, I'm listening for an answer here." The point, of course, is that Charlie was *giving* the first fellow an answer: he

---

[464] Ehrman, *Jesus, Interrupted: Revealing the Hidden Contradictions in the Bible (and Why We Don't Know About Them)* (HarperOne, 2009), 2.

just wasn't ready to hear it. And the answer is that the problem of evil is at least in part a problem that rests squarely on the shoulders of the church. In short, before we ask why God allows evil, perhaps we should ask ourselves: *why do we?*

The same can be said of the problem variously described as miscommunication or massive theological disagreement. Rather than focus only on the question of whether God has done enough to disambiguate the Bible, perhaps we should ask: have we? It could be that one important reason that God has allowed the degree of ambiguity that exists is precisely so the church can undertake the responsibility of faithful pastoral and community disambiguation of the text. Perhaps there is intrinsic value in the church as a corporate body wrestling with Scripture in this manner as Jacob wrestled with the angel.

With that in mind, I would make an appeal to Christians everywhere and church leaders in particular who are persuaded by my argument: if you believe that it is wrong and harmful to read the Canaanite conquest as historical for the reasons I gave, or if you just believe that it is wrong for Christians to feel *obliged* to read it as historical, then I believe you have an obligation to your church community to share your views and your reasons for them. Even if you don't know precisely what the satisfactory solution is (and I agree that it is easier to say how these texts should not be read than to say how they should be read), you owe it to yourself and to the wider Christian community to introduce the conversation and speak out of your convictions.

As you can imagine, those will not be easy conversations. In some circumstances, you can expect to experience fear, confusion, anger, and pushback. This is to be expected given that many of the people you will encounter will have learned decades ago to read these texts by way of omission, misrepresentation, distraction, and blunted affect. And even if you are simply raising difficult questions that every thinking person should be asking, remember that people will not necessarily see things that way: it remains, as ever, perilously easy to shoot the messenger.

I would add this caution to the would-be prophet: it is best to wait to raise the most difficult questions for the time when there is a preexisting relationship of trust. The more that people trust you, the more willing they will be to hear you out and the less threatened they will likely be by the challenges you present. It is also important to remember that Rome wasn't built in a day. Nor, for that matter, does a paradigm shift overnight.

Also, don't be unnecessarily dogmatic in pushing your opinion: give people the space to disagree. Let's say that you accept, as I do, that belief in the historical conquest with all its genocidal implications is inconsistent with Christian faith not least because it leads Christians to seek to resolve cognitive dissonance by dehumanizing and othering their neighbors. Even if that is your view, it will be far more effective to present your perspective as one position among others. Don't try to force others to adopt your view: just aim to have them concede that your view deserves a place at the table. If people prefer to believe in divinely commanded genocide, then we should not try to force them to give up their opinions. It should be enough for them to recognize that others can be full Christians while conscientiously disagreeing with them. Let them sit with the cognitive dissonance until they are ready to address it.

Although it won't be easy, honest discussions about biblical violence could be a catalyst for growth within your church community. M. Scott Peck describes four stages of growth toward community: pseudocommunity, chaos, emptiness, and finally true or genuine community. In the first stage, pseudocommunity, members of the group are typically 'faking' it for they are uncomfortable to broach difficult topics which carry with them the risk of conflict: "The members attempt to be an instant community by being extremely pleasant with one another and avoiding all disagreement."[465] Forcing your church to con-

---

465 M. Scott Peck, *The Different Drum: Community Making and Peace* (Touchstone, 1987), 86.

front the problem of biblical genocide is a challenge to move beyond pseudocommunity, through the chaos and emptiness of an honest wrestling with Scripture and on to true community where we either come to read the text differently, or at least we become aware of how other Christians can reasonably and in good conscience disagree with our reading. Indeed, I do believe that one of God's many reasons for biblical ambiguation is precisely to catalyze such maturation in Christian community.

But what if people are unwilling to grant that space at the table? What if they insist that spiritualizing and providential errancy views are unorthodox, impious, or even dangerous? What if they disregard the appeal to conscience? What if they believe that those who disagree do not belong in their community any longer, that they have no place at the table?

In cases like that, the next step may be to reframe the disagreement and place your interlocutor on the defensive. Over the years, I have occasionally experienced just that kind of pushback and I have responded, when necessary, by offering precisely that kind of reframing. For example, for many years I have defended a hopeful inclusivist soteriology: that is, I am very optimistic that some people will be saved by Christ without ever having prayed a sinner's prayer or otherwise verbally assented to the Lordship of Christ in this life. One gentleman challenged me on this position, insisting that my theological endorsement of hopeful inclusivism was inconsistent with our denominational confessional statement, the North American Baptist Statement of Beliefs. The problem, in his view, arose with the following passage on the centrality of Christ in salvation: "It is offered as a free gift by God to all and must be received personally through repentance and faith in Jesus Christ (I Timothy 2:4; Ephesians 2:8-9; Acts 20:21)." [466] This gentleman insisted that by allow-

---

466 North American Baptist Statement of Beliefs, https://nabconference.org/wp-content/uploads/2019/02/2.-NAB-Statement-of-Beliefs-and-Affirmation-of-Marriage-ADOPTED-by-Triennial-Delegates-July-5-2012_0-1.pdf

ing for inclusive salvation, I was contradicting the statement's description of salvation as coming by way of personal reception through repentance and faith.

When a person faces a challenge like this to their orthodoxy, they are automatically placed on the defensive. So it is important in that moment to turn the tables by reframing the issue so that it is your interlocutor who is forced to defend *their* position. To be clear, at this point I am not proposing some disingenuous, obfuscatory debating strategy. Rather, I am proposing a way to drill down to the main issue. And that is what I did with this challenge over inclusivism. There are many things I could have said in reply to that gentleman. For example, I could have discussed the function of confessional statements like the North American Baptist Statement of Beliefs and their complex relation to soul competency. Or I could have talked about the many different inclusivist and second chance theologies in the history of the church. Or I could have simply reasoned from the love and mercy of God. But focusing on any one of those issues would risk appearing to skirt the central concern of my interlocutor and would then oblige me to argue for that additional claim (inclusivism or second-change theology, or whatever). So instead, I responded to that gentleman with a simple but blunt question: "A 10-year-old Jewish girl dies in Auschwitz. Are you saying that in order to teach at this seminary, that in order to accept the North American Baptist Statement of Beliefs, *I need to believe that little girl went to hell?*"

The gentleman offered no reply and he chose not to raise that issue again. By reframing the issue in those stark terms, I effectively turned the tables and shifted the power differential. Rather than remain on the defensive I placed my interlocutor in the hot seat by forcing him to confront the implications of *his* position. If he really believes that inclusivism, as defined, is false then it follows that the Jewish girl who dies in Auschwitz really does go to hell forever. He's free to take that view if he likes, but I believe he is quite wrong to suggest that every person who assents to the North American Baptist Statement of Beliefs should likewise be compelled to accept that conclusion. By his silence, he seemed to concede the point.

So when you encounter cases where Christians challenge your orthodoxy for questioning the historicity of the Canaanite conquest, don't allow yourself to be put on the defensive, attempting to identify which events in the biblical narrative you consider to be historical and which not. That is a lose-lose proposition. Instead, you can turn the challenge back on your interrogator with a question: "are you saying that in order to be a member in good standing of this community, that I must believe that God commanded the Israelites to hack children and infants into pieces?" You might be thinking: Is that too blunt? I don't think so. I don't think we do anyone any favors when we continue to shield ourselves and others from the true horror of biblical genocide. People need to come to terms with the extraordinary implications of the doxastic demands they are placing on others. They need to understand the full implications of what it is they are requiring others to believe. If they don't, they will never truly understand why other people in good conscience cannot agree with them. It is one thing to insist that you must reject inclusivism or accept the historicity of Joshua. It is quite another thing to insist that you must believe a Jewish girl who dies in Auschwitz goes to hell or that the Israelites were commanded by God to hack children and infants into pieces in order to protect the spiritual purity of the Israelite people. I believe that one of the main reasons these stark positions are allowed to proliferate in the church unchallenged year after year is because they are not reframed in precisely the forthright and honest manner that I am proposing.

The Book Ends But the Conversation Continues

Twenty-five years ago, I shed tears of anger for a child killed because of his father's distorted perception of the divine will. In the foreword I described those tears as seeds and this book as the harvest. If the harvest is a good one, it will prompt readers to facilitate crucial conversations about biblical violence in their communities of faith while boldly seeking new ways of reading the text that do not violate our most basic moral intuitions.

This book may be concluded but I am happy to say that the conversation will continue. Year by year, I find there is a growing chorus of Christians from laypeople to church leaders to trained theologians who are questioning the interpretations of the Genocide Apologists and Just War Interpreters. That fact leaves me hopeful that in a generation or two, such interpretations of Joshua will have become as unthinkable as the pro-slavery interpretations of Scripture which were widely assumed just a few generations ago. The Bible is not the book I would have written. But that's as it should be: God knew what he was doing even if we don't. Our call as Christian readers is always to read the text in order that we may love God with everything we have and to love our neighbor as ourselves, even, and perhaps especially, our neighbor the Canaanite.

Also Available from 2 Cup Press

Deep down, every Christian has an 'inner atheist', a still small voice of doubt and questioning.

For many, that voice is viewed as a threat, one to be silenced if at all possible.

But what if the inner atheist has something important to say? What if it could provide the way not to a weakened faith but to a deepened one?

"Do I agree with everything Randal Rauser says and with every way he put things? I do not.

Do I think that what he says and how he says it is so sensible and so helpful that I am going to buy copies of this book to give to relatives, friends, students—even my own sons? I do."

John G. Stackhouse, Jr.
Samuel J. Mikolaski Professor of Religious Studies, Crandall University

Both available for purchase (print and e-book) at major online retailers including Amazon and Barnes & Noble.

www.ingramcontent.com/pod-product-compliance
Lightning Source LLC
Chambersburg PA
CBHW070136100426
42743CB00013B/2720